Keep this book. You will need it and use it throughout your career.

About the American Hotel & Lodging Association (AH&LA)

Founded in 1910, AH&LA is the trade association representing the lodging industry in the United States. AH&LA is a federation of state lodging associations throughout the United States with 11,000 lodging properties worldwide as members. The association offers its members assistance with governmental affairs representation, communications, marketing, hospitality operations, training and education, technology issues, and more. For information, call 202-289-3100.

LODGING, the management magazine of AH&LA, is a "living textbook" for hospitality students that provides timely features, industry news, and vital lodging information.

About the Educational Institute of AH&LA (EI)

An affiliate of AH&LA, the Educational Institute is the world's largest source of quality training and educational materials for the lodging industry. EI develops textbooks and courses that are used in more than 1,200 colleges and universities worldwide, and also offers courses to individuals through its Distance Learning program. Hotels worldwide rely on EI for training resources that focus on every aspect of lodging operations. Industry-tested videos, CD-ROMs, seminars, and skills guides prepare employees at every skill level. EI also offers professional certification for the industry's top performers. For information about EI's products and services, call 800-349-0299 or 407-999-8100.

About the American Hotel & Lodging Educational Foundation (AH&LEF)

An affiliate of AH&LA, the American Hotel & Lodging Educational Foundation provides financial support that enhances the stability, prosperity, and growth of the lodging industry through educational and research programs. AH&LEF has awarded hundreds of thousands of dollars in scholarship funds for students pursuing higher education in hospitality management. AH&LEF has also funded research projects on topics important to the industry, including occupational safety and health, turnover and diversity, and best practices in the U.S. lodging industry. For information, call 202-289-3180.

FOOD SAFETY
Managing the HACCP Process

Educational Institute Books

FOOD SAFETY
Managing the HACCP Process

Ronald F. Cichy, NCE, CHA, CFBE, CHE

EDUCATIONAL INSTITUTE
American Hotel & Lodging Association

Disclaimer

This publication is designed to provide accurate and authoritative information in regard to the subject matter covered. It is sold with the understanding that the publisher is not engaged in rendering legal, accounting, or other professional service. If legal advice or other expert assistance is required, the services of a competent professional person should be sought.
　　—From the Declaration of Principles jointly adopted by the American Bar Association and a Committee of Publishers and Associations

The author, Ronald F. Cichy, is solely responsible for the contents of this publication. All views expressed herein are solely those of the author and do not necessarily reflect the views of the Educational Institute of the American Hotel & Lodging Association (the Institute) or the American Hotel & Lodging Association (AH&LA).

Nothing contained in this publication shall constitute a standard, an endorsement, or a recommendation of the Institute or AH&LA. The Institute and AH&LA disclaim any liability with respect to the use of any information, procedure, or product, or reliance thereon by any member of the hospitality industry.

Printed in the United States of America
1 2 3 4 5 6 7 8 9 10 10 09 08 07 06 05 04

ISBN 0-86612-263-X

Editor: George Glazer

DEDICATION

Service is an honorable profession. If you have the gift of serving others, concentrate on serving others. Extend your hospitality to strangers as well as to those you know. This book is dedicated to my family and students, who provide me with countless opportunities to practice hospitality service.

Contents

Hard Floors • Resilient Floors • Wood Floors • Carpeting •
Recommended Floors for Food Establishments

Toilet and Lavatory Facilities

The Housekeeping Department • Waste Collection and Disposal •
The On-Premises Laundry

About the Author

Ronald F. Cichy is the Director of and a Professor in *The* School of Hospitality Business at Michigan State University. Previously, he was the Director of Educational Services for the Educational Institute of the American Hotel & Lodging Association. Dr. Cichy has also served on the faculties of the University of Denver and Lansing Community College. He earned a Ph.D. (1981) from MSU's Food Science and Human Nutrition, and an MBA (1977) and a BA (1972) from MSU's School of Hotel, Restaurant and Institutional Management.

In 2003, Dr. Cichy earned the designation of NAMA Certified Executive (NCE) from the National Automatic Merchandising Association. He also earned the designations of Certified Food and Beverage Executive (CFBE) and Certified Hotel Administrator (CHA) in 1983, and Certified Hospitality Educator (CHE) in 1992, from the Educational Institute of AH&LA. In 1996, he was named an Outstanding Alumnus by MSU's College of Human Ecology. He was inducted into the School of Hospitality Business Alumni Association's Wall of Fame in 2001, and was honored as one of the school's 75th Anniversary Distinguished Alumni in 2002. In 2003, he received MSU's Eli Broad College of Business Distinguished Alumnus Award.

Dr. Cichy's industry experience includes leadership positions in lodging and food service operations as a hotel manager, food and beverage manager, banquet chef, and sales representative. He has written more than 125 articles for food service and lodging audiences, and, because of his hospitality leadership research, has been identified as one of the top 50 most influential scholars in hospitality management. In addition to authoring *Managing Service in Food and Beverage Operations,* Third Edition, Dr. Cichy is the author or co-author of seven other books, including *Managing Beverage Service* with Dr. Lendal Kotschevar.

Dr. Cichy is a member of AH&LA's Educational Foundation's Board of Trustees, the National Automatic Merchandising Association's Foundation's Board of Directors, the President's Academy Board of Regents, and the Michigan Hotel, Motel and Resort Association's Board of Directors. He is a frequent speaker at annual conferences, meetings, and institutes for businesses ranging from Fortune 500 companies to organizations in the hospitality industry. He has delivered seminars and workshops in Australia, Canada, Europe, Japan, Mexico, and the United States. Dr. Cichy resides in Okemos, Michigan, with his wife Shelley, daughter Grace, and son John.

Chapter 1 Outline

Competencies

1. Define the term *control points,* and identify the ten control points in the food service system. (pp. 3–7)

2. Explain the focus of the food safety risk management program discussed in this chapter. (pp. 7–9)

3. Describe the responsibilities of executive managers, mid-level managers, staff members, and regulatory authorities with respect to an establishment's food safety risk management program. (p. 9)

4. Identify the benefits of a food safety risk management program. (p. 10)

5. Describe the Hazard Analysis Critical Control Point (HACCP) system and how it relates to a food safety risk management program. (pp. 10–12)

6. Identify the seven HACCP principles, and explain how they are used to establish a HACCP plan. (pp. 13–22)

7. Identify the purposes of food establishment inspections, define the types of inspections, and describe how a HACCP inspection should be conducted. (pp. 22–33)

8. Define the term "imminent health hazard." (p. 30)

1

Food Safety Risk Management and the HACCP System

Sᴇʀᴠɪɴɢ ꜱᴀꜰᴇ ꜰᴏᴏᴅ ᴛᴏ ᴛʜᴇ ᴘᴜʙʟɪᴄ is a major responsibility of food service owners and staff members. Food establishments that do not have effective food safety programs run the risk of initiating an outbreak of foodborne illness—one that could have dire consequences for the business as well as its guests, staff members, and owners. Consider the following newspaper and magazine excerpts:

Toxic Tuna on the Rise

Tuna, mackerel, and salmon contain omega-3 acids and can reduce the risk of heart disease. Restaurants are adding these items to their menus in response to rising demand from health-conscious guests. These new menu items also bring new food safety concerns. Tuna burgers have been linked to outbreaks of histamine poisoning. When tuna is held at improper temperatures, bacteria in the fish convert the fish enzyme histidine to histamine. Histamine poisoning results in immediate reactions that may include diarrhea, headache, rash, strange metallic or peppery taste, throat tightening, and vomiting.

Salmonella Linked to Imported Cantaloupes

Forty-seven cases and two deaths resulted from consuming contaminated cantaloupes from South America. *Salmonella Poona* was identified in the lab tests. Since 1990, over 1,000 outbreaks of *Salmonella* have been linked to imported cantaloupes.

School Outing Spoiled due to E. coli Outbreak

During a school picnic, one teacher and 14 out of 22 seventh graders contracted foodborne illness from meat containing *Escherichia coli*. The barbecued meat was undercooked.

Ill Cook Serves *Shigella* to Customers at a Mexican Restaurant

A cook working while infected with *Shigella flexneri* served this pathogen to customers. Forty customers at the Mexican restaurant became sick as a result of this food handler working while ill. Also, improper use of the same knife to cut meat and fresh produce led to cross contamination.

Restaurant Chain Pays Each Hepatitis Victim $25,000 to $75,000

More than 1,400 customers of a restaurant chain were affected by a Hepatitis A (HEPA) scare. The restaurant company paid for the inoculation of 1,400 people and paid each $200 for the time and anxiety spent receiving the HEPA treatment. Four people tested positive, sued the restaurant chain, and received between $25,000 and $75,000 to settle their law-suit. The outbreak was caused by food handlers working while they had diarrhea.

Customer Finds Fried Chicken Head in Chicken Wings

After returning home with a take-out order of chicken wings, a customer screamed when she saw a battered and fried chicken head in with the chicken wings. She phoned the restaurant and was offered a full refund or a replacement order. Instead, she phoned a local TV station and the incident was broadcast on the evening news. The amount of the eventual legal settlement was not reported.

Guests and potential guests of the food establishments named in these articles read the reports. How do you think they reacted? What effects do you think these reports had on staff members?

The operation of a food establishment is an inherently risky business. As you read this book, you will learn that food safety hazards are among the most critical risks food service managers must control. Failing to understand and manage these risks can quickly ruin a business. A comprehensive food safety risk management program is thus essential to the long-term success of a food service operation.

Food Safety Risk Management Program

A food service organization can be thought of as a system of basic operating activities or **control points.** Each control point is a miniature system with its own recognizable structure and functions (see Exhibit 1). The overall success of the operation depends upon the success of each of these interrelated activities and controlling the food safety risks throughout the entire process.

A food safety risk management program focuses on managing risks at each of the ten control points. This approach systematizes the otherwise overwhelming task of managing the food safety risks of the entire establishment. The program involves identifying the risks at each control point and implementing procedures for reducing those risks in the course of daily operations. By thus reducing risks at each control point, managers can successfully reduce the overall risks of operating a food establishment. The food safety risk management program also incorporates food quality and food cost control procedures. The end result is satisfaction for guests, staff members, and owners.

Control Points

Menu planning is the initial control point in the food service system. Because the menu influences the remaining control points, managers must understand all the

Exhibit 1   **Control Points in a Food and Beverage Operation**

```
      Staff Satisfaction                                    Owner Satisfaction

                        Guest Satisfaction

                          Cleaning and
                          Maintenance

                            Serving
                                                              Production
                            Holding                           Activities

                            Cooking

                           Preparing

                            Issuing

                            Storing

                           Receiving

                          Purchasing

                         Menu Planning
```

control points before developing the menu. For example, the menu affects purchasing, receiving, storing, issuing, preparing, cooking, and serving procedures because these procedures vary with the food product in question. The menu also affects and, in some cases, may be affected by the facility's design and layout, equipment requirements, and labor needs. A properly designed food safety program must begin with the menu.

Purchasing is important for maintaining the value and quality of products, minimizing the investment in inventory, and strengthening the operation's competitive position. Sound purchasing techniques can protect profits, control costs, and reduce risks. A sound purchasing system is essential to the operation's food safety program.

Receiving is a critical control point because at this point the operation assumes ownership of the products. The receiving function involves checking quality, quantity, and price. Proper receiving practices, when combined with skillful purchasing, can maximize the benefits of a carefully planned menu.

Storing serves to prevent deterioration and theft of valuable food products before the operation uses them. Food products are valuable assets that must be protected from contamination, spoilage, and theft in order to minimize costs and risks and maximize profits. Standards for the different types of storage (dry, refrigerated, and frozen) provide this protection.

Issuing is the control point at which food products are released from storage. The objective of issuing controls is to ensure that products are only released to the production department with proper authorization. A poorly designed issuing system can undermine an operation's food safety efforts, increase risks, and jeopardize profits.

Preparing is the series of activities performed on food products before cooking. Cleaning and peeling vegetables, trimming meat, and assembling raw ingredients are examples of preparing activities. Food is exposed to food safety hazards during preparing; food safety standards are therefore important at this control point.

Cooking is the control point at which heat is applied to food in order to change its color, odor, texture, taste, appearance, and nutritional value. Food products are further exposed to food safety hazards during cooking, so this control point must be carefully monitored.

Holding is a critical control point, particularly in food service operations that prepare products well in advance of service. Menu items may be held hot or cold. Holding times should be as short as possible to maintain product quality and reduce food safety hazards. Holding temperatures must also be monitored carefully.

Serving involves physically transferring finished menu items from the production department to guests. This control point should be designed to deliver quality products to guests quickly and efficiently. Serving standards should focus on protecting food safety and quality.

Cleaning and maintenance is the final control point; it is also one of the most important. Cleanliness is intimately related to every other basic operating activity. Many of the standards at other control points are standards of cleanliness and relate to food safety and maintenance.

These ten control points are the foundation of any food establishment. A comprehensive food safety program must address each point. Specific standards and operating procedures will vary among individual operations. However, a food safety program based on these control points can be adapted to any food establishment.

Reducing Risks

The program described in this book focuses on reducing overall risks by identifying the risks at each control point in a food service operation. This approach is a modified version of the Hazard Analysis Critical Control Point (HACCP—pronounced "HAH-sep") approach developed jointly by the Pillsbury Company, the United States Natick Laboratories, and the National Aeronautics and Space Administration in 1974.

HACCP is a systematic approach to identifying, evaluating, and controlling food safety hazards. Food safety **hazards** are biological, chemical, or physical agents that are reasonably likely to cause injury or illness in the absence of their control. HACCP systems are designed to prevent the occurrence of potential food safety hazards. The food safety risk management program presented here incorporates HACCP and also includes controls for maintaining food quality and managing food costs.

Hazard analysis serves as the basis for establishing critical control points. **Critical control points (CCPs)** are those activities or procedures in a specific food system where loss of control may result in an unacceptable health risk. **Critical limits** establish appropriate standards that must be met at each CCP. The final step in HACCP is to monitor and verify that potential hazards are controlled. All of this information is documented in the **HACCP plan**—a written document that delineates the formal procedures for following HACCP principles.

The food safety program presented here is a HACCP-based approach which focuses on essentials: the ten control points common to most food establishments. Standards and procedures for each control point are presented as they relate to the four resources under a manager's control: inventory, people, equipment, and facilities. A resource evaluation is necessary for each of the ten control points. The result is a systematic approach to managing risks. Exhibit 2 presents a control points diagram for baked chicken. The left side of the diagram indicates the ingredients that are added to the chicken as it passes the control points. The right side of the diagram indicates the appropriate actions that reduce risks at each control point.

Inventory is an essential management resource because it is converted into revenue and, ultimately, into profits. Inventory in a food service operation normally consists of food products, beverages, and non-food items such as linens and cleaning chemicals. Inventory control is a vital link in an operation's cost and quality control systems. Inventory items are assets which must be protected from spoilage, contamination, pilferage, and waste.

Because the hospitality industry is labor-intensive—that is, it relies on large staffs—people are an important resource. It is management's responsibility to train staff members in proper food safety practices. Failing to control this important resource undermines the food safety program and jeopardizes the establishment's bottom line.

The food establishment's equipment represents a substantial investment. Equipment selection is important to a food safety program, as is the proper

Exhibit 2   Control Points Diagram for Baked Chicken

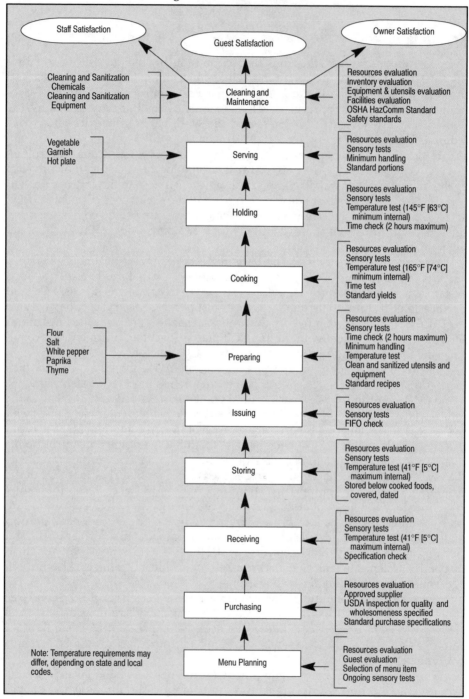

Staff Satisfaction

Guest Satisfaction

Owner Satisfaction

Cleaning and Sanitization
Chemicals
Cleaning and Sanitization
Equipment

Cleaning and
Maintenance

Resources evaluation
Inventory evaluation
Equipment & utensils evaluation
Facilities evaluation
OSHA HazComm Standard
Safety standards

Vegetable
Garnish
Hot plate

Serving

Resources evaluation
Sensory tests
Minimum handling
Standard portions

Holding

Resources evaluation
Sensory tests
Temperature test (145°F [63°C]
   minimum internal)
Time check (2 hours maximum)

Cooking

Resources evaluation
Sensory tests
Temperature test (165°F [74°C]
   minimum internal)
Time test
Standard yields

Flour
Salt
White pepper
Paprika
Thyme

Preparing

Resources evaluation
Sensory tests
Time check (2 hours maximum)
Minimum handling
Temperature test
Clean and sanitized utensils and
   equipment
Standard recipes

Issuing

Resources evaluation
Sensory tests
FIFO check

Storing

Resources evaluation
Sensory tests
Temperature test (41°F [5°C]
   maximum internal)
Stored below cooked foods,
   covered, dated

Receiving

Resources evaluation
Sensory tests
Temperature test (41°F [5°C]
   maximum internal)
Specification check

Purchasing

Resources evaluation
Approved supplier
USDA inspection for quality and
   wholesomeness specified
Standard purchase specifications

Note: Temperature requirements may
differ, depending on state and local
codes.

Menu Planning

Resources evaluation
Guest evaluation
Selection of menu item
Ongoing sensory tests

cleaning and maintenance of each piece of equipment. A food service operation's facilities also represent a sizable investment, and their design and layout have a great impact on the success of a food safety program.

Program Responsibility

The responsibility for the food safety program should be accepted throughout a food service operation, shared alike by top management/owners, mid-level managers, and staff members. Regulatory authorities also share this responsibility by virtue of their positions.

The program must start at the top of a food service organization. Owners, chief executive officers, presidents, and corporate executives must be genuinely committed to making food safety a top priority. The program should be addressed in the mission statement, corporate policies, and operating philosophies. It should be clearly documented with written comprehensive food safety standards and procedures. Top management is responsible for enforcing these standards and ensuring regulatory compliance, as well as for developing and implementing training materials for use at lower levels.

Mid-level managers include individual operation managers and supervisors. These managers must also accept responsibility for the food safety program at their levels. Like top managers and owners, mid-level managers must provide leadership by demonstrating their commitment to food safety risk management.

Mid-level managers are responsible for planning and conducting staff member training programs and for monitoring the food safety program on a day-to-day basis. Mid-level managers must make many decisions in the course of daily operations; the program helps them make these decisions by providing guidelines at each control point.

Staff members share the responsibility for the program; in some ways, they are most important to its success. Making every staff member in a food service operation aware of his or her role in the food safety program helps ensure the program's effectiveness and build staff member commitment to the program. An overview of the food safety program should be part of every staff member's orientation. The overview should cover the objectives and major components of the program. Training should address concepts, procedures, and policies that help reduce risks. Follow-up training should review each individual's role in the overall program.

Staff members should participate in the development of food safety standards. This participation will reinforce the importance of the program and encourage stronger commitment to it. Staff members should also be expected to report food safety risks and guest complaints to management.

Regulatory authorities, by the very nature of their profession, are committed to reducing risks in food service operations. They are therefore an important resource for food service managers and share the responsibility for the success of a food safety program. Their primary role is to protect the safety of the food supply by enforcing regulations. Their inspections serve to identify risks to the public health. Regulatory authorities can also help train staff members and managers and provide suggestions for reducing risks.

Program Benefits

A formalized program ensures a continuous effort toward better food safety. It guarantees that important points are not overlooked or forgotten in the course of daily operations and personnel changes. Naturally, a comprehensive program costs money. However, it provides an immediate payback to the business by performing the following functions:

- Meeting guest expectations, upon which the establishment's success (and everyone's job) depends

- Protecting guest and staff health, thereby reducing staff member absences

- Reducing the operation's liability for accidents, injuries, or deaths

- Increasing the useful life of the operation's facilities and equipment

- Increasing the effectiveness and reducing the cost of cleaning procedures with the proper use of chemicals

- Reducing the risks associated with the storage and application of toxic chemicals by standardizing products and procedures

- Simplifying supervision with the use of checklists

- Eliminating product waste and simplifying work methods through the use of written cleaning procedures

- Establishing management objectives which can be used to measure the progress of the business toward reducing risks

- Providing an acceptable return on investment for the owners of the business

- Reducing the risks of operating a food establishment

As this list of benefits indicates, a comprehensive food safety program does not cost as much as it pays. However, the return on this investment depends on how well management communicates the food safety standards and how well everyone performs to uphold these standards. Management must make food safety part of daily operations and make all staff members aware of its importance.

The HACCP System

The remainder of this chapter addresses two key issues: the HACCP system and the food establishment inspection. They are integrated and interrelated.

Recall that the food safety risk management program is a HACCP-based system that goes beyond issues of food safety. The program uniquely presents not only safety but also quality and cost control concerns. The program has as its very core HACCP and the reduction of risks. Risks not only apply to food safety hazards, they also affect cost control and quality implications. The program goal is achieved when the unique blend of safety, quality, and cost issues is integrated, resulting in staff member, guest, and owner satisfaction. It is possible to control risks and maximize satisfaction at the same time. Each complements the other, resulting in a system that works.

Consider poker, a game of chance played according to specific rules. It is a game of chance because players are not guaranteed to win or lose. Whether a player wins or loses depends on the cards he or she is dealt, on the cards dealt to other players in the game, and on each player's skill level in playing each hand. While it is possible to define the probability of winning given a particular poker hand, it may not be possible to entirely prevent oneself from losing.

Consider managing a food establishment. It is somewhat like playing a poker game in that there are rules, and managers are not guaranteed to win or lose. The manager's skill level and the skill of the other players (employees, for example) directly affect the success or failure of the food establishment. It is possible to control the risks of losing through the implementation of a food safety program. HACCP is the program that helps control such risks.

The HACCP system is prevention-based. It is designed to prevent potential food safety problems. Risks are reduced by, first, assessing the risks of a product or food production process, and, second, determining the steps that must be taken to control these risks. The reader must fully understand the following definitions before reading the discussion of the HACCP system:

(1) *Acceptable level* means the presence of a hazard that does not pose the likelihood of causing an unacceptable health risk.

(2) *Control point* means any point in a specific food system at which loss of control does not lead to an unacceptable health risk.

(3) *Critical control point* means a point at which loss of control may result in an unacceptable health risk.

(4) *Critical limit* means the maximum or minimum value to which a physical, biological, or chemical parameter must be controlled at a critical control point to minimize the risk that the identified food safety hazard may occur.

(5) *Deviation* means failure to meet a required critical limit for a critical control point.

(6) *HACCP plan* means a written document that delineates the formal procedures for following the HACCP principles.

(7) *Hazard* means a biological, chemical, or physical property that may cause an unacceptable consumer health risk.

(8) *Monitoring* means a planned sequence of observations or measurements of critical limits designed to produce an accurate record and intended to ensure that the critical limit maintains product safety. Continuous monitoring means an uninterrupted record of data.

(9) *Preventive measure* means an action to exclude, destroy, eliminate, or reduce a hazard and prevent recontamination through effective means.

(10) *Risk* means an estimate of the likely occurrence of a hazard.

(11) *Sensitive ingredient* means any ingredient historically associated with a known microbiological hazard that causes or contributes to production of a potentially hazardous food.

(12) *Verification* means methods, procedures, and tests used to determine if the HACCP system in use is in compliance with the HACCP plan.

The HACCP system identifies and monitors specific foodborne hazards. The hazard analysis establishes critical control points (CCPs), which identify those points in the process that must be controlled to ensure food safety. In addition, critical limits are established that document the appropriate parameters that must be met at each CCP. CCPs are monitored and verified in subsequent steps to ensure that risks are controlled. All of this information is specified in the HACCP plan.

HACCP plans must include flow diagrams, product formulations, training plans, a corrective action plan, and a verification plan. These HACCP plans enable food managers and staff members to assess whether the food establishment has a system of controls that will sufficiently ensure safety of the products. The plan must include enough detail to facilitate staff member and management understanding of the operation and the intended controls.

When used properly, HACCP is an important food protection tool. The key to success is staff member training. Staff members must know which control points are critical and what the critical limits are at these points—for each preparation step they perform. Management must routinely follow up to verify that all staff members are controlling the process by complying with the critical limits.

HACCP is a system of preventive controls that effectively and efficiently ensures that food products are safe in a food establishment. It emphasizes the food service industry's role in continuous improvement: rather than relying only on periodic facility inspections by regulatory agencies to point out deficiencies, food service operations should engage in ongoing problem-solving and prevention. HACCP clearly identifies the food establishment as the final party responsible for ensuring the safety of the food it sells. It requires the food establishment to analyze its preparation methods in a rational, scientific manner to identify CCPs and to establish critical limits and monitoring procedures. The establishment is responsible for maintaining records that document adherence to the critical limits that relate to the identified critical control points; this results in continuous self-inspection.

A food establishment's use of HACCP requires development of a plan to prepare safe food. The plan must be shared with the regulatory agency, which must have access to CCP monitoring records and other data necessary to verify that the HACCP plan is working. With conventional inspection techniques, a regulatory agency can only determine conditions that exist during the time of the inspection. However, both current and past conditions can be determined when a HACCP approach is used. Therefore, the regulatory agency can more effectively ensure that processes are under control. The HACCP approach to ensuring food safety is preventive, while traditional inspection is reactive.

The National Advisory Committee on Microbiological Criteria for Foods (NACMCF) consists of regulatory officials, academicians, consumer groups, state government, and the food industry. NACMCF has developed seven widely accepted HACCP principles. They are listed in Exhibit 3 and each is discussed in the following sections of the chapter.

Exhibit 3   The Seven HACCP Principles

1. Conduct a hazard analysis.
2. Determine the critical control points (CCPs).
3. Establish critical limits for preventive measures associated with each identified CCP.
4. Establish procedures to monitor CCPs.
5. Establish corrective actions to be taken when monitoring shows that a critical limit has been exceeded.
6. Establish effective verification procedures that document the HACCP plan.
7. Establish recordkeeping and documentation procedures to verify that the HACCP plan is working.

Hazard Analysis

The hazard analysis process identifies significant hazards, provides a risk basis for selecting likely hazards, and develops preventive measures for a process or product to ensure or improve food safety. HACCP's focus is high-risk hazards that are likely to occur. HACCP includes an analysis of ingredients, processing, distribution, and the intended use of the product. Such an analysis would state that sensitive ingredients (such as raw eggs) can create microbiological, chemical, and/or physical hazards in food.

Hazard analysis includes flow diagrams that depict control points or basic operating activities (see Exhibits 1 and 2). The significant hazards associated with each control point are listed, but, more important, preventive measures to control the hazards should be highlighted by management and staff members. In Exhibit 2, for example, preventive actions are listed to the right of the control points. A food safety risk management program is more comprehensive than HACCP, since its results transcend food safety and ultimately integrate quality and cost control with safety concerns to achieve staff, guest, and owner satisfaction. Each flow diagram should be constructed by a HACCP team that has knowledge about all control points on the product, the process, and likely hazards.

Hazards. Hazards can be categorized as biological, chemical, and physical. Biological hazards include bacterial, viral, and parasitic organisms. Refer to Exhibit 4 for a summary of hazardous microorganisms and parasites grouped on the basis of risk severity. Chemical hazards may be naturally occurring or may be added during food processing. Exhibit 5 lists types of chemical hazards and examples. Physical hazards are hard foreign objects found in food; sources are presented in Exhibit 6.

Level of Risk. An assessment of the risk of each hazard must consider the likelihood of occurrences and severity. The estimate is based on experience, epidemiological data, and technical information. When hazard identification and risk estimation are combined, significant hazards can be highlighted and addressed in the HACCP plan.

Exhibit 4   Hazardous Microorganisms and Parasites Grouped By Severity of Risk

Severe Hazards

Clostridium botulinum types A, B, E, and F
Shigella dysenteriae
Salmonella typhi; paratyphi A, B
Hepatitis A and E
Brucella abortis; B. suis
Vibrio cholerae 01
Vibrio vulnificus
Taenia solium
Trichinella spiralis

Moderate Hazards: Potentially Extensive Spread[2]

Listeria monocytogenes
Salmonella spp.
Shigella spp.
Enterovirulent *Escherichia coli* (EEC)
Streptococcus pyogenes
Rotavirus
Norwalk virus group
Entamoeba histolytica
Diphyllobothrium latum
Ascaris lumbricoides
Cryptosporidium parvum

Moderate Hazards: Limited Spread

Bacillus cereus
Campylobacter jejuni
Clostridium perfringens
Staphylococcus aureus
Vibrio cholerae, non-01
Vibrio parahaemolyticus
Yersinia enterocolitica
Giardia lamblia
Taenia saginata

Hazard Analysis Process. In this step, management must answer a series of questions for each control point in the flow diagram. The questions are listed in Exhibit 7. Once these questions are answered, preventive measures (which may be physical or chemical) can be taken to control hazards. For example, cooking sufficiently to kill pathogens is a physical preventive measure that can eliminate enteric pathogens.

Critical Control Points (CCPs)

Recall that a critical control point is a step or procedure at which control can be applied and a food safety hazard prevented, eliminated, or reduced to acceptable levels. Some CCPs are cooking, chilling, product formulation (recipe) control, prevention of cross-contamination, and certain aspects of environmental and staff

Exhibit 5   Types of Chemical Hazards and Examples

Naturally Occurring Chemicals

    Mycotoxins (e.g., aflatoxin) from mold
    Scombrotoxin (histamine) from protein decomposition
    Ciguatoxin from marine dinoflagellates
    Toxic mushroom species
    Shellfish toxins (from marine dinoflagellates)
    Paralytic shellfish poisoning (PSP)
    Diarrhetic shellfish poisoning (DSP)
    Neurotoxic shellfish poisoning (NSP)
    Amnesic shellfish poisoning (ASP)
    Plant toxins
    Pyrrolizidine alkaloids
    Phytohemagglutinin

Added Chemicals

    Agricultural chemicals: pesticides, fungicides, fertilizers, insecticides,
        antibiotics, and growth hormones
    Polychlorinated biphenyls (PCBs)
    Industrial chemicals
    Prohibited substances (21 CFR 189)
        Direct
        Indirect
    Toxic elements and compounds: lead, zinc, arsenic, mercury, and cyanide
    Food additives:
        Direct—allowable limits under GMPs
            Preservatives (nitrite and sulfiting agents)
            Flavor enhancers (monosodium glutamate)
            Nutritional additives (niacin)
            Color additives
        Secondary direct and indirect
            Chemicals used in establishments (e.g., lubricants, cleaners,
              sanitizers, cleaning compounds, coatings, and paints)
    Poisonous or toxic chemicals intentionally added (sabotage)

member hygiene. While there may be many control points in a food process (as shown in Exhibits 1 and 2), few may be *critical* control points.

CCPs differ with the layout of a facility as well as the equipment, ingredients, and processes used. They vary with the staff members, too. Exhibit 8 presents a CCP decision tree used to help identify CCPs.

Critical Limits for Preventive Measures

A critical limit is a boundary of safety. Some preventive measures have upper and lower critical limits. For example, the temperature danger zone (TDZ) is 41°F (5°C) to 140°F (60°C); potentially hazardous foods should not be held within this range of temperatures. Both critical limits must be met for this preventive measure.

Consider the cooking of freshly ground beef patties. Critical limit criteria in this instance would include temperature, time, and patty thickness. Each patty

Exhibit 6   Physical Hazards

Material	Injury Potential	Sources
Glass fixtures	Cuts, bleeding; may require surgery to find or remove	Bottles, jars, lights, utensils, gauge covers
Wood	Cuts, infection, choking; may require surgery to remove	Fields, pallets, boxes, buildings
Stones, metal fragments	Choking, broken teeth, cuts, infection; may require surgery to remove	Fields, buildings, machinery, wire, staff members
Insulation	Choking; long-term if asbestos	Building materials
Bone	Choking, trauma	Fields, improper plant processing
Plastic	Choking, cuts, infection; may require surgery to remove	Fields, plant packaging materials, pallets, staff members
Personal effects	Choking, cuts, broken teeth; may require surgery to remove	Staff members

should be cooked to a minimum internal temperature of 155°F (68°C) for a minimum of 15 seconds if a broiler set at 400°F (207°C) is used. Patty thickness should not exceed $1/2$ inch (2.6 cm). These three critical limit criteria—temperature, time, and patty thickness—must be evaluated and monitored regularly. Other critical limit criteria include humidity, water activity (a_w)—the amount of available water in the food product, pH—the acidity or alkalinity of the food product, preservatives, salt concentration, available chlorine, and viscosity (the thickness of the food product).

Monitoring Critical Control Points

Monitoring comprises a planned sequence of measurements or observations taken to ascertain whether a CCP is under control. Monitoring procedures establish an accurate record for future verification. Monitoring procedures should: (1) track the system's operation so that a trend toward a loss of control can be identified and corrective action taken to bring the process back into control before a deviation occurs; (2) indicate when a loss of control and a deviation have actually occurred, and corrective action must be taken; and (3) provide written documentation for use in verification of the HACCP plan. Examples of measurements for monitoring include sensory observations (such as sight, smell, touch), temperature, time, pH, and a_w.

Monitoring procedures must be effective to avoid unsafe food. Continuous monitoring is always preferable when feasible. Instruments used for measuring critical limits must be carefully calibrated and used accurately, and calibration records must be maintained as part of HACCP-plan documentation. When it is not possible to monitor continuously, sampling systems or statistically designed data collection should be used. The most appropriate staff member should be assigned responsibility for monitoring each CCP, and must be trained to be accurate. If an

Exhibit 7   Questions For Hazard Analysis

1. **Ingredients**
   - Does the food contain any sensitive ingredients that are likely to present microbiological hazards (e.g., *Salmonella, Staphylococcus aureus*), chemical hazards (e.g., aflatoxin, antibiotic, or pesticide residues), or physical hazards (stones, glass, bone, metal)?

2. **Intrinsic factors of food**
   Physical characteristics and composition (e.g., pH, type of acids, fermentable carbohydrate, a_w, preservatives) of the food during and after the process can cause or prevent a hazard.
   - Which intrinsic factors of the food must be controlled to ensure food safety?
   - Does the food allow survival or multiplication of pathogens and/or toxin formation before or during the process?
   - Will the food allow survival or multiplication of pathogens and/or toxin formation during subsequent control points, including storage or consumer possession?
   - Are there similar products in the marketplace? What has been the safety record for these products?

3. **Procedures used for the process**
   - Does the procedure or process include a controllable step that destroys pathogens or their toxins? Consider both vegetative cells and spores.
   - Is the product subject to recontamination between production (e.g., cooking) and packaging?

4. **Microbial content of the food**
   - Is the food commercially sterile (i.e., low acid, canned food)?
   - Is it likely that the food will contain viable spore-forming or nonspore-forming pathogens?
   - What is the normal microbial content of the food stored under proper conditions?
   - Does the microbial population change during the time the food is stored before consumption?
   - Does that change in microbial population alter the safety of the food?

5. **Facility design**
   - Does the layout of the facility provide an adequate separation of raw materials from ready-to-eat foods?
   - Is positive air pressure maintained in product packaging areas? Is this essential for product safety?
   - Is the traffic pattern for people and moving equipment a potentially significant source of contamination?

6. **Equipment design**
   - Will the equipment provide the time/temperature control that is necessary for safe food?
   - Is the equipment properly sized for the volume of food that will be prepared?
   - Can the equipment be sufficiently controlled so that the variation in performance will be within the tolerances required to produce a safe food?
   - Is the equipment reliable or is it prone to frequent breakdowns?
   - Is the equipment designed so that it can be cleaned and sanitized?
   - Is there a chance for product contamination with hazardous substances, e.g., glass?
   - What product safety devices such as time/temperature integrators are used to enhance consumer safety?

(continued)

Exhibit 7   *(continued)*

---

7. Packaging
- Does the method of packaging affect the multiplication of microbial pathogens and/or the formation of toxins?
- Is the packaging material resistant to damage, thereby preventing the entrance of microbial contamination?
- Is the package clearly labeled "Keep Refrigerated" if this is required for safety?
- Does the package include instructions for the safe handling and preparation of the food by the consumer?
- Are tamper-evident packaging features used?
- Is each package legibly and accurately coded to indicate production lot?
- Does each package contain the proper label?

8. Sanitation
- Can the sanitation practices that are employed adversely affect the safety of the food that is being produced?
- Can the facility be cleaned and sanitized to permit the safe handling of food?
- Is it possible to provide sanitary conditions consistently and adequately to ensure safe foods?

9. Staff member health, hygiene, and education
- Can staff member health or personal hygiene practices adversely affect the safety of the food being produced?
- Does the staff understand the food production process and the factors it must control to ensure safe foods?
- Will the staff inform management of a problem that could negatively affect food safety?

10. Conditions of storage between packaging and the consumer
- What is the likelihood that the food will be improperly stored at the wrong temperature?
- Would storage at improper temperatures lead to a microbiologically unsafe food?

11. Intended use
- Will the food be heated by the consumer?
- Will there likely be leftovers?

12. Intended consumer
- Is the food intended for the general public, i.e., a population that does not have an increased risk of becoming ill?
- Is the food intended for consumption by a population with increased susceptibility to illness (e.g., infants, the elderly, the infirm, and immunocompromised individuals)?

---

operation or product does not meet critical limits, immediate corrective action should be taken. All records used for monitoring must be initialed or signed and dated by the person doing the monitoring.

Corrective Action

Although some say that practice makes perfect, perfection is rarely achieved. A corrective action plan determines the disposition of any food produced while a

Exhibit 8   Critical Control Point Decision Tree

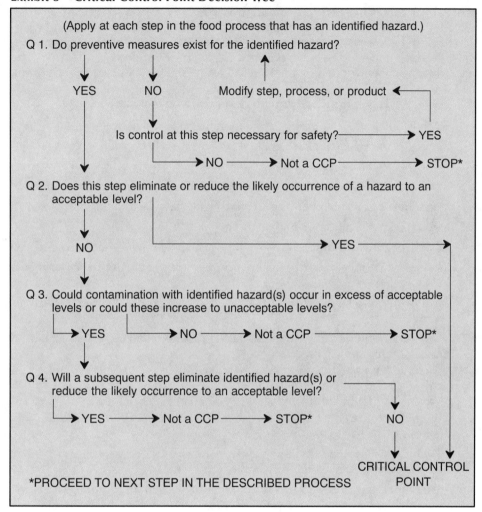

(Apply at each step in the food process that has an identified hazard.)

Q 1. Do preventive measures exist for the identified hazard?

YES   NO   Modify step, process, or product

Is control at this step necessary for safety? ⟶ YES

NO ⟶ Not a CCP ⟶ STOP*

Q 2. Does this step eliminate or reduce the likely occurrence of a hazard to an acceptable level?

NO   YES ⟶

Q 3. Could contamination with identified hazard(s) occur in excess of acceptable levels or could these increase to unacceptable levels?

YES   NO ⟶ Not a CCP ⟶ STOP*

Q 4. Will a subsequent step eliminate identified hazard(s) or reduce the likely occurrence to an acceptable level?

YES ⟶ Not a CCP ⟶ STOP*   NO

CRITICAL CONTROL POINT

*PROCEED TO NEXT STEP IN THE DESCRIBED PROCESS

deviation is occurring, corrects the cause of the deviation and ensures that the CCP is under control, and maintains records of corrective actions.

Specific corrective action plans are required for each CCP. Corrective action procedures should be well documented in the HACCP plan. When a deviation occurs and is corrected, more frequent monitoring may be temporarily required to ensure that it has indeed been corrected.

Verification

The first phase of the verification process involves the scientific or technical verification that critical limits at CCPs are satisfactory. This can be complex and may require outside expert help. The second phase of verification ensures that the

HACCP plan is functioning effectively. This involves frequent reviews of the HACCP plan, verification that the plan is correctly followed, review of CCP records, and determination that appropriate risk management decisions and product dispositions are made when production deviations occur. The third phase comprises documented periodic revalidations, independent of audits. The revalidations are performed by the HACCP team. The fourth phase is verification by the regulatory authority.

HACCP plan verification procedures may include the following:

- Establishment of appropriate verification inspection schedules
- Review of the HACCP plan
- Review of CCP records
- Review of deviations and their resolutions, including the disposition of food
- Visual inspections of operations to observe if CCPs are under control
- Random sample collection and analysis
- Review of critical limits to verify that they can adequately control hazards
- Review of verification inspection records certifying compliance with the HACCP plan
- Review of any deviations from the HACCP plan, and the corrective actions taken
- Validation of the HACCP plan, including on-site review and verification of flow diagrams and CCPs
- Review of modifications of the HACCP plan

HACCP verification inspections should be conducted:

- Routinely or on an unannounced basis, to ensure that selected CCPs are under control
- When it is determined that intensive coverage of a specific food is necessary because of new information concerning food safety
- When foods prepared at the establishment have been implicated as a vehicle of foodborne disease
- When established criteria have not been met
- To verify that changes have been implemented correctly after a HACCP plan has been modified

HACCP verification reports should include information about:

- The existence of a HACCP plan and the person(s) responsible for administering and updating the plan
- The status of records associated with CCP monitoring
- Direct monitoring of the CCP while in operation
- The certification of monitoring equipment as properly calibrated and in working order

- Deviations and corrective actions
- Any samples analyzed to verify that CCPs are under control; analyses may involve physical, chemical, microbiological, or sensory methods
- Modifications to the HACCP plan
- The training and knowledge of individuals responsible for monitoring CCPs
- Training reinforcement (reminders and refresher training) for continued motivation of staff members

Staff member training is a very important element in the success of HACCP in a food establishment. HACCP works best when it is integrated into each staff member's duties and not seen as an "add-on." The fundamental training goal should be to make staff members and managers proficient in the specific tasks that the HACCP plan requires them to perform. Managers need a deeper understanding of HACCP than staff members do. The training plan should be specific to the establishment. Remember that each time the menu changes, the HACCP plan should be reevaluated. The HACCP plan should include a feedback loop for employees to suggest what additional training is required.

Recordkeeping

The preparation and maintenance of the written HACCP plan is the responsibility of the food establishment's managers. The plan must detail hazards, identify CCPs and critical limits, specify CCP monitoring and recordkeeping procedures, and outline the implementation strategy.

Recordkeeping makes the system work. The level of sophistication of recordkeeping depends on the complexity of the food establishment. The simplest effective recordkeeping system is the best.

The approved HACCP plan and associated records must be on file at the food establishment. The following information should be included:

- List of the HACCP team and assigned responsibilities
- Description of each food product and its intended use
- Flow diagram indicating CCPs
- Hazards associated with each CCP and preventive measures
- Critical limits
- Monitoring system
- Corrective action plans for deviations from critical limits
- Recordkeeping procedures
- Procedures for verification of HACCP system

Other information in the HACCP plan can be tabulated using the format shown in Exhibit 9. Some examples of records obtained during the operation of the HACCP plan are described in Exhibit 10.

Exhibit 9   HACCP Information Reporting Form

Process Step	CCP	Chemical/ Physical/ Biological Hazards	Critical Limit	Monitoring Procedures/ Frequency/ Person(s) Responsible	Corrective Action(s)/ Person(s) Responsible	HACCP Records	Verification Procedures/ Person(s) Responsible

Food Establishment Inspections

The overall desired result of **food establishment inspections** is to prevent food-borne illness. Inspections are the primary means by which food establishment management and staff members and the regulatory authority detect procedures and practices that may be hazardous. Once deficiencies are found, management and staff members can take action to correct them.

Food establishment inspections serve as educational sessions regarding specific requirements as they apply to a particular establishment. Inspections also convey new food safety information and provide opportunities to ask questions. In addition, inspections provide a written report, so that the responsible person can bring the establishment into compliance.

Even though this discussion of food establishment inspections will focus at times on the role of the regulatory authority, it can be applied directly to managers, staff members, and owners. For example, jurisdictions must consider the number of hours required to perform inspections when allocating resources. So must a food establishment's management team consider resources (i.e., people, food, equipment, facilities, time, and money) and the worth of activities in relation to the amount of resources used. Other factors affecting resources are inspection frequency for each category of establishment, any variations over time in inspection violations or scores, and training provided to inspection staff.

Inspectors must have the correct equipment, including necessary forms, thermocouple or thermistor, alcohol swabs, flashlight, sanitizer test kit, 160°F (73°C)

Exhibit 10   Types of HACCP-Plan Records

1. **Ingredients**
   - Supplier certification documenting compliance with establishment's specifications.
   - Establishment audit records verifying supplier compliance.
   - Storage temperature record for temperature-sensitive ingredients.
   - Storage time records of limited shelf-life ingredients.

2. **Processing**
   - Records from all monitored CCPs.
   - Records verifying the continued adequacy of the food processing procedures.

3. **Packaging**
   - Records indicating compliance with specifications of packaging materials.
   - Records indicating compliance with sealing specifications.

4. **Finished product**
   - Sufficient data and records to establish the efficacy of barriers in maintaining product safety.
   - Sufficient data and records establishing the safe shelf life of the product, if age of product can affect safety.
   - Documentation of the adequacy of the HACCP procedures from an authority with knowledge of the hazards involved and necessary controls.

5. **Storage and distribution**
   - Temperature records.
   - Records showing no product shipped after shelf-life date on temperature-sensitive products.

6. **Deviation and corrective action**
   - Validation records and modification to the HACCP plan indicating approved revisions and changes in ingredients, formulations, preparation, packaging, and distribution control, as needed.

7. **Staff member training**
   - Records indicating that food staff members responsible for implementing the HACCP plan understand the hazards, controls, and procedures.

maximum registering indicators for verifying mechanical warewasher sanitization, pressure gauge, and light meter. If the food process flow is complicated, the inspector may also need a pH meter, a_w meter, and time-temperature data loggers.

Risk Categorization of Food Establishments. The establishments with the highest risks are targeted for inspection by regulatory authorities, based on the types of food served, the process flow the foods require, the volume of food produced and served, the population served, and the establishment's previous compliance history. All of these variables can affect the probability of a foodborne illness outbreak

Exhibit 11   Risk Categorization of Food Establishments

RISK TYPE	RISK TYPE CATEGORY DESCRIPTION	FREQUENCY #/YR
1	Pre-packaged nonpotentially hazardous foods only. Limited preparation of nonpotentially hazardous foods only.	1
2	Limited menu (1 or 2 main items). Pre-packaged raw ingredients are cooked or prepared to order. Retail food operations exclude deli or seafood departments. Raw ingredients require minimal assembly. Most products are cooked/prepared and served immediately. Hot and cold holding of potentially hazardous foods is restricted to single meal service. Preparation processes requiring cooking, cooling, and reheating are limited to 1 or 2 potentially hazardous foods.	2
3	Extensive handling of raw ingredients. Preparation process includes the cooking, cooling, and reheating of potentially hazardous foods. A variety of processes require hot and cold holding of potentially hazardous food. Advance preparation for next-day service is limited to 2 or 3 items. Retail food operations include deli and seafood departments. Establishments doing food processing at retail.	3
4	Extensive handling of raw ingredients. Preparation processes include the cooking, cooling, and reheating of potentially hazardous foods. A variety of processes require hot and cold holding of potentially hazardous foods. Food processes include advanced preparation for next-day service. Category would also include those facilities whose primary service population is immunocompromised.	4
5	Extensive handling of raw ingredients. Food processing at the retail level, e.g., smoking and curing; reduced oxygen packaging for extended shelf-life.	4

in a food establishment. Exhibit 11 presents the risk categorization of food establishments.

Types of Inspections. In some countries, access to a retail establishment for inspection is a condition of the acceptance and retention of the food establishment permit. Inspections are generally unannounced to obtain a more accurate assessment of normal operating conditions and practices. Inspections determine compliance and are of five types: preoperational, routine, follow-up, HACCP, and complaint.

Preoperational inspections are conducted to ensure that the establishment is built or remodeled in accordance with the plans and specifications approved by the regulatory authority. *Routine* inspections are full reviews of operations and facilities and their impact on food safety. The frequency of these inspections is usually determined by the risk category of the food operation. Routine inspections include assessment of the health, practices, and food safety knowledge of staff members and managers; food flows, storage, thawing preparation (including cooking temperatures and times) and post-preparation processes; equipment and facility construction; cleaning and sanitizing processes; water sources; sewage disposal; and vermin control. *Follow-up* inspections concentrate on correction of critical violations uncovered during routine inspections. *HACCP* inspections review critical limits, required records, and corrective actions outlined in the establishment's HACCP plan. *Complaint* inspections follow consumer complaints and may involve the regulatory agency's medical staff.

Staff Training

Staff training is the key to reducing risks and increasing staff, management, guest, and owner satisfaction. Food establishments should begin with a well-defined training process and use the resources of local and national regulatory agencies.

The first phase of staff training should provide information on the establishment's HACCP-program's history and structure, and should emphasize specific goals and objectives. The study of the epidemiology of foodborne illness—including organisms, foods, contributing factors, case studies, and all aspects of basic microbiology—is critical for both the inspector as well as the inspected. The second phase of training is on-site training conducted by trainers familiar with HACCP inspecting. The trainees should demonstrate expertise in data gathering and analysis before moving to the third phase of training, which is standardization. In this phase, points of violation are fully discussed and differentiated from similar conditions that are not violations. The final phase of training—lifelong or continuing education—is ongoing. Managers and staff members must remain current in this rapidly changing world through seminars and workshops offered by colleges and universities, professional associations, regulatory agencies, and private companies. Food service training programs offer excellent opportunities for acquiring, reinforcing, and retaining food safety knowledge.

Conducting the Inspection

The HACCP inspection views a food establishment and its operations as a total process by identifying CCPs in an attempt to prevent food safety hazards. Regulatory agencies may take individual program, personnel, establishment, and jurisdiction differences into account when establishing procedures for assigning food establishments and preparing for and conducting inspections.

The menu and the food product flow are the places to start the review for the HACCP inspection. Full food-flow diagrams should be reviewed by the regulatory authorities even though only a portion of the steps will take place during the inspection. The focus during the inspection must be, first and foremost, the food.

The sources of food, storage practices, and process flow steps all should be noted. Risk assessment data guide the allocation of time and focus during the inspection. Complex, higher-risk food processes that involve multiple ingredients, potentially hazardous foods, long holding times, foods to be cooled, and reheating steps should be given a high priority. Foods that have been implicated in foodborne illness should receive high priority, too. Other high risk indicators are foods prepared in large volumes and those requiring manual assembly and manipulation during preparation or portioning.

Accurate measurements during inspections are essential. Accuracy of measurements depends on at least two variables: calibration of the equipment and procedures followed by the person making the measurements. Critical limits to be measured include temperature, pH, a_w, food additive concentrations, warewashing processes, wash/rinse/heat sanitization, sanitizer concentrations, pressure and time measurements, light distribution, and insect and rodent infestations.

Temperature measurements. Food product internal temperatures should be taken in the geometric center of the product. Additional measurements (taken at points farthest from the heat source) may be necessary when foods are held hot on steam tables. Ambient temperature monitoring devices should be used as indicators of where further temperature investigations are warranted. Temperatures monitored between packages of food, such as milk cartons or packages of meat, also indicate the need for further examination. However, the temperature of a potentially hazardous food itself, rather than the temperature between packages, is usually necessary for regulatory citations.

The three dimensions of bacterial load, temperature, and time must be considered when inspecting the cooking process. Temperature measurement should take into account post-cooking heat rise (which allows the temperature to reach equilibrium throughout the food), particularly for foods cooked in a microwave oven. Product cooking temperatures and times should be carefully evaluated during inspections.

Modern thermometers that measure temperature electrically, rather than bimetal types that rely on thermal expansion of two different metals, are recommended by regulatory authorities. Such modern thermometers yield faster responses and provide greater overall accuracy. Before internal food temperatures are taken, the probe must be cleaned and sanitized. Boiling water, alcohol swabs, or sanitizers can destroy pathogens on the probe. When a series of temperatures is taken, it is important that the probe be thoroughly cleaned and sanitized between uses to prevent cross-contamination.

pH measurements. The pH measurement is important in determining if a food is potentially hazardous. The closer the food approaches the critical limit of 4.6, the more precise the measurement should be.

Water activity measurements. Water activity (a_w) is another factor used to determine if a food is considered potentially hazardous. The a_w is measured with a laboratory or field a_w meter.

Food additive concentrations. Samples of food are sometimes collected and sent to a laboratory for analysis.

Warewashing process evaluation. Because proper cleaning and sanitization of food-contact surfaces are important safeguards of public health, the washing, rinsing, and sanitizing processes must be verified to ensure that they meet regulatory provisions.

Mechanical warewashers are required to have data plates that indicate acceptable parameters for temperatures and cycle times for particular machines.

Wash/rinse/heat sanitization measurement. Devices used for measuring food product temperature can also be used for determining the critical limits of washing, rinsing, and sanitization. Three-compartment sinks and many mechanical warewashers have vats for water that can be checked with a probe thermometer and compared to the installed thermometer readings.

Sanitizer concentration. Sanitizer test kits are used.

Pressure measurements. The hot water sanitizing rinse pressure of mechanical warewashing machines is an important factor.

Time measurements. Time is significant in the evaluation of warewashing operations, as are temperature and concentration. Time should be measured with a watch that has a second hand or readout.

Light distribution. Portable light meters are used to take measurements of the amount of light. The measurements should be taken 30 inches (76 cm) above the floor.

Insect and rodent infestation. Physical evidence of insect and rodent infestation can take the form of dead vermin, droppings, nesting, gnawings, and grease marks on the walls. A bright flashlight, a magnifying lens, and an ultraviolet light to detect rodent urine stains can reveal infestations.

Inspection Documentation

It is essential that accurate notes be taken during a HACCP inspection. One acceptable format is the HACCP Inspection Data form shown in Exhibit 12. This form consists of an administrative section, a food flow section, a section for recording temperatures that are spot-checked, and categorical sections to record other data.

Note that the administrative section identifies the date and time of the inspection. The food flow section is used to record detailed information regarding as many as four food items identified as having the most potential for presenting problems. Additional sheets can be used if more than four food items are tracked. The foods are listed horizontally across the top, and steps from source to reheat are listed down the left side of the form. Under each food identified, space is provided for recording information observed such as time and temperature for each of the steps. A shaded column is provided for each of the foods to identify any critical limits that exist for each of the steps.

The entire production and service cycle might not take place while the food establishment is being inspected. Therefore, it should be clearly delineated on the form at which point the observations began and ended.

The food temperature recording section can list both acceptable and violative temperatures.

The back of the form asks for data relating to other areas of the operation.

Many violations found during inspection can be corrected immediately if the person in charge accompanies the inspector. Immediate correction does not negate the original violation, but should be recognized as part of the inspection documentation. The inspector will note violations and corrections on the official inspection report.

Inspection Report

The inspection report is the official regulatory agency document. It is completed for routine, follow-up, and complaint inspections. A copy should be kept in the food establishment's files.

The inspection report is usually completed at the end of the inspection. Not every item recorded on the HACCP Inspection Data form is included in the inspection report. The HACCP Inspection Data form may include some information,

Exhibit 12   HACCP Inspection Data Form

DEPARTMENT OF HEALTH AND HUMAN SERVICES
PUBLIC HEALTH SERVICE
FOOD AND DRUG ADMINISTRATION

HACCP INSPECTION DATA

EST. NAME:	PERMIT NO.	INSPECTOR:	
DATE:	TIME IN:	:AM / PM TIME OUT:	:AM/ PM

Record all observations below - transfer violations to Inspection Report

FOOD TEMPERATURES / TIMES / OTHER CRITICAL LIMITS
Use Additional Forms If Necessary

FOOD / STEP	1.	CRITICAL LIMIT	2	CRITICAL LIMIT	3	CRITICAL LIMIT	4	CRITICAL LIMIT
A. SOURCE								
B. STORAGE								
C. PREP BEFORE COOK								
D. COOK								
E. PREP AFTER COOK								
F. HOT/COLD HOLD								
G. DISPLAY/ SERVICE								
H. COOL								
I. REHEAT								

OTHER FOOD TEMPERATURES OBSERVED   Use steps from above for location

FOOD	TEMP. °C/°F	STEP	FOOD	TEMP. °C/°F	STEP	FOOD	TEMP. °C/°F	STEP

Page 1 of 2

Exhibit 12   *(continued)*

MANAGEMENT / PERSONNEL OBSERVATIONS	

OTHER FOOD OBSERVATIONS	

EQUIPMENT, UTENSILS, AND LINEN OBSERVATIONS	

WATER, PLUMBING, AND WASTE OBSERVATIONS	

PHYSICAL FACILITIES	

POISONOUS OR TOXIC MATERIALS OBSERVATIONS	

HACCP Inspection Data Page 2 of 2

Source: U.S. Food and Drug Administration.

such as documentation of acceptable holding temperatures, that is not necessary for the final report.

The final score indicates how well an establishment is complying with the regulatory agency's food safety rules. Compliance with provisions is oftentimes the basis for retaining the permit to operate the food establishment. Certain violations are called **imminent health hazards** and require immediate action or closure of the affected part of the food establishment. Sewage backing up in a food preparation area is an example of an imminent health hazard.

Critical items are violations that may contribute to food contamination, illness, or environmental degradation and represent substantial public health hazards. The inspector can use professional judgment regarding some of the violations to determine how serious the violations are—that is, how critical or non-critical—based on the likelihood of food contamination, illness, or environmental degradation.

The final score, which is the number of items in violation, is significant as an indicator of the food establishment's overall control of hazards; however, there is no defined point at which a score translates into a significant health hazard. A jurisdiction can choose the method it will use to score its food establishments.

One method might employ statistical process control to focus on continuous quality improvement. This method uses percentile rank to judge compliance against a range of compliance levels of similar establishments within the category. The *fixed categorization method* uses a fixed number of critical violations selected for each category of establishment. The *fixed without categorization method* is the simplest method. It sets a single level of compliance for all types and complexities of establishments.

Food Establishment Inspection Report

Exhibit 13 shows the Food Establishment Inspection Report. The introduction and administrative data clearly ask for key information, including inspection type and time.

It is essential that regulatory officials standardize the inspection process within an agency. Inspectors mark violations on the inspection report when they clearly exist in the food establishment. Each violation is recorded as a separate item on the report.

Critical violations are indicated with an X in the first column. Critical violations are always listed first for emphasis. Repeat items are those that were in violation on the previous inspection and are indicated in the second column, "Repeat," with an X. Specific code references are recorded in the third column. Inspectors use the fourth column, "Violation Description/Remarks/Corrections," to briefly record the specifics of the observed violation. Any additional information or explanation should be recorded here, including, if appropriate, that the person in charge corrected a violation during the inspection.

Once the inspection form has been completed, a closing conference is held to give the inspector the opportunity to clearly and firmly convey the compliance status to the person in charge. It may be beneficial to include other members of the food establishment management team in the closing conference. The written report

Exhibit 13   Food Establishment Inspection Report

FD\/\

DEPARTMENT OF HEALTH AND HUMAN SERVICES
PUBLIC HEALTH SERVICE
FOOD AND DRUG ADMINISTRATION

FOOD ESTABLISHMENT INSPECTION REPORT

Violations cited in this report shall be corrected within the time frames specified below, but within a period not to exceed 10 calendar days for critical items (§ 8-405.11) or 90 days for noncritical items (§ 8-406.11).

VIOLATIONS: CRITICAL _____   NONCRITICAL_____

ESTABLISHMENT:	PERMIT NUMBER:	DATE:

ADDRESS:	CITY:	STATE:	ZIP:

PERSON IN CHARGE / TITLE:	TELEPHONE:

INSPECTOR / TITLE:

INSPECTION TYPE: ROUTINE   FOLLOW-UP   COMPLAINT   OTHER: TIME:

Critical (X)	Repeat (X)	Code Reference	Violation Description / Remarks / Corrections

Food Establishment Inspection Report Page __ of __

(continued)

Exhibit 13 *(continued)*

FOOD ESTABLISHMENT INSPECTION REPORT

ESTABLISHMENT:			PERMIT NUMBER:	DATE:

Critical (X)	Repeat (X)	Code Reference	Violation Description / Remarks / Corrections	

Source: U.S. Food and Drug Administration.

is the focus of the closing conference. The listing of the results with the critical violations listed first helps focus the discussion on violations that could directly lead to a foodborne illness.

The closing conference gives management the opportunity to ask questions of the inspector. A detailed discussion of the establishment's plans for correcting violations revealed during the inspection must be included in the closing conference. Some jurisdictions require establishments to return a notice to the agency that violations cited during the inspection have been corrected.

Record Maintenance System

A detailed record maintenance system supports the HACCP program and tracks potential compliance actions. The following documents should be included in the food establishment's active files: records related to initial plan review, permit application and issuance, inspection reports, complaints, investigations, management training and certification, correspondence, and compliance actions.

Key Terms

cleaning and maintenance—The final control point; also one of the most important. It involves upkeep and cleaning associated with the other basic operating activities (i.e., purchasing, receiving, storing, issuing, preparing, cooking, holding, and serving), as well as cleaning and maintenance of equipment and facilities.

control points—A system of basic operating activities in a food service operation. Each control point is a miniature system with its own recognizable structure and functions.

cooking—The control point at which heat is applied to food in order to change its color, odor, texture, taste, appearance, and nutritional value.

critical control point—A point or procedure in a specific food system where loss of control may result in an unacceptable health risk.

critical limit—The maximum or minimum value to which a physical, biological, or chemical parameter must be controlled at a critical control point to minimize the risk that the identified food safety hazard may occur.

food establishment inspection—The primary means by which food establishment management and staff members and the regulatory authority detect hazardous procedures and practices. Inspections serve as educational sessions regarding requirements as they apply to a particular establishment. They also convey new food safety information, provide opportunities to ask questions, and provide a written record to the person in charge, who can bring the establishment into compliance with regulations.

HACCP plan—A written document that delineates the formal procedures for following the Hazard Analysis Critical Control Point principles.

hazard—A biological, chemical, or physical property that may cause an unacceptable consumer health risk.

holding—A critical control point in which menu items are maintained either hot or cold after cooking and in advance of service.

imminent health hazard—A serious health threat that may cause a regulatory inspector to order food operations to cease immediately; examples are sewage backups, complete lack of refrigeration, or evidence of a communicable disease outbreak such as hepatitis.

issuing—The control point at which food products are released from storage; issuing controls ensure that products are only released to the production department with proper authorization.

menu planning—In the food service industry, the initial control point, which influences all the remaining control points. It includes considering trends and other marketing factors, deciding what items to offer, pricing, image-projection, knowledge of preparation and production methods, inventory and equipment concerns, and guest and staff member concerns.

preparing—The critical point comprising the functions that must take place after food is issued and before food is cooked or otherwise readied for serving.

purchasing—The control point important in maintaining the value and quality of products, minimizing the investment in inventory, and strengthening the operation's competitive position.

receiving—A control point that involves checking the quality, quantity, and price of incoming purchased products; a critical control point wherein a food service operation assumes ownership of purchased products.

serving—The control point in which finished menu items are transferred from the production department to guests.

storing—The control point that protects valuable food products from deterioration and theft; standards for different types of storage (dry, refrigerated, and frozen) provide this protection.

Review Questions

1. What are control points?

2. What are the ten control points in the food service system?

3. Why is menu planning of special importance?

4. What is a food safety risk management program and how does it work?

5. How should responsibility for the food safety risk management program be handled?

6. What are the benefits of a food safety risk management program?

7. What are the definitions of *critical control point, critical limit, hazard, risk,* and *sensitive ingredient*? How does an understanding of these terms affect the HACCP plan?

8. What are the seven HACCP principles? How are they used to establish a HACCP plan?

9. How does a HACCP inspection differ from a food establishment inspection? What are the similarities?

10. What are critical violations? How can they be reduced?

Chapter 2 Outline

Competencies

1. Distinguish between pathogens and spoilage organisms, and list four types of microorganisms responsible for most food contamination. (pp. 37–40)

2. Explain the four factors affecting bacterial reproduction. (pp. 38–39)

3. Explain why the temperature danger zone (TDZ) is important to food safety. (p. 39)

4. Briefly describe food infections and intoxications. (pp. 40–41)

5. Explain how to prevent cross-contamination. (pp. 41–42)

6. List common chemical poisons and foodborne physical hazards, and briefly describe control measures. (pp. 43–44)

7. Describe personal health and hygiene practices necessary in a food establishment. (pp. 44–45)

8. Describe the steps that managers should take when handling a foodborne illness complaint. (pp. 45–48)

9. Identify the common causes of food spoilage in a food establishment. (pp. 48–49)

10. Define the three ranges of low-temperature food preservation and describe low-temperature food preservation techniques and their benefits. (p. 49)

11. Describe high-temperature food preservation techniques and their benefits. (pp. 49–50)

12. Describe dehydration food preservation techniques and their benefits. (pp. 50–51)

2

Food Contamination and Spoilage

FOOD SERVICE MANAGERS AND STAFF MEMBERS are responsible for serving safe food to the public. Moreover, guests *expect* food service businesses to provide them with safe, wholesome food. The publicity generated by an outbreak of foodborne illness (when two or more people become sick from eating the same food) can be disastrous for a business.

Managers of food service businesses can protect the public health, as well as the establishment's reputation and profits, by making sure that all staff members understand the fundamentals of food contamination and foodborne illness and how to prevent them. This chapter covers food contamination and spoilage.

Microorganisms Responsible for Food Contamination ———

A microorganism (or microbe) is a small living organism. Most microorganisms consist of a single cell. Microorganisms are ubiquitous in our environment: they are found in and on humans, animals, plants, water, air, and soil. Most microorganisms need organic matter (matter containing carbon) to survive and often obtain this "food" from our own food supply.

The majority of microorganisms are beneficial. Some serve as food for humans or animals, while others provide or help produce special nutrients and enzymes. There are, however, many harmful microorganisms. These can be divided into two broad categories: pathogens and spoilage organisms. **Pathogens** are disease-causing agents; they are the source of the foodborne diseases described later in this chapter. Spoilage organisms do not cause disease, but they make food products unusable. These microbes render food products unfit for human consumption by altering their color, odor, texture, taste, and appearance. Appendix A at the end of this chapter presents a summary of pathogenic microorganisms and a pronunciation guide.

Four types of microorganisms are responsible for most food contamination: bacteria, parasitic worms, fungi, and viruses. Food service managers and staff members should understand these four groups and their characteristics, factors affecting their reproduction, common food sources, incubation periods, symptoms produced when they are ingested by humans, and methods of control.

Exhibit 1   The pH Scale and Some Representative Foods

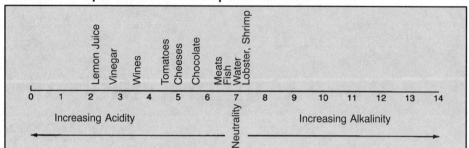

Bacteria

Bacteria are single-celled organisms. Most bacteria possess cell walls which give them their characteristic shape. Bacteria take in nutrients and expel waste products through their cell walls. Bacterial cells contain all the genetic material necessary for reproduction. Most are able to reproduce asexually through a process called binary fission, in which a single cell divides itself into two equal-sized cells. Bacterial growth refers to an increase in the number, not the size, of bacterial cells.

Environmental conditions influence the rate of bacterial reproduction. Bacteria differ in the environmental conditions they require, and food products also differ in the degree to which they provide favorable conditions for bacterial growth. The most important conditions affecting bacterial reproduction are moisture, oxygen, the level of acidity, time, and temperature.

Moisture. All bacteria need moisture in a usable form to grow and reproduce. The amount of water available to microorganisms in an environment is expressed as its **water activity** value or a_w. The amount of water in a food product can be reduced in several ways. Water can be removed by drying. Because they have a reduced a_w, food products which have been dried generally have a longer shelf life than do food products in their original moist state. Food may be frozen, making the water unavailable (bacteria cannot use water unless it is in liquid form). Sugar or salt added to food also binds water and reduces the a_w. When water is added to dried or reconstituted foods, the rehydrated foods can again support bacterial growth.

Oxygen. The availability of oxygen also greatly influences microbial growth rates. Oxygen requirements of bacteria vary with the species.

Acidity or Alkalinity. The acidity or alkalinity of the environment is an important influence on bacterial activity. The standard measure of acidity or alkalinity is **pH.** The pH scale ranges from 0 to 14. Food products with pH values less than 7 are acidic; those with pH values greater than 7 are basic or alkaline. A pH of 7 is considered neutral. Exhibit 1 shows the pH values of several common foods. In general, microorganisms reproduce best in food products with a pH between 6.6 and 7.5. *Clostridium botulinum,* the microorganism which causes botulism poisoning, produces its toxins at pH values of 4.7 and higher. This fact, coupled with information about a_w, led to a definition for potentially hazardous foods.

A **potentially hazardous food** means a food that is natural or synthetic and requires termperature control because it is in a form capable of supporting the rapid and progressive growth of infectious or toxigenic microorganisms and the growth and toxin production of *Clostridium botulinum* or, in raw shell eggs, the growth of *Salmonella Enteritidis*. Potentially hazardous food includes an animal food (a food of animal origin) that is raw or heat-treated; a food of plant origin that is heat-treated or consists of raw seed sprouts; cut melons; and garlic and oil mixtures. Potentially hazardous food does not include:

- An air-cooled hard-boiled egg with shell intact.

- A food with a water activity (a_w) value of 0.85 or less.

- A food with a pH level of 4.6 or below when measured at 24°C (75°F).

- A food, in an unopened hermetically sealed container, that is commercially processed to achieve and maintain commercial sterility under conditions of nonrefrigerated storage and distribution.

- A food for which laboratory evidence that is the basis of a variance granted by the regulatory authority demonstrates that rapid and progressive growth of infectious and taxigenic microorganisms or the growth of *Salmonella Enteritidis* in eggs or the slower growth of *Clostridium botulinum* cannot occur.

Examples of potentially hazardous foods include animal products such as fish, meat, and poultry. Also included are some plant products, such as refried beans, cooked rice, seed sprouts (germinated soybeans, mung beans, alfalfa sprouts), processed garlic in oil, and tofu and other moist soy protein products. In some jurisdictions, potentially hazardous foods do not include clean, whole, uncracked, odor-free shell eggs. Other jurisdictions include such eggs as potentially hazardous foods. Check your state and local codes for the specifics in your area.

Time and Temperature. Time and temperature requirements are interrelated. Fluctuating temperatures are hazardous to food products because they can favor food spoilage or the proliferation of foodborne illness microbes. The temperature at which raw ingredients are stored influences later bacterial activity; thus storage at intermediate temperatures must be kept to a minimum. The temperature range of 41°F (5°C) to 140°F (60°C) is the **temperature danger zone (TDZ).** The TDZ can vary from one location to another. It is critical that you find out the exact TDZ applicable to your food service operation, and minimize the amount of time food spends in the TDZ during storing, preparing, and serving. Most foodborne pathogens move from place to place by "hitchhiking" on humans, dust, air, food, clothing, or sneezes and coughs.

Parasitic Worms

Foodborne parasitic worms (or nematodes) are found in the intestines of animals; humans become infected when they consume the flesh of infected animals. Most parasitic worms can be destroyed by cooking or freezing. Trichinosis is a disease caused by a parasite known as *Trichinella spiralis*, found in infected hogs and the flesh of some wild animals (such as bear and walrus). Other foodborne parasites are found in both freshwater and saltwater fish. Freshwater fish (salmon, for example) are frequently contaminated with the live larvae of *Diphyllobothrium latum,* a fish tapeworm. *Anisakis spp.* are nematodes that infect saltwater fish such as salmon, striped bass, and Pacific snapper. Since foodborne parasites are likely to be present in both freshwater and saltwater fish, fresh fish that has never been frozen must be cooked thoroughly to internal temperatures of at least 140°F (60°C). Restaurants serving sushi (raw fish) may only serve fish that has been frozen and thawed. It is a good idea to obtain a guarantee from the fish supplier that the product has been properly frozen (at –31°F [–35°C] or below for 15 hours in a blast freezer, or at –4°F [–20°C] for 168 hours—7 days).

Foodborne Fungi

Molds and yeasts are fungi, and some species are foodborne. Although these foodborne fungi are generally beneficial, some are harmful microorganisms. Molds and yeasts do not usually cause foodborne illness, but they can cause food spoilage. Yeasts are single-celled organisms which are abundant in nature and are often found on fruit. The importance of yeasts to people lies in their ability to ferment carbohydrates. Yeasts are used in the production of wine, beer, alcoholic spirits, cheese, bread and other baked products, and enzymes. Yeasts break down glucose to form ethanol (ethyl alcohol) and carbon dioxide. Molds often cause food spoilage. *Fusarium spp.*, for example, are responsible for fruit and vegetable spoilage. *Penicillium* molds are used in the production of antibiotics and cheese. *Penicillium roqueforti* is used to make a blue-veined cheese; if produced in certain caves in France, the cheese is called Roquefort.

Viruses

Viruses are microorganisms that are even smaller than bacteria. They are always parasites of other living cells, since they cannot grow, feed, or reproduce in isolation. Viruses do not reproduce in food products, though some viruses can be transmitted through food products.

Foodborne Diseases ───────────────────────────────

A foodborne disease results when food containing infectious, toxic, or toxigenic (toxin-producing) agents is eaten. Some groups of people (e.g., the immunocompromised, elderly, and preschool-age children) are highly susceptible to foodborne disease. As Exhibit 2 shows, foodborne diseases are of two general types: infections and poisonings. **Infections** are caused by bacteria and viruses that are transmitted in food and later reproduce inside the body. These agents of food infection invade the gastrointestinal system of humans and can affect other organs. **Poisonings** result: (1) when harmful chemicals are ingested, (2) when poisonous plants or animals are eaten, or (3) when food contaminated with the poisonous waste products (toxins) of toxigenic bacteria or fungi is consumed. The illnesses that result

Exhibit 2   A Classification for Foodborne Diseases

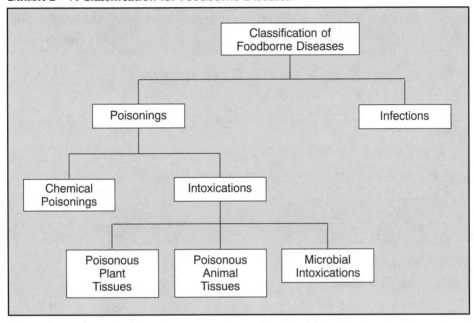

from the ingestion of poisonous plants or animals or of toxin-contaminated food are referred to as **intoxications.**

Both infections and microbial intoxications produce similar symptoms: nausea, vomiting, intestinal cramps, and diarrhea. However, microbial intoxications usually have a much shorter **incubation time**—the amount of time between consumption of the contaminated food and the first symptoms of illness—than infections. This is because the agents of infection require time to reproduce in the body.

Bacterial Infections

Bacterial infections result when relatively large numbers of bacteria are consumed, entering the body through contaminated food. Once inside the body, the infectious microorganisms multiply in the intestines. They can also move to other tissues in the body and reproduce.

Human carriers are a major source of bacterial infections. Therefore, food handlers should adhere to rules of good personal hygiene. **Cross-contamination,** which occurs when a food product comes into contact with a contaminated non-food source (knives, cutting boards, thermometers, and other equipment) or with raw food, can be prevented by:

- Separating raw animal foods during storing, preparing, holding, and display from raw ready-to-eat food and cooked ready-to-eat food

- Separating types of raw animal foods from each other

- Cleaning and sanitizing equipment and utensils

- Storing food in packages, covered containers, or wrappers
- Cleaning hermetically sealed containers of food of visible soil before opening
- Protecting food containers that are received packaged together in a case or overwrap from cuts when the case or overwrap is opened
- Storing damaged, spoiled, or recalled food separately
- Separating fruits and vegetables before they are washed

Appendix A at the end of this chapter presents details about bacterial infections including:

- *Salmonella spp.*
- *Shigella spp.*
- *Vibrio parahaemolyticus*
- *Escherichia coli*
- *Listeria monocytogenes*
- *Yersinia enterocolitica*
- *Campylobacter jejuni*

Because of technological advances and better methods of detecting pathogens, other bacterial agents might be identified in the next few years as sources of food-borne illness.

Viral Infections

Although not usually a source of foodborne infections, two infectious viruses have been found in a limited number of foods, particularly those consumed raw: virius infectious hepatitis (or HEPA), found in the blood, urine, and feces of human and animal carriers; and the Norwalk virus, an intestinal pathogen. Additional food-borne viruses may be positively linked to outbreaks of foodborne illness as refined isolation and culture techniques improve detection. Whenever handling potentially hazardous foods, use good personal hygiene and food handling techniques, practice time and temperature control, and vigilantly guard against contamination by any pathogen.

Food Poisoning

Toxic chemicals, poisonous plants and animals, and bacterial and fungal toxins all cause food poisoning when consumed.

Bacterial Intoxications. There are several sources of bacterial intoxication:

- *Staphylococcus aureus*
- *Clostridium botulinum*
- *Clostridium perfringens*
- *Bacillus cereus*

Appendix A at the end of this chapter presents details on these bacterial intoxications.

Poisonous Plants and Animals. A wide variety of plants and animals are toxic if consumed. Most people have read about the fatal hemlock that Socrates was forced to drink. Poisonous plants have long been the cause of accidental (and intentional) deaths.

Toxic plants implicated in food poisoning are usually poisonous mushrooms of the genus *Amanita*. Many other plants have been identified as poisonous. Therefore, the practice of foraging for edible plants should be left to experts—it is an extremely risky way to obtain food. *Never serve food obtained this way in a food establishment.*

Several types of fish cause food poisoning when consumed. Scombroid poisoning results from eating infected scombroid fish (tuna, bonito, and mackerel). Toxic species of puffer fish (such as fugu, blowfish, and balloonfish) should be avoided. Ciguatera poisoning is carried by many marine fish, as well as clams and oysters.

To minimize the risks posed by poisonous plants and animals, purchase food products only from approved sources.

Chemical Poisonings and Other Toxic Effects. The adulteration of food with undesirable chemicals can occur at any point in the chain of distribution or production. Mislabeling and mishandling must be closely guarded against. In food establishments, it is especially important that all equipment and utensils be made of corrosion-resistant materials.

Zinc poisoning can occur when food products are cooked or stored in galvanized (zinc-coated) containers. Antimony poisoning can occur when antimony-glazed enamel containers are used to store or cook acidic foods. Copper is a heavy metal that can enter the food supply from copper pipes, containers, and cake decorating tools. When carbonated beverages and acidic foods come into contact with copper, they can carry copper poisoning. Lead poisoning comes from lead pipes, pesticide sprays, and utensils. Lead poisoning has been linked to the storage and service of acidic liquids (tomato juice, orange juice, coffee) in earthenware glazed with lead-based glazes.

Other food products can cause allergic reactions in some guests. Some individuals are sensitive to eggs, fish and shellfish, flavors, food colors, milk, peanuts, or preservatives. It is wise to train staff members to be able to answer questions about food preparation techniques and ingredients. In addition, the surfaces of all preparation equipment and utensils should be thoroughly cleaned and sanitized after each changed use.

Toxic chemicals sometimes enter the food supply accidentally. Most of these toxins are insecticides, soil fumigants, roach and rat poisons, and weed killers. Others are present in a food service operation in the form of cleaning and sanitization compounds. These necessary chemicals are potentially poisonous if consumed. They should be used only according to the manufacturer's recommendations.

Cleaners and compounds used for sanitization should be stored separately from other chemicals and may be stored in the area of use, such as under or above sinks or on shelves.

You must obtain all food and beverage products from approved sources. In addition, proper food handling techniques, personal hygiene and cleanliness, acceptable cleaning and sanitization procedures, and caution and common sense can prevent a tragedy.

Foodborne Physical Hazards

Physical hazards present in food service businesses should never be allowed to endanger the safety of guests. The possible hazards are numerous. Metal fragments can end up in foods if can openers are not cleaned frequently and if knives, forks, spoons, pots, and pans are used and cleaned carelessly. Glass is frequently used for food and beverage containers. When handled or stacked carelessly, glass fragments can find their way into food products. Cigarette butts and matches, when discovered in food, are a nauseating turn-off. Hair in food is unsanitary, distasteful, and the greatest dissatisfier for many restaurant guests. All staff members must wear approved hair restraints. Physical hazards can be minimized if staff members are made aware of the hazards and take steps to reduce the risks. As with the other forms of food contamination, specific controls must be built into the operation's food safety risk management program.

The Importance of Health and Hygiene

Good health and personal cleanliness are important for every staff member in the food service business. Strict sanitation standards are necessary throughout the operation to prevent the contamination of food and food-contact surfaces with diseases or pathogenic organisms. These standards should be adapted to the individual operation and presented to all staff members during orientation and training. Management should follow up to ensure that each staff member upholds the standards.

All staff members must practice good personal hygiene. Food service staff members must also be in good health; some operations require job applicants to pass a physical examination before considering them for employment. Staff member uniforms must be clean and well-maintained; if possible, staff members should change into their uniforms after arriving at the workplace, thus minimizing possible contamination from street clothes. Frequent handwashing while working is especially important.

Food staff members must keep their hands and exposed portions of their arms clean. The hands and exposed portions of the arms must be cleaned by vigorously rubbing together the surfaces of the lathered hands and arms for at least 20 seconds and thoroughly rinsing with clean water. Special attention should be paid to areas beneath the fingernails and between the fingers.

After defecating, contacting body fluids and discharges, or handling waste containing fecal matter, body fluids, or body discharges, and before beginning or returning to work, staff members should wash their hands *twice*, using a nailbrush during the first washing to clean their fingertips, under their fingernails, and between their fingers. Food staff members are required to clean their hands and exposed portions of their arms at the following times:

- After touching bare human body parts other than clean hands and clean, exposed portions of arms;

- After using the toilet room;

- After caring for or handling animals;

- After coughing, sneezing, using a handkerchief or disposable tissue, using tobacco, eating, or drinking;

- After handling soiled equipment or utensils;

- During food preparation, as often as necessary to remove soil and contamination and prevent cross-contamination when changing tasks;

- When switching between working with raw foods and working with ready-to-eat foods;

- Before donning gloves for working with food; and

- After engaging in other activities that contaminate the hands.

An alcohol-based instant hand sanitizer lotion or a chemical hand sanitizing solution should be applied to the clean hands.

A food service operation must have adequate facilities to ensure compliance with these sanitation standards. Proper handwashing and restroom facilities must be available to all staff members. Usually, staff members should not share restroom facilities with guests, although the number of restrooms required depends on the seating capacity of the food establishment's serving area. If staff members change into uniforms at the workplace, they should have adequate dressing areas and lockers. These areas should be used for no other purpose.

Staff members who regulatory authorities have reasonable cause to believe have transmitted a foodborne disease may be interviewed and/or required to have appropriate medical examinations. As a result, an infected staff member may be restricted or excluded from the food establishment.

Handling a Foodborne Illness Complaint

Assume you are a food service manager and a guest calls to inform you that she and her husband became ill after eating in your establishment. What will you say, and what action will you take? How will you handle the guest's accusation that your facility might be a source of foodborne illness? What steps will you take to close this complaint with the guest? The answers to these questions might depend on whether or not your operation has an established procedure for dealing with suspected outbreaks of foodborne illness.

If you have a written procedure detailing what to do and when, you will probably respond to this potential crisis in a logical and systematic way. If no set of procedures exists, your response is likely to be rash and disorganized. Having a detailed procedure can save you time when you need it most. In such an emergency situation, prompt action will prevent further problems and will minimize the likelihood of other outbreaks. With your reputation, your guest's health, and the image of your operation at stake, you cannot afford to be unprepared.

Regulations and recommendations for properly handling, preparing, and serving food are aimed at preventing the situation just described from occurring. But with so many potential sources of food contamination, it is only sensible to be ready to deal with a foodborne disease outbreak. Such readiness is not a sign that the operation is negligent; rather, it shows that management is realistic and follows the principles of food safety risk management.

The following 11-step procedure for handling guest foodborne illness complaints should prove valuable to food service and lodging managers in their risk management programs.

Step 1—Just one person in the operation, usually the manager, should be responsible for the investigation. It is important that this person keep accurate, detailed records, since these records may be beneficial during a health department investigation. If public statements are necessary, the responsible person should also act as the only authoritative spokesperson for the establishment.

Step 2—Listen to the complaint. The interviewer should be courteous and should avoid arguing with the complainant. The responsible person should not talk about similar problems which have occurred in the past. When listening, focus all of your attention on the guest who is complaining. Never argue, defend, or try to explain away the guest's concerns.

Step 3—Get the facts. The person designated as the complaint investigator should keep a supply of complaint forms on hand. By using a standard form such as the one shown in Exhibit 3, the investigator is sure to get all of the essential information.

Step 4—Promptly and properly evaluate the guest complaint. The investigator should then contact the people who dined with the complainant to determine whether these guests have experienced similar symptoms. If so, the investigator should sort through the other guest checks to identify those who also consumed the same food. By matching credit card receipts to guest checks, the person in charge can gather the information necessary to contact these other guests. Detailed records should be kept on every conversation related to the suspected outbreak.

Step 5—The health department should be promptly notified if the complaint appears to be valid. It is the obligation of the health department to investigate foodborne illness outbreaks. An outbreak is a situation in which more than one person becomes ill from eating the same food.

Step 6—Isolate the suspected food products, if samples are still available. By this time the responsible person should have an idea of what food caused the suspected outbreak. The person in charge should promptly take possibly contaminated ingredients or batches of finished menu items out of circulation. These samples should be placed in clean, sanitized containers and then covered, dated, and labeled "DO NOT USE—SUSPECTED SOURCE OF FOODBORNE ILLNESS."

Exhibit 3   Sample Food-Related Complaint Record

Name of Complainant		
Address		
Telephone Number		
Summary of the Complaint		
Number Affected	**Date of Meal**	**Time Eaten**
Food and Beverages Consumed		

Symptoms

_____	Nausea	_____	Abdominal Cramps
_____	Diarrhea	_____	Prolonged loss of appetite
_____	Fever		(more than 3 days)
_____	Jaundice	_____	Other (specify) _____
_____	Vomiting		_____

Did others consume the same food and beverage?

Names, Telephone Numbers, and Addresses of Other Consumers

Management Action to Resolve the Complaint

Date _____   Signature _____

Step 7—Cooperate with the health department. Cooperation with health department officials is essential. Tell them everything, accurately and quickly. They will be able to determine whether guests who could not be identified or located have filed similar complaints with the health department office.

Step 8—Take corrective action to reduce future risks. The manager of a business implicated in an outbreak of foodborne disease has a powerful incentive to evaluate the operation's staff member training, its system of food handling, and its overall sanitation risk management program. The results of this evaluation should be improvements which will minimize the risk of another outbreak. Corrective action should address the four resources under the manager's control and the problems associated with them—that is, human hazards, product hazards, equipment hazards, and facilities hazards.

Step 9—Close the complaint with the guest. When the investigation is completed, it is time to contact the complainant and apologize. Some operations have a policy of offering a gift, a free meal, a coupon, or a small check.

Step 10—Index all complaints. The person responsible for the investigation should maintain a file of complaint record forms.

Step 11—Follow up to ensure that corrective action has been taken. Regardless of who handles the in-house investigation of a suspected foodborne illness outbreak, management is ultimately responsible for preventing a recurrence. Thus, the operation's manager should conduct an in-house follow-up inspection. This inspection should be documented in the complaint file. The manager should also periodically spot-check the critical areas associated with past problems to make sure they are under control.

Food Spoilage

Almost all food products are composed largely of organic material (material containing carbon compounds). Once the food is harvested or slaughtered, the organic material in it begins to break down chemically. Two distinct processes occur during food breakdown: autolysis and spoilage. **Autolysis** is the chemical breakdown of food products caused by substances (primarily enzymes) within the food. **Enzymes** are proteins that catalyze this chemical reaction; that is, they speed up the rate of autolysis. Food spoilage occurs primarily through the action of bacteria, molds, and yeasts. Spoilage organisms break down the complex organic substances in foods into their simple, inorganic components. This process is responsible for the changes in the odor, color, texture, appearance, and taste of food products which indicate spoilage. Spoiled food is unfit for human consumption.

The spoilage of food products in a food establishment is often linked to one or more of the following causes:

- Improper storage temperatures

- Incorrect or excessive storage times

- Unacceptable levels of ventilation in storage areas

- Failure to segregate foods in storage

- Excessive delays between the receiving and storing of food products

- Inadequate or unacceptable sanitation standards resulting in exposure of food products to contaminants

As this list suggests, most food spoilage occurs when foods are at the storing control point. Storage area standards must be designed to prevent or minimize food spoilage and exposure of food products to pathogenic organisms.

Food Preservation

There are four main objectives of food preservation. Some preservation methods are designed to lengthen the lag phase of bacterial growth. Another objective of food preservation is to delay undesirable autolysis. This is achieved by destroying enzymes or preventing enzymatic action. The third objective is to minimize the damage caused by insects, rodents, and physical trauma. The fourth objective, the prevention of microbiological breakdown of food, is probably the most important. All methods of food preservation are designed to achieve one or more of these objectives.

Low-Temperature Food Preservation

Low temperatures preserve food products during their flow through the control points of a food service operation. They slow the growth of spoilage organisms and decrease the rate of chemical reactions and enzyme activity. The rate of microbial reproduction decreases as the temperature drops, and eventually stops altogether. There are three kinds of low-temperature food preservation: chilled storage, refrigerated storage, and freezer storage.

Chilled Storage. Temperatures for chilled storage are lower than room temperature but higher than those for refrigerated temperatures. A typical range for chilled storage is between 50°F (10°C) and 59°F (15°C).

Refrigerated Storage. Temperatures for refrigerated storage range from 32°F (0°C) to 41°F (5°C). Check your local regulations. Most food products that are classified as perishable are best stored at refrigerator temperatures. Storage at these temperatures slows the growth rate of spoilage organisms and most pathogenic bacteria.

Freezer Storage. Freezer storage temperatures are generally 0°F (–18°C). These very low temperatures reduce the growth rate of microorganisms even further. One advantage of freezing over refrigeration is that freezing also reduces the a_w (water activity) of food products: when water is converted from liquid to solid form, microbes can no longer use it.

Quick freezing reduces the temperature of a product to –4°F (–20°C) in 30 minutes or less, while slow freezing takes 3 to 72 hours. Quick freezing is more desirable than slow freezing because it better preserves product quality.

High-Temperature Food Preservation

High temperatures are effective in food preservation because they control the growth of microorganisms. When most microbial cells are heated, they are either injured and deactivated or destroyed. There are two methods of high-temperature food preservation: **pasteurization** and **sterilization.**

Pasteurization. Pasteurization temperatures are used either to extend the shelf life of food by reducing spoilage organisms or to destroy all pathogenic microorganisms present in the food. Pasteurization may be done in one of two ways. The holder process of pasteurization involves heating the food product to 145°F (63°C) for 30 minutes. In the **high temperature–short time (HTST)** method of pasteurization, the product is heated to 161°F (72°C) for 15 seconds. Both techniques require the heated food to be immediately cooled to 50°F (10°C) or less. The most common example of pasteurized food is fluid milk. In addition to milk, governments generally require that ice cream mixes and liquid egg products (such as shelled whole eggs) be pasteurized. Canned hams are also pasteurized.

Sterilization. Sterilization destroys virtually all microorganisms and their spores. Once the food is batch-sterilized, or before it is individually sterilized, it must be stored in a hermetically sealed container, such as a can, glass bottle, or jar. With advances in food technology, flexible plastic containers can also be used for sterilized food products as well. Because the food is sterilized and hermetically sealed, it need not be refrigerated until the containers are opened.

Food Preservation by Dehydration

Food **dehydration** may be the oldest method of food preservation. Dehydration is an effective method of preservation because it reduces the a_w of food and thus inhibits microbial activity. There are four methods of drying food: sun drying, mechanical drying, freeze-drying, and drying during smoking.

Sun Drying. This is effective in areas with low humidity and high temperatures.

Mechanical Drying. Food products are prepared for mechanical drying by trimming, washing, and removing the inedible parts. Then heat is applied, usually in combination with moving air.

Freeze-Drying. This technique uses a process known as sublimation—the direct conversion of solid water (ice) to water vapor without the usual intermediate step of melting into a liquid. To freeze-dry a product, the product must first be frozen.

Drying During Smoking. This method is quite slow compared to other means of drying, but its results are unique. Smoking alters the odor, color, appearance, texture, and taste of food products. It also has a tenderizing effect.

Chemical Food Preservation

Chemical food additives have been approved for food preservation applications. These chemical preservatives inhibit the activity of selected pathogens and spoilage organisms. The categories of chemical preservatives are nitrites and nitrates, sugar and salt, sulfur dioxides and sulfites, ethylene and propylene oxides, alcohol, organic acids and their salts, and spices and other condiments. Nitrites, nitrates, and their salts are used in the preservation of meat products. Salt is used in brines in which canned fish, meats, and vegetables are packed, and enhances their flavor. Sugar is found in the syrups in which canned fruits are packed; it also contributes to their flavor.

Sulfiting agents have been used to retard oxidative or enzymatic browning of fruits and vegetables, to inhibit "black spot" on shrimp, and to control gray mold on table grapes. Ethylene and propylene oxides are used to sterilize containers, for example wine bottles and juice packages. Ethanol (ethyl alcohol) is produced by fermentation in wine, beer, and spirits. Organic acids and their salts are sometimes added to food products as preservatives. Spices and other condiments constitute the last class of chemical preservatives.

Food Preservation by Radiation

The use of radiation in food preservation is called "irradiation" and involves exposing food to ultraviolet light, gamma rays, or X rays to destroy harmful organisms. Food irradiation can help extend shelf life by keeping grains from sprouting, deactivating molds, and killing spoilage bacteria. It can also make food safer.

Preservation Methods for Various Types of Foods ─────

Appendixes B through H at the end of the chapter indicate the recommended storage, temperatures, and times for food product categories. The characteristics of each category of food provide insight into the spoilage problems food service companies might encounter. Appendix I at the end of the chapter covers the characteristics, spoilage potential, and control methods for each group of food products.

☞ Key Terms ─────────────────────────

cross-contamination—The process in which a food product becomes contaminated by its contact with a bacteria-carrying non-food source (knives, cutting boards, thermometers, and other equipment).

dehydration—An effective method of preservation that reduces the a_w of food and thus inhibits microbial activity.

enzymes—Proteins that catalyze the breakdown of food products; that is, speed up the rate of autolysis.

high temperature–short time (HTST) pasteurization—The process in which a food product is heated to 161°F (72°C) for 15 seconds, then immediately cooled to 50°F (10°C) or less.

incubation time—The amount of time between consumption of contaminated food and the first symptoms of illness.

infection—A foodborne disease caused by bacteria and viruses that are transmitted in food and later reproduce inside the body.

intoxication—A foodborne disease that results from the ingestion of poisonous plants or animals or of toxin-contaminated food.

pasteurization—A method of high-temperature food preservation in which the product is heated to 145°F (63°C) for 30 minutes or 161°F (72°C) for 15 seconds; it is then immediately cooled to 50°F (10°C) or less.

pathogen—Disease-causing microorganisms; the source of many foodborne diseases.

pH—The standard measure of acidity or alkalinity—the hydrogen ion concentration; an important influence on bacterial activity. Food products with pH values less than 7 are acidic; those with pH values greater than 7 are basic or alkaline. A pH of 7 is neutral.

poisoning—A type of foodborne disease caused by ingesting harmful chemicals, poisonous plant or animal products, or food contaminated with the poisonous waste products (toxins) of toxigenic bacteria or fungi.

potentially hazardous food—Any food or ingredient, natural or synthetic, in a form capable of supporting the rapid and progressive growth of *Clostridium botulinum* or the slower growth of *Salmonella Enteritidis*. Includes any food of animal origin, either raw or heat-treated, and any food of plant origin which has been treated or which is raw seed sprouts.

sterilization—A process that destroys virtually all microorganisms and their spores. Heating for sterilization usually takes place in a large container which is pressurized according to the food product, its ability to withstand heat, and packaging.

temperature danger zone (TDZ)—The temperature range of 41°F (5°C) to 140°F (60°C). The TDZ can vary from one location to another. It is critical that you find out the exact TDZ applicable to your food service operation, and minimize the amount of time food spends in the TDZ during storing, preparing, and serving.

water activity (a_w)—The amount of water available to microorganisms. The water activity value is the ratio of the water vapor pressure in the food to the vapor pressure of pure water at the same temperature.

Review Questions

1. How do pathogens differ from spoilage organisms?

2. What are the four types of microorganisms responsible for most food contamination?

3. What are the two general types of foodborne diseases and their causes?

4. What personal health and hygiene practices must be observed in a food establishment?

5. What are the 11 steps that should be followed in handling a foodborne illness complaint?

6. What are the common causes of food spoilage in a food establishment?

7. What are the four objectives of food preservation?

8. Low-temperature food preservation comprises what three types of storage?

9. What are the two methods of high-temperature food preservation?

10. Why is dehydration an effective method of food preservation? What are the four methods of dehydration?

Appendix A

A Summary of
Pathogenic Microorganisms

Name of Microorganism	Environmental and Food Sources	Incubation Time
Anisakis spp. (Ann-is-ah-kiss)	Saltwater fish (e.g., salmon, striped bass, Pacific snapper)	(Several days)[b]
Bacillus cereus (Bah-sill-us seer-ee-us)	Soil, dust, grains, vegetables, cereal products, puddings, custards, sauces, soups, meatloaf, meat products, boiled or fried rice	15 minutes to 16 hours[a] (1 to 5 hours)[b]
Campylobacter jejuni (Camp-ill-oh-back-ter jeh-june-knee)	Intestinal tract of infected cattle, swine, chickens, turkeys, and other animals. Raw or inadequately cooked or processed foods of animal origin (milk, poultry, clams, hamburger), unchlorinated water	(1 to 7 days or longer)[b]
Clostridium botulinum (Claws-trid-ee-um botch-you-line-um)	Soil, contaminated water, dust, fruits, vegetables, animal feed and manure, honey, sewage, inadequately processed or heated low-acid canned foods, inadequately processed fermented foods, and smoked fish	2 hours to 14 days[a] (12 to 36 hours)[b]
Clostridium perfringens (Claws-trid-ee-um per-frin-jens)	Soil, dust, animal manure, human feces, cooked meat and poultry, meat pies, gravies, stews, soil-grown vegetables, food cooked and cooled slowly in large quantities at room temperatures	6 to 24 hours[a] (8 to 12 hours)[b]
Diphyllobothrium latum (Die-file-oh-bo-three-um late-um)	Freshwater fish (e.g., salmon)	(3 to 6 weeks)[b]
Escherichia coli (Es-cher-ee-chee-ah coal-eye)	Feces of infected humans; air; sewage-contaminated water; cheese; shellfish; watercress, ground beef	8 to 24 hours[a] (11 hours)[b]
Listeria monocytogenes (Lis-teer-ee-ah mon-oh-site-oh-jean-ees)	Widely distributed; contaminated feces, coleslaw, domestic and imported cheeses, chickens, dry sausages, contaminated meat and meat products	(4 days to 3 weeks)[b]
Norwalk virus (Nor-walk)	Fish and shellfish harvested from contaminated waters, infected humans	(24 to 48 hours)[b]

Symptoms	Controls
Irritation of the throat and digestive tract, diarrhea, abdominal pain	1. Purchase food from approved sources. 2. Cook thoroughly. 3. Heavy salting. 4. Freeze food at -4°F (-20°C) for 168 hours.
Nausea, abdominal pain, vomiting, diarrhea	1. Hold foods out of the TDZ. 2. Chill leftover hot foods rapidly to less than 41°F (5°C). 3. Reheat all leftovers to a minimum of 165°F (74°C) for 15 seconds prior to service. (Add 25°F/14°C for microwave cooking.) 4. Serve and eat foods immediately after cooking.
Diarrhea, abdominal pain, fever, malaise, sometimes nausea, headache, urinary tract infection, reactive arthritis	1. Cook foods thoroughly. 2. Properly handle foods. 3. Dry or freeze food products. 4. Add acids.
High fever, dizziness, dry mouth, respiratory difficulties including paralysis, loss of reflexes	1. Destroy the toxin with correct time-temperature combinations. 2. Add acids. 3. Store foods under refrigeration. 4. Add salts during curing. 5. Destroy all bulging cans and their contents. 6. Refuse to serve home-canned foods.
Acute abdominal cramps, diarrhea, dehydration, and prostration (occasionally)	1. Thoroughly clean, cook, and chill food products. 2. Reheat all leftovers to a minimum of 165°F (74°C) for 15 seconds prior to service. (Add 25°F/14°C for microwave cooking.) 3. Hold foods out of the TDZ. 4. Enforce rules of good personal hygiene.
Hard to detect (sometimes anemia)	1. Purchase food from approved sources. 2. Cook thoroughly.
Abdominal pain, diarrhea, fever, chills, headache, blood in the feces, nausea, dehydration, prostration	1. Heat and chill food products rapidly. 2. Enforce rules of good personal hygiene. 3. Control flies. 4. Prepare all food products in a sanitary manner.
Mild and flu-like, headache, vomiting. More severe and possibly death in pregnant women and those with compromised immune systems.	1. Pasteurize or heat-process food products. 2. Avoid recontamination. 3. Refrigerate or freeze dairy products. 4. Properly clean and sanitize equipment.
Fever, headache, abdominal pain, diarrhea, vomiting	1. Purchase food from approved sources. 2. Cook shellfish by steaming for a minimum of 4 minutes. 3. Enforce rules of good personal hygiene and cleanliness. 4. Freeze at -4°F (-20°C) for 168 hours.

Name of Microorganism	Environmental and Food Sources	Incubation Time
Salmonella spp. (Sell-mon-ell-ah species)	Intestinal tract of humans and animals; turkeys, chickens, hogs, cattle, dogs, cats, frogs, turtles, and birds; meat products; egg and poultry products; coconut; yeast; chocolate candy; smoked fish; raw salads; fish; shellfish	5 to 72 hours[a] (12 to 48 hours)[b]
Shigella spp. (Shig-ell-ah species)	Feces of infected humans; direct contact with carriers; contaminated water; uncooked food that is diced, cut, chopped, and mixed; moist and mixed foods (tuna, shrimp, turkey, macaroni and potato salads); milk; beans; apple cider; contaminated produce	1 to 7 days[a] (less than 4 days)[b]
Staphylococcus aureus (Staff-low-cock-us or-ee-us)	In and on human nose and throat discharges, hands and skin, infected wounds and burns, pimples and acne, hair, feces; cooked ham; poultry and poultry dressing; meat products; gravies and sauces; cream-filled pastries; milk; cheese; hollandaise sauce; bread pudding; fish, potato, ham, poultry, and egg salads; high-protein leftover foods	1 to 8 hours[a] (2 to 4 hours)[b]
Trichinella spiralis (Trick-in-ell-ah spur-el-is)	Infected hogs, flesh of bear and walrus	4 to 28 days[a] (9 days)[b]
Vibrio parahaemolyticus (Vib-ree-oh para-heemo-lit-ick-us)	Marine life, sea water, raw foods of marine origin, saltwater fish, shellfish, fish products, salty foods, cucumbers	2 to 48 hours[a] (10 to 20 hours)[b]
virus of infectious hepatitis (in-feck-shus hep-a-tie-tis)	Blood, urine, and feces of human and animal carriers; water; rodents; insects; shellfish; milk; potato salad; cold cuts; frozen strawberries; orange juice; whipped cream cakes; glazed doughnuts; sandwiches	10 to 50 days[a] (30 days)[b]
Yersinia enterocolitica (Your-sin-ee-ah enter-oh-coal-it-ah-kah)	Contaminated raw pork and beef, drinking water, ice cream, raw and pasteurized milk, tofu (soy bean curd)	(3 to 7 days)[b]

[a]Range of reported incubation times.
[b]Usual, average, or most frequently reported incubation time.

Symptoms	Controls
Abdominal pain, diarrhea, fever, chills, vomiting, dehydration, headache, prostration	1. Cook food products thoroughly. 2. Rapidly chill all hot foods. 3. Guard against cross-contamination. 4. Enforce rules of good personal hygiene.
Abdominal pain, diarrhea, fever, chills, headache, blood in feces, nausea, dehydration, prostration	1. Chill and heat food products rapidly. 2. Enforce rules of good personal hygiene. 3. Control flies. 4. Prepare all food products in a sanitary manner.
Vomiting, abdominal cramps, diarrhea, nausea, dehydration, sweating, weakness, prostration	1. Remove ill staff members from food production and handling activities. 2. Enforce rules of good personal hygiene. 3. Handle food products with the utmost care. 4. Thoroughly cook and reheat foods. 5. Rapidly chill and properly refrigerate food products.
Muscle invasion and soreness, weakness, swelling of muscles	1. Heat pork to an internal temperature of 155°F (68°C) or above for 15 seconds. (Add 25°F/14°C for microwave cooking.) 2. Freezing pork will destroy the parasite. 3. Store at 5°F (-15°C) or lower for not less than 20 days.
Abdominal cramps, diarrhea, nausea, vomiting, mild fever, chills, headache, prostration	1. Cook and chill food products properly. 2. Separate raw and cooked foods. 3. Do not rinse food products with sea water.
Fever, nausea, abdominal pain, tired feeling, jaundice, liver infection	1. Purchase all food products from approved sources. 2. Enforce rules of good personal hygiene. 3. Cook foods thoroughly.
Varies with the age of the victim. Digestive upset and acute abdominal pain (children). Acute abdominal disorders, diarrhea, fever, arthritis (adults). Skin and eye infections (both groups).	1. Pasteurize or heat-process food products. 2. Avoid recontamination. 3. Practice proper personal hygiene. 4. Properly clean and sanitize equipment. 5. Obtain food from approved sources.

Appendix B

Recommended Storage Conditions
for Fresh and Frozen Meats

PRODUCT	STORAGE TEMPERATURES	RELATIVE HUMIDITY (Percent)	STORAGE TIMES
Refrigerated Storage			
Beef			
Wholesale Cuts	34 to 36°F (1 to 2°C)	85	1-2 weeks
Portion Cuts	34 to 36°F (1 to 2°C)	85	4-6 days
Ground Beef	34 to 36°F (1 to 2°C)	85	1-2 days
Pork			
Wholesale Cuts	34 to 36°F (1 to 2°C)	85	5 days
Portion Cuts	34 to 36°F (1 to 2°C)	85	3 days
Ground Pork	34 to 36°F (1 to 2°C)	85	1-2 days
Lamb			
Wholesale Cuts	34 to 36°F (1 to 2°C)	85	1 week
Portion Cuts	34 to 36°F (1 to 2°C)	85	3-4 days
Veal			
Wholesale Cuts	34 to 36°F (1 to 2°C)	90	5 days
Portion Cuts	34 to 36°F (1 to 2°C)	90	3 days
Cured Meats	34 to 36°F (1 to 2°C)	75	2 weeks
Variety Meats	34 to 36°F (1 to 2°C)	85	3-5 days
Freezer Storage			
Beef			
Wholesale Cuts	-10 to 0°F (-23 to -18°C)	—	6-10 months
Portion Cuts	-10 to 0°F (-23 to -18°C)	—	4-8 months
Ground Beef	-10 to 0°F (-23 to -18°C)	—	4-6 months
Pork			
Wholesale Cuts	-10 to 0°F (-23 to -18°C)	—	4-8 months
Portion Cuts	-10 to 0°F (-23 to -18°C)	—	2-6 months
Cured/Smoked	-10 to 0°F (-23 to -18°C)	—	1-2 months
Lamb			
Wholesale Cuts	-10 to 0°F (-23 to -18°C)	—	6-10 months
Portion Cuts	-10 to 0°F (-23 to -18°C)	—	4-8 months
Veal			
Wholesale Cuts	-10 to 0°F (-23 to -18°C)	—	4-8 months
Portion Cuts	-10 to 0°F (-23 to -18°C)	—	2-6 months

Appendix C

Recommended Storage Conditions for Fresh and Frozen Poultry

PRODUCT	STORAGE TEMPERATURES	RELATIVE HUMIDITY (Percent)	STORAGE TIMES
Refrigerated Storage			
Chickens			
Whole	28 to 32°F (-2 to 0°C)	85	2-4 days
Pieces	28 to 32°F (-2 to 0°C)	85	1-2 days
Turkeys			
Whole	28 to 32°F (-2 to 0°C)	85	2-4 days
Pieces	28 to 32°F (-2 to 0°C)	85	1-2 days
Ducks	28 to 32°F (-2 to 0°C)	85	2-4 days
Geese	28 to 32°F (-2 to 0°C)	85	2-4 days
Freezer Storage			
Chickens			
Whole	-10 to 0°F (-23 to -18°C)	—	4-10 months
Pieces	-10 to 0°F (-23 to -18°C)	—	3-6 months
Turkeys	-10 to 0°F (-23 to -18°C)	—	4-10 months
Ducks	-10 to 0°F (-23 to -18°C)	—	4-10 months
Geese	-10 to 0°F (-23 to -18°C)	—	4-10 months

Appendix D

Recommended Storage Conditions for Fresh and Frozen Fish and Shellfish

PRODUCT	STORAGE TEMPERATURES	RELATIVE HUMIDITY (Percent)	STORAGE TIMES
Refrigerated Storage			
Finfish			
Fatty	28 to 32°F (-2 to 0°C)	95	1-2 days
Lean	28 to 32°F (-2 to 0°C)	95	1-3 days
Shellfish			
Mollusks	34 to 36°F (1 to 2°C)	85	1-7 days
Crustaceans	30 to 34°F (-1 to 1°C)	90	1-3 days
Freezer Storage			
Finfish			
Fatty	-10 to 0°F (-23 to -18°C)	—	2-6 months
Lean	-10 to 0°F (-23 to -18°C)	—	2-6 months
Shellfish			
Mollusks	-10 to 0°F (-23 to -18°C)	—	2-6 months
Crustaceans	-10 to 0°F (-23 to -18°C)	—	2-6 months

Appendix E

Recommended Storage Conditions for Fresh and Frozen Eggs

PRODUCT	STORAGE TEMPERATURES	RELATIVE HUMIDITY (Percent)	STORAGE TIMES
Refrigerated Storage			
Shell Eggs*	29 to 35°F (-2 to 2°C)	80-85	2-4 weeks
Dried Eggs	35°F (2°C)	minimum	6-12 months
Reconstituted Eggs	29 to 35°F (-2 to 2°C)	80-85	2-4 weeks
Freezer Storage			
Whole Eggs	-10 to 0°F (-23 to -18°C)	—	6-8 months

*Some states do not consider clean, whole, uncracked, odor-free shell eggs potentially hazardous.

Appendix F

Recommended Storage Conditions for Dairy Products

PRODUCT	STORAGE TEMPERATURES	RELATIVE HUMIDITY (Percent)	STORAGE TIMES
Refrigerated Storage			
Butter	32 to 36°F (0 to 2°C)	85	2-4 weeks
Cheese, Hard	38 to 40°F (3 to 4°C)	75	4-6 months
Cheese, Soft	38 to 40°F (3 to 4°C)	75	13-14 days
Fluid Milk	36 to 38°F (2 to 3°C)	85	6-14 days
Reconstituted Dried Milk	36 to 38°F (2 to 3°C)	85	5-8 days
Freezer Storage			
Ice Cream and Frozen Desserts	0 to 10°F (-18 to -12°C)	—	2-4 months
Dry Storage			
Condensed Milk	50 to 70°F (10 to 21°C)	50-60	2-4 months
Evaporated Milk	50 to 70°F (10 to 21°C)	50-60	8-10 months
Dried Milk	50 to 70°F (10 to 21°C)	50-60	8-10 months

Appendix G

Recommended Storage Conditions for Fruits

PRODUCT	STORAGE TEMPERATURES	RELATIVE HUMIDITY (Percent)	STORAGE TIMES
Fresh Fruits			
Apples	30 to 32°F (-1 to 0°C)	85	2-6 months
Grapefruits	32 to 45°F (0 to 7°C)	85	1-2 months
Lemons	46 to 50°F (8 to 10°C)	85	1-4 months
Limes	46 to 50°F (8 to 10°C)	85	1-2 months
Melons	40 to 45°F (4 to 7°C)	85	2-4 weeks
Oranges	32 to 36°F (0 to 2°C)	85	2-3 months
Peaches	30 to 32°F (-1 to 0°C)	85	2-4 weeks
Berries	30 to 32°F (-1 to 0°C)	85	1-2 weeks
Grapes	30 to 32°F (-1 to 0°C)	85	1-2 months
Strawberries	30 to 32°F (-1 to 0°C)	85	4-8 days
Canned Fruits	50 to 72°F (10 to 22°C)	50-60	8-12 months
Frozen Fruits	-10 to 0°F (-23 to -18°C)	—	6-12 months

Appendix H

Recommended Storage Conditions for Vegetables

PRODUCT	STORAGE TEMPERATURES	RELATIVE HUMIDITY (Percent)	STORAGE TIMES
Fresh Vegetables			
Asparagus	32 to 34°F (0 to 1°C)	90	2-4 weeks
Beans	40 to 45°F (4 to 7°C)	85	7-10 days
Cabbage	32 to 34°F (0 to 1°C)	90	2-3 months
Carrots	32 to 34°F (0 to 1°C)	90	1-3 weeks
Cauliflower	32 to 34°F (0 to 1°C)	85	2-3 weeks
Corn	31 to 32°F (-1 to 0°C)	85	4-7 days
Cucumbers	45 to 48°F (7 to 9°C)	90	1-2 weeks
Lettuce	32 to 34°F (0 to 1°C)	90	2-4 weeks
Onions	32 to 34°F (0 to 1°C)	75	5-8 months
Potatoes	50 to 55°F (10 to 13°C)	85	2-4 months
Spinach	32 to 34°F (0 to 1°C)	90	1-2 weeks
Squash, Zucchini	32 to 36°F (0 to 2°C)	85	1-2 weeks
Tomatoes, Ripe	32 to 34°F (0 to 1°C)	85	7-10 days
Canned Vegetables	50 to 70°F (10 to 21°C)	50-60	8-12 months
Frozen Vegetables	-10 to 0°F (-23 to -18°C)	—	6-10 months

Appendix I

A Summary of Food Spoilage

Type of Food	Type of Spoilage/ Indicators	Causative Agents	Control Method(s)
Bakery Products	Rope - odor of ripe melons - yellow crumbs - color change - sticky crumbs - slimy thread-like material	*Bacillus* bacteria (Bah-sill-us)	1. Add acid before baking 2. Fast cooling 3. Freezing 4. Proper and prompt wrapping
	Black color change	*Rhizopus nigricans* mold (Rye-zoe-pus nie-gri-kans)	1. Add propionates before baking 2. Fast cooling 3. Proper and prompt wrapping
	Green color change	*Penicillium expansum* mold (Pen-ah-sill-ee-um ek-spans-um)	1. Add propionates before baking 2. Fast cooling 3. Proper and prompt wrapping 4. Freezing
Dairy Products	Protein breakdown	*Bacillus* bacteria (Bah-sill-us) *Clostridium* bacteria (Claws-trid-ee-um) *Pseudomonas* bacteria (Sood-oh-moan-ahs)	1. Commercially sterilize 2. Pasteurize and refrigerate 3. Dry
	Souring	*Streptococcus lactis* bacteria (Strep-toe-cock-us lack-tis) *Lactobacillus bulgaricus* bacteria (Lack-toe-bah-sill-us bul-gar-ih-kus) *Lactobacillus thermophilus* bacteria (Lack-toe-bah-sill-us therm-ah-fill-us)	1. Commercially sterilize 2. Pasteurize and refrigerate 3. Dry
Eggs	Microbial - green rot (whites) - colorless rot (whole eggs) - black rot (whole eggs)	bacteria	1. Refrigerate 2. Freeze 3. Dry
	Non-microbial - loss of moisture - addition of oxygen - thinning of albumen - weakening of yolk membrane - increase in pH from 7.6 to 9.5	environment (addition of oxygen)	1. Coat shells with colorless, odorless, tasteless mineral oil 2. Refrigerate

Type of Food	Type of Spoilage/ Indicators	Causative Agents	Control Method(s)
Fats and Oils	Autoxidation - oxidative rancidity - addition of oxygen - increased with light, heat, heavy metals, salt - off-odors and flavors	environment (addition of oxygen)	1. Add BHA and/or BHT before baking 2. Wrap properly and promptly
	Hydrolytic rancidity - flavor, odor, taste changes	lipase enzyme (Lie-pays)	1. Heat to destroy
	Flavor reversion - oxidative rancidity - unsaturated vegetable oils - linolenic fatty acid - beany, fishy, paint-like odor	environment (addition of oxygen)	1. Partially hydrogenate
Fruits and Vegetables, canned	Carbon dioxide gas spoilage - swollen cans due to gas production - frothy and slimy contents	*Micrococcus spp.* bacteria (Mike-row-cock-us) *Streptococcus thermophilus* bacteria (Strep-toe-cock-us therm-ah-fill-us)	1. Proper sealing of cans 2. Proper heating during processing
	Flat sour spoilage - flavor change	*Bacillus coagulans* bacteria (Bah-sill-us coe-ag-you-lans)	1. Sufficient time-temperature combination during processing
	Thermophilic gas spoilage - swollen cans due to gas production - flipper, springer, soft swell, hard swell	*Clostridium sporogenes* bacteria (Claws-trid-ee-um spore-ah-jen-ees) *Clostridium putrefaciens* bacteria (Claws-trid-ee-um pyut-rah-face-yens) *Clostridium thermosaccharolyticum* bacteria (Claws-trid-ee-um thermo-sack-ah-roe-lit-ah-cum)	1. Sufficient time-temperature combination during processing
Fruits and Vegetables, fresh	Black rot - color change - sour, bitter flavors - softening	Molds	1. Low temperatures (refrigeration, freezing) 2. Commercial sterilization 3. Dry 4. Use rapidly
	Blue rot - color change - sour, bitter flavors - softening	*Penicillium* mold (Pen-ah-sill-ee-um)	1. Low temperatures (refrigeration, freezing) 2. Commercial sterilization 3. Dry 4. Use rapidly

Type of Food	Type of Spoilage/ Indicators	Causative Agents	Control Method(s)
	Gray rot - color change - flavor change - softening	*Botrytis cinerea* mold (Bow-trite-is sin-er-ee-ah)	1. Low temperatures (refrigeration, freezing) 2. Commercial sterilization 3. Dry 4. Use rapidly
	Soft rot - flavor change - softening - mushy - odorous	*Pseudomonas* bacteria (Sood-oh-moan-ahs)	1. Low temperatures (refrigeration, freezing) 2. Commercial sterilization 3. Dry 4. Use rapidly
Meats	Souring - flavor change - odor change - color change	*Pseudomonas* bacteria (Sood-oh-moan-ahs)	1. Carefully handle 2. Quickly slaughter 3. Rapid chilling 4. Avoid contamination 5. Clean and sanitize equipment
	Surface color/texture changes - fuzziness - stickiness - unacceptable odor, color, taste, texture	*Penicillium* and other molds (Pen-ah-sill-ee-um)	1. Can (commercially sterilize) 2. Pasteurize and store refrigerated 3. Low temperatures (freeze and refrigerate) 4. Carefully wrap
Poultry	Chemical changes and deterioration - stickiness - sliminess - objectionable odor	*Pseudomonas* bacteria (Sood-oh-moan-ahs) *Flavobacterium* bacteria (Flave-oh-back-tear-ee-um) Enzymes Molds	1. Rapid slaughter, then wash with chlorinated water 2. Immediate chilling 3. Low temperatures (refrigerate or freeze) 4. Carefully wrap 5. Commercially sterilize 6. Add organic acids
Seafood	Ammonia-like odor	*Pseudomonas* bacteria (Sood-oh-moan-ahs) *Proteus* bacteria (Pro-tee-us)	1. Immediate chilling 2. Low temperatures (refrigerate or freeze) 3. Carefully wrap 4. Commercially sterilize
	Fruity or unpleasant sweet odor	*Acinetobacter* bacteria (Ah-seen-oh-back-ter) *Aeromonas* bacteria (Air-oh-moan-ahs)	1. Immediate chilling 2. Low temperatures (refrigerate or freeze) 3. Carefully wrap 4. Commercially sterilize

Chapter 3 Outline

The Menu Planning Control Point
    Menu Planning and Inventory
    Menu Planning and People
    Menu Planning and Equipment
    Menu Planning and Facilities
    Changing the Menu
    Truth-in-Menu Regulations
    Menu Planning and Food Safety
The Purchasing Control Point
    Purchasing and Inventory
    Purchasing and People
    Purchasing and Equipment
    Purchasing and Facilities
    Purchasing and Change
    Purchasing and Food Safety

Competencies

1. Describe the relationship between menu planning and inventory, and note the effects of rationalization, diversification, and convenience foods. (pp. 67–69)

2. Identify important staff member considerations at the menu planning control point. (pp. 69–70)

3. Identify important equipment and facilities considerations at the menu planning control point. (pp. 70–72)

4. Identify factors that influence menu changes. (pp. 72–75)

5. Identify factors that influence purchasing needs, and list the functions of the purchasing control point. (pp. 75–76)

6. Explain the relationship between purchasing and inventory. (pp. 76–81)

7. Outline the skills of a successful buyer, including what one should know about dealing with suppliers. (pp. 81–88)

8. Explain how a buyer can reduce risks at the purchasing control point. (p. 88)

3

The Menu Planning and Purchasing Control Points

IN THIS CHAPTER we will discuss the menu planning and purchasing control points of the food safety risk management program, including truth-in-menu regulations, food safety concerns, and how inventory, people, equipment, and facilities affect these control points.

The Menu Planning Control Point

Menu planning is the first control point in the food service system. In many respects, the menu is the mission statement for a food establishment. It defines the operation's concept and communicates that concept to guests. The menu attempts to provide what guests expect from their overall hospitality experience. It also serves as a plan for the entire food service system. The success of menu planning determines the success of the other basic operating activities.

When a menu is presented to a guest, a sales transaction begins. If properly designed, the menu can stimulate sales and increase the guest check average. The menu also presents an image of the establishment. Therefore, the appearance of the menu should be in harmony with the image the food establishment wants to project. The image may be elegant, businesslike, fun, ethnic, or trendy, depending on the target markets. The physical condition of the menu is also important. Dirty, worn, out-of-date, or unattractive menus indicate management's lack of concern for the establishment's image. Because they create a negative first impression, such menus should be discarded. Someone should be responsible for checking the condition of each menu before each meal period begins.

Guests are influenced by visual cues provided by the menu, such as design and layout, artwork, and type styles. As with other communication tools, the way the information is conveyed is as important as the information itself. For example, fast-food restaurants offer a limited number of menu items but sell these items in large quantities. Since guests are served at a common sales counter, separate menus are not needed. Most guests are familiar with the standardized menu offerings, so long, elaborate descriptions are unnecessary; they would only slow down the guests' decision-making process. Fast-food restaurants simply post the names and prices of their products near the sales counter. Enlarged color photographs of menu items show their color and texture and thus may contribute to increased sales. (However, it is important that the items served look like the pictured items.) The overall effect is to convey simplicity, speed, and a limited selection of products prepared the same way at every unit.

On the other hand, a specialty restaurant catering to wealthy, sophisticated guests would have an altogether different menu. To project an image of elegance, such a restaurant might have a menu as large as a book, with detailed descriptions of a wide range of food products. This type of menu offers guests a feeling of endless possibilities. Since the establishment's guests probably seek a leisurely and pleasurable dining experience, the time it takes them to peruse a large menu is no problem.

Another element distinguishes the menu of an elegant restaurant from that of a fast-food restaurant: prices. Prices are sometimes omitted from extensive menus due to seasonal fluctuations in the cost of some items. In such cases, the management assumes either that money is no object or that, if it is, guests will inquire about current prices. When setting menu prices, it is important to remember that today's sophisticated guest is searching for the best price-value relationship. If an operation's prices far exceed the perceived value of its menu items, guests are unlikely to return.

To draw attention to daily specials and highlight signature items, some restaurants box these items on the menu. Another way to increase sales of featured items is to write them on an illuminated board near the entrance. Some restaurants specializing in fresh seafood use a chalkboard to list the flight arrival times of the jet-fresh catch of the day. While this approach sacrifices a degree of elegance, it provides convincing evidence of the freshness and variety of the operation's offerings.

Generally, dynamic menus are preferable to static menus. However, menu variability depends on the seasonal availability of raw ingredients, the number and kinds of courses offered, the potential for using leftovers and local ingredients, the operation's image, and the demands of its target markets. In many respects, the menu is never complete; menu planning is an ongoing process.

Menu Planning and Inventory

Inventory is the total supply of items an operation has in stock. The menu helps create demand for the finished food products prepared from the items in inventory. The guest's order depletes the inventory on hand. The operation must periodically replenish the inventory if it is to continue offering the items guests are buying. It is important to keep detailed records on the relative popularity of every menu item. This information is useful at the purchasing control point, the next step of the food service system.

The menu directly affects the establishment's purchasing, receiving, and storage requirements. The size of storage areas needed for raw ingredients and finished menu items depends on the menu. One of the primary advantages of a limited menu is that it reduces storage area requirements.

In the past, food service managers attempted to diversify their menus, offering a wide variety of items. Since most items were made on-site, the number and variety of raw ingredients needed increased significantly with each new item.

Today, there is a trend toward **rationalization** of menu items: the creation of a simplified, balanced menu for the sake of operational efficiency and guest satisfaction. Although this strategy frequently results in a limited menu, the operation can offer several menu items which use the same raw ingredients. The objective of this **cross-utilization** is to prepare and serve as many menu items as possible with a limited number of raw ingredients. Planning the menu to ensure a balance of menu selections in each category helps streamline the purchasing, receiving, and storing functions.

The decision of whether or not to diversify the menu is driven to a great extent by guest demands. Guests who dine out frequently are looking for diversity in menu choices. Some food service operators reason that, due to increased competition, they must diversify in order to build guest loyalty and repeat business, expand business into new meal periods, and draw on a wider guest base. However, while a constantly changing menu offers variety, it can cause confusion in the operation and result in lowered food safety and quality standards. Alternatives to extensive diversification include highlighting items on the existing menu and adding a few daily specials.

Proponents of menu rationalization say that a food establishment should discover what it does best and continually refine it. Menu diversification requires additional staff training and additional time for taking orders and answering guest questions. Perhaps the best strategy is to create a balanced menu by choosing items from a limited inventory—in other words, create a rational, consolidated menu that maximizes cross-utilization.

The proliferation of high-quality **convenience foods** has made it easier for food service operations to offer new items without buying additional raw ingredients or elaborate equipment. High-quality convenience products can be purchased in semi- or fully-prepared forms. These products reduce in-house labor requirements. Of course, convenience food products usually have a higher AP (as-purchased) price than the raw ingredients from which they are made.

It is always best to base initial menu plans on the needs and expectations of the target markets. Several other factors may influence the selection of menu items as well. Among these factors are recommended storage conditions; staff member skill levels; product availability and seasonality; the stability of quality and price levels; and the operation's ability to purchase, prepare, and serve the menu item safely.

Menu Planning and People

An operation's staff members are important to the success of its menu. Before management begins menu planning, the skill levels of production and service staff must be assessed. It may be helpful to consider the production staff and service staff separately, although their functions are closely related in practice.

The production staff produces menu items within the confines of the kitchen. In planning the operation's menu, the objective is to avoid overloading any one person or work station. A well-planned menu features items that the operation's kitchen staff can consistently produce while maintaining the operation's quality, cost, and food safety standards.

Management should be realistic in determining what can be accomplished with the existing staff. For example, consider a kitchen in a metropolitan hotel where every menu item is prepared from scratch. If all meats are received in the wholesale-cut form (which is less expensive than the retail- or portion-cut form), the staff has to do the retail butchering. If the production staff is not properly trained in butchering wholesale cuts into retail cuts of meat, a lot of time and money will be wasted, and unnecessary food safety hazards will abound. Rather than saving the business money, this poorly conceived arrangement increases the food cost, adds to the labor cost, and destroys the quality control system. Such problems can be avoided by organizing the menu planning function with personnel limitations in mind.

The service staff transfers the menu items from the production staff to the guests. In order to properly serve guests, servers should be ready to answer their questions. For example, servers should know what items are on the menu, the portion sizes offered, how the items are prepared, and the prices. Even if the menu contains all of this information, a server can provide a personal touch by answering guests' questions directly. Servers should also know the meanings of all terms used on the menu so they can explain them to any guests who are puzzled. This is particularly important if the menu includes ethnic foods, since these items may be unfamiliar to the average guest.

Again, staff training is critical. In addition to thoroughly training new servers, some managers call a five- to ten-minute **line-up meeting** with production and/or service staff members before each meal period. These brief meetings are informal training sessions. They give the chef and the manager an opportunity to explain daily specials, and they give the staff members the opportunity to sample portions of new menu items and to ask questions.

Like the skill levels of production staff, the skills of service staff must be considered in menu planning. This is particularly true if management is considering menu items to be prepared in the dining room, such as tossed salads and flambéed desserts. Whether an operation uses tableside preparation methods depends, in part, on the image it seeks. Whatever style of service an operation offers, the service staff must be trained in the skills dictated by the menu.

Suppliers must also be considered when planning a menu. Although suppliers are not, strictly speaking, under the manager's control, they can contribute to the success of the business. Particularly at the menu planning control point, their input and suggestions can help make the business more profitable while enhancing the guests' satisfaction. For example, suppliers can offer preparation and merchandising suggestions for various menu items. Excellent food service operations view their suppliers as partners and use their suppliers as sources of market trend information, new promotion ideas, and informal competitive analyses.

Menu Planning and Equipment

Any food service operation must make a large investment in equipment before it can open for business. Naturally, the amount and type of production and service equipment owned by the business determines what items it can produce and place on the menu. It is imperative to select equipment based on capacity, skill levels of staff members, energy and maintenance costs, and initial purchase price. Equipment should be constructed according to nationally recognized food safety standards and/or be listed by accredited testing and listing organizations. But above all, it is critical that equipment be easy to clean and sanitize.

Adding a new menu item may require purchasing new production equipment. Such purchases should not be made without an analysis of the flow of products and people through the work area. This analysis helps management anticipate where cross-traffic may create hazards. Many operations use equipment on wheels or casters which can be moved easily when necessary. In addition to allowing for adjustments to the product and staff traffic patterns, this mobility facilitates cleaning. Before a new menu item is added, the proper equipment should be available to reduce food safety hazards. For example, if the proposed menu change involves adding a soup bar to the dining room, the kitchen must have adequate steam-table, steam-jacketed kettle, or range equipment to reach and maintain safe product temperatures during preparing and cooking.

A change in menu may also have implications for the operation's service equipment. Again, the food safety hazards must be considered beforehand. In the case of the soup bar, for example, the dining room should be equipped with suitable hot-holding equipment before these new items are added to the menu.

A dramatically modified menu can have a devastating effect on the system if proper equipment is not available. Consider what might happen if the owner of a bar that serves a wide selection of drinks and cold snack foods decides to add hot barbecued meatballs to the snack food menu. She realizes that equipment to produce and hold the product is necessary; however, she fails to realize the significance of the serving containers. She chooses reusable dishes, thinking that these will be less expensive in the long run than disposable containers. Making a hasty decision on cost alone, the owner neglects to consider the fact that if the meatballs are served in reusable containers, proper provisions must be made for washing, sanitizing, and storing the dishes. It is not acceptable to wash the sauce-laden meatball dishes in the bar's glass-washing equipment. In the end, she realizes that the addition of this new food item is an expensive endeavor.

The addition of banquet service to a traditional food service operation must also be carefully considered in light of the additional constraints banquets place on menu planning and equipment. For example, if a hotel is planning to serve a banquet for 800, all of the food items cannot be dished for all 800 guests immediately prior to service. Therefore, extra hot-holding and cold storage equipment is essential. The hotel must also limit its banquet menu to items which can safely withstand the extra handling and holding times involved.

Menu Planning and Facilities

Both indoor and outdoor facilities affect the image of an establishment. The layout and design of the facilities are also important considerations in menu planning, because they establish the physical limits within which food preparation and service take place. The facilities must be adequate for the purchasing, receiving, storing, issuing, preparing, cooking, holding, and serving of every item on the menu. Thus, a major change in the menu may necessitate remodeling the physical facilities. By the same token, a change in facilities may force an operation to revise its menu. This mutual influence can be illustrated by the following examples.

Consider a country club food service operation in which 80 percent of the space is allocated to the dining room and 20 percent to the kitchen. Since the kitchen generally prepares menu items from scratch, the production facilities are often pushed to the limit. The kitchen facilities are almost always overtaxed during the summer, when there are more parties and special functions.

Suppose the country club manager decides to expand the dining and banquet facilities by adding a 90-seat patio service area with a clear glass roof. He is convinced that this area will appeal to guests planning parties and banquets because it offers a breathtaking view of the golf course. However, the manager has not considered the production capabilities of the kitchen; to increase the dining facilities without adding to the production area would be a critical error. Such a decision would likely result in lower productivity and morale among production staff. A corresponding reduction in guest satisfaction could be expected to follow.

Another hotel decides to add room service in an attempt to generate more revenue. Again, the size and layout of the facility have an impact on the success of the effort. For example, the kitchen might produce a beautiful and tasty eggs Benedict entrée for breakfast, but by the time room service delivers the order to the farthest wing of the hotel, the product is cold and unappealing. Room service menus must be limited to those items that can be successfully and safely delivered to the guest.

Yet another problem occurs when an overly ambitious hotel sales force convinces meeting planners that special entrées or desserts will add a touch of elegance to their banquets. These salespeople sometimes fail to consider the limitations of the hotel's production and service facilities. Likewise, an outdoor barbecue for 500 people in the hotel's gardens may sound like an exciting affair, but if the kitchen or service staff cannot deliver the products, the guests will not be satisfied.

In all of these examples, the unfortunate results could be prevented. An operation must design its menu around what the physical facilities can realistically handle. Menu planning is a complex process, but it can be successful when the establishment's resources are taken into consideration.

Changing the Menu

Because conditions change, a food service operation's menu must also change. Menu changes are influenced by both external and internal factors.

External factors include guest demands, economic factors, the competition, supply levels, and industry trends. Guest demands are perhaps the most important factor to consider in changing a menu. Management should first decide which potential markets it wants to attract with a modified menu. The proposed menu change should then be evaluated in light of its potential impact on the current markets.

Economic factors include the cost of ingredients and the potential profitability of new menu items. The competition's menu offerings can also influence menu decisions. For example, a hotel food service operation located next door to a restaurant offering the "best Chinese food in town" might elect not to serve Chinese cuisine. Supply levels affect the price and the quality and quantity of the proposed menu items. Supply levels are highly variable for some seasonal raw ingredients such as fresh fruits and vegetables. Industry trends are general observations about how the industry is responding to new demands. At present, the overall trend is to attempt to satisfy a more sophisticated, value-conscious guest.

Internal factors that may result in a proposed menu change are the facility's meal pattern, concept and theme, operational system, and menu mix. The typical meal pattern is breakfast, lunch, and dinner. Management must decide if existing meal periods should be continued or altered. The target markets' expectations directly influence this decision. Any menu change must also be compatible with the establishment's concept and theme; a restaurant that is known as the best steakhouse in the city may do itself a disservice by offering fewer steak selections in order to add fresh fish and shellfish to the menu. An establishment's image may also rule out certain foods which do not blend with its theme and decor.

Menu changes are also modified by the establishment's operational system. For example, a menu change may raise both food and labor costs to unacceptable levels. The production and service staff members may lack the necessary skills to produce and present the new menu item. If extensive new equipment is crucial to the successful production and service of a new item, the change may be too costly. Many operations deal with this factor by designing flexible kitchens with multi-purpose equipment. For example, a combination convection oven/steamer can bake, roast, and steam. Tilt skillets can be used for baking, braising, frying, griddling, or steaming.

An operation's existing menu has a certain overall combination or mix of items. This menu mix will be affected by any change in individual items. All of these factors should be evaluated before menu changes are finalized.

Truth-in-Menu Regulations

Due to rising consumerism, **truth-in-menu regulations** are an increasingly important menu planning consideration around the globe. According to truth-in-menu regulations, accurate descriptions of raw ingredients and finished menu items are essential. For example, the correct quality or grade of food products must be stated; care must be exercised when grades are printed on the menu. It is also important that items billed as "fresh" have not been frozen, canned, or preserved in any way. A product's point of origin must also be represented accurately; for example, "fresh Lake Superior whitefish" should indeed be fresh whitefish from Lake Superior. A sample list of common points of origin is presented in Exhibit 1.

The size, weight, and portion advertised on the menu must also be accurate. A bowl of soup should contain more than a cup of soup. Descriptions like "extra tall" drinks or "extra large" salads can open the door to possible guest complaints. "All you can eat" implies that the guest is entitled to exactly that: as much as he or she can eat. For meat items, it is a generally accepted practice to list the precooked weight.

The preparation technique must be accurately described. If there are additional charges for extras (such as substitutions or coffee refills), such charges must be clearly stated on the menu. Any pictures of food products should be accurate.

Exhibit 1 Typical Representations of Point of Origin

Dairy Products

Danish Bleu Cheese
Domestic Cheese
Imported Swiss Cheese
Roquefort Cheese
Wisconsin Cheese

Fish and Shellfish

Cod, Icelandic (North Atlantic)
Crab
    Alaskan King Crab
    Florida Stone Crab
    North Atlantic Crab
    Snow Crab
Frog Legs
    Domestic Frog Legs
    Imported Frog Legs
    Louisiana Frog Legs
Lobster
    Australian Lobster
    Brazilian Lobster
    Maine Lobster
    South African Lobster
Oysters
    Blue Point Oysters
    Chesapeake Bay Oysters
    Olympia Oysters
Salmon
    Nova Scotia Salmon
    Puget Sound Sockeye Salmon
    Salmon Lox
Scallops
    Bay Scallops
    Sea Scallops

Scrod, Boston
Shrimp
    Bay Shrimp
    Gulf Shrimp
Trout
    Colorado Brook Trout
    Idaho Brook Trout
Whitefish, Lake Superior

Meats

Beef, Colorado
Ham
    Country Ham
    Danish Ham
    Imported Ham
    Smithfield Ham
    Virginia Style Ham
Pork, Iowa

Poultry

Long Island Duckling
Maryland Milk-Fed Chicken

Vegetables and Fruits

Orange Juice, Florida
Pineapples
    Hawaiian Pineapples
    Mexican Pineapples
Potatoes
    Idaho Potatoes
    Maine Potatoes

Dietary or nutritional claims, if used, must be precise. "Low calorie," for example, is vague because it implies that the product is lower in calories but does not specify what the product is being compared to. Servers' descriptions should also accurately portray the menu selections.

Some chains (for example, KFC and McDonald's) have developed descriptive brochures and pamphlets that provide nutritional information on their products. This information is available upon request; however, most participating chains report little guest interest. While such brochures may be useful and interesting to only a relatively small number, the information should be available to those who request it. Some people use this information to avoid allergenic foods; others simply like to know exactly what they are eating.

The food service industry argues that package labeling is too time-consuming and expensive because of the space it requires. For example, a pizza restaurant offering four sizes and twelve different toppings would need over 4,000 different package labels. The industry also questions the ability of a "typical customer" to analyze scientific data (for example, milligrams of sodium). The government and private interest groups argue that it is time to provide consumers with information that could help them improve their health. In addition, labeling would enable individuals who are allergic to certain foods to avoid them.

Whether you are for or against mandatory labeling of fast food or food in all restaurants, your guests will ultimately decide how important this information is to them. Be aware of their needs and expectations, and consider what might happen if you ignore them: they may choose to spend their money elsewhere.

Menu Planning and Food Safety

Menu planning sets the direction for each of the other control points. Thus, the food safety risk management program begins with menu planning. Management must consider each menu item in light of possible food safety hazards at every control point. Once potential hazards are identified, risks can be reduced. Several questions must be considered before the menu planning process is complete. Can the operation procure the necessary raw ingredients from safe, approved sources? Can the raw ingredients be received and stored easily? Is the production staff able to prepare the menu items efficiently and safely? Can the finished products be served safely? All of these factors are important in menu planning decisions.

The Purchasing Control Point

Once menu planning is completed, purchasing is the next step in the flow of basic operating activities. The menu determines what ingredients must be purchased and in what amounts. One of the major objectives of purchasing is to obtain the right quality and quantity of items at the right price from the right supplier. The goals are to maintain quality and value, strengthen the establishment's competitive position, and minimize the investment in inventory.

Purchasing is one of the most important control points for cost and quality controls. Most food service businesses spend 30 to 50 percent of their total sales revenues on product purchasing. Reducing purchasing costs can translate directly to the operation's bottom line. Failing to properly control food costs can have a more devastating effect than overspending in most other cost categories. It is not surprising that the primary concern of many operators is their food costs. Rising food costs often force management to re-examine the operation's purchasing needs.

In addition to the menu, several other factors dictate purchasing needs. The forecasted sales volume is an estimate of how much business a facility will have on a given day. This information, along with the operation's standard recipes, can be used to calculate the amounts of ingredients needed. Certain external factors also affect purchasing needs. The size and frequency of orders, for example, are affected by how much lead time the supplier requires before a delivery can be made. The facility's distance from the supplier may also affect quantities purchased. For example, a steakhouse located high in the mountains or in a rural area would probably receive less frequent deliveries than a steakhouse in a downtown metropolitan area. More frequent deliveries usually mean smaller orders, which results in less money tied up in inventory.

Of course, the quantities of food ordered and the money invested in inventory are not the only purchasing concerns. Quality and food safety standards must also be considered at this control point. A low-quality or unsafe product is never a bargain, no matter how inexpensive it is. It can unnecessarily increase the operation's risks.

The factors affecting purchasing needs are directly related to the functions of the purchasing control point. These purchasing functions are:

- Establishing and maintaining an adequate supply of food and non-food products

- Minimizing the operation's investment in inventory

- Maintaining the operation's quality, food safety, and cost standards while reducing risks

- Maintaining the operation's competitive position

- Buying the product, not the deal

Each of these purchasing objectives will be discussed as it relates to the four resources under a manager's control.

Purchasing and Inventory

Many functions of the food service operation can be delayed or stopped entirely if the necessary quantity and quality of inventory is not available. As Exhibit 2 illustrates, the purchasing department plays a major role in the flow of products through the food service facility. The overall goal of purchasing is to obtain quality food and non-food items in the proper quantities at a reasonable price. To reach this goal, buyers have many tools at their disposal. The first tool is a set of standard purchase specifications.

Standard purchase specifications precisely define the quality, quantity, and other characteristics of the products an establishment buys. Standard purchase specifications are communication tools. They require management to define exactly what is needed; thus they eliminate supplier confusion and facilitate the bidding process. A sample standard purchase specification format is presented in Exhibit 3. Note that the form calls for precise details in describing the product. These specifications can be developed by a management team consisting of the food and beverage director, the executive chef, the buyer, and other users. Although it might take this team some time to develop standard purchase specifications for all products normally purchased by the operation, the results are well worth the investment of time. Once they are developed, the specifications can be used over and over again and are especially useful for new suppliers, menu changes, and quality control.

Exhibit 2   Overview of Purchasing Activities

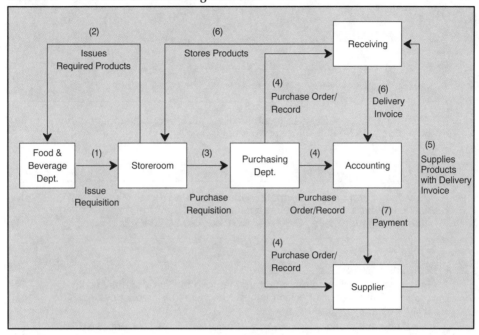

The standard purchase specification defines quality with government grades or brand names. For example, the "fancy" or "A" government grade indicates a certain quality level in fruits and vegetables. Likewise, the quality of Heinz tomato ketchup, Swift's Premium ham, and Minor's beef base are implied by their brand names. Quantity may be indicated as the number of units per container, box, or case, and by the size of standardized containers (for example, #10 cans). Other descriptions complete the standard purchase specification, telling the supplier exactly what kind of product is desired.

Standard purchase specifications are only useful if they accurately reflect the particular needs of the operation. Although several specification manuals are available, the general specifications in these references should be modified as necessary. In-house kitchen or performance tests can be used to alter general specifications to fit the establishment's needs. Market conditions which affect availability may also modify an operation's specifications. Ultimately, standard purchase specifications for each product must be based on the intended use of the product.

A second tool available to buyers is the **food sample data sheet** (see Exhibit 4). This form helps standardize the evaluations of products that an operation is considering for purchase. It can be used to record purchasing, storing, preparing, and serving information about such products. Note that this sheet can also be used to request nutritional and ingredient analysis information. The food sample data sheet makes product selection more objective and less likely to be the result of a buyer's personal preferences.

Exhibit 3   Purchase Specification Format

(Name of food and beverage operation)

1. Product name: _____

2. Product used for:

> Clearly indicate product use (such as olive garnish for beverage and hamburger patty to be grilled for sandwich).

3. Product general description:

> Provide general quality information about desired product. For example, "iceberg lettuce; heads to be green, firm without spoilage, excessive dirt, or damage. No more than 10 outer leaves; packed 24 heads per case."

4. Detailed description:

> Purchaser should state other factors that help to clearly identify desired product. Examples of specific factors, which vary by product being described, may include:
>
> | | | |
> |---|---|---|
> | • Geographic origin | • Product size | • Medium of pack |
> | • Variety | • Portion size | • Specific gravity |
> | • Type | • Brand name | • Container size |
> | • Style | • Density | • Edible yield, trim |
> | • Grade | | |

5. Product test procedures:

> Test procedures occur at time product is received and as or after product is prepared or used. For example, products to be at a refrigerated temperature upon delivery can be tested with a thermometer. Portion-cut meat patties can be randomly weighed. Lettuce packed 24 heads per case can be counted.

6. Special instructions and requirements:

> Any additional information needed to clearly indicate quality expectations can be included here. Examples include bidding procedures, if applicable, labeling and packaging requirements, and special delivery and service requirements.

Once standard purchase specifications are developed and suppliers are selected, a third tool—the **purchase order**—assists in maintaining purchasing control. The purchase order contains the details of an order placed with a supplier.

Exhibit 4   Food Sample Data Sheet

1. Product: _____

2. Brand Name: _____

3. Presented By: _____   Date:_____

4. Varieties Available: _____

5. Shelf Life: (Frozen) _____   (Thawed, Refrigerated, Dry)_____

6. Preparation and Sanitation Considerations:_____

_____

_____

_____

7. Menu Suggestions: _____

8. Merchandising Aids Available (Poster, Table Tents, etc.): _____

9. Case Size (Number of Portions): _____

10. Portion Size:_____

11. Distributed By: _____

12. Minimum Order: _____

13. Any Additional Ordering Information: _____

_____

14. Lead Time: _____

15. Approximate Price Per Serving:_____

NOTE: Were the following information sheets received with products?

    a. Nutritional and Ingredient Analysis: Yes _____   No _____

    b. Specification Sheet: Yes _____   No _____

This standard form is filled in by the operation's buyer and sent to the supplier. A copy of the purchase order is retained to facilitate in-house recordkeeping. A sample purchase order is displayed in Exhibit 5.

Government agencies provide guidelines for obtaining food supplies. These guidelines serve to prevent both food spoilage and contamination. For example, in the United States, home-canned products such as fruits, vegetables, and meats may not be stored in or served by a food service business because home-canned products are not prepared by processors licensed and inspected by governmental agencies. Unpasteurized (raw) milk cannot be served in a food service facility. Fish and shellfish may be purchased only from sources approved by the United States government. Egg products are expected to undergo preservation processing and

Exhibit 5   Purchase Order

Purchase Order Number: _____		Order Date: _____

Purchase Order
Number: _____

Order Date: _____

Payment Terms: _____

To: _____
(supplier)

From/
Ship to: _____
(name of food service operation)

_____

_____

_____
(address)

_____
(address)

Delivery Date: _____

Please Ship:

Quantity Ordered	Description	✓	Units Shipped	Unit Cost	Total Cost

Total Cost _____

Important: This Purchase Order expressly limits acceptance to the terms and conditions stated above, noted on the reverse side hereof, and any additional terms and conditions affixed hereto or otherwise referenced. Any additional terms and conditions proposed by seller are objected to and rejected.

_____
Authorized Signature

handling under carefully controlled conditions. Rigorous requirements are imposed on all of these products because they are common food sources of pathogenic bacteria.

An operation should never purchase a product after the expiration date printed on the package has passed. Suppliers should employ the **first-in, first-out (FIFO) inventory system;** however, once a food service operation buys, uses, and sells a bad product, it is liable for any resulting damages.

Another important inventory item is water. While it is used in more food recipes than any other item purchased by a food service business, the quality of water is often taken for granted in developed countries. Check with your regulatory authorities for additional regulations affecting your food service operation.

Purchasing and People

A number of people have responsibilities related to the purchasing control point; however, purchasing itself is a management function. Hotels often have a full-time purchasing agent, or, if the hotel is large, a purchasing department responsible for all food and non-food buying. Of course, not all operations need a full-time buyer. In smaller operations, the manager or a key assistant (such as the assistant manager, executive chef, steward, or food and beverage director) might serve as a part-time buyer. The buyer is responsible for the operation's purchasing control point.

The Successful Buyer. To be successful, the buyer must possess many skills, including managerial and technical skills and knowledge. Managerial skills are necessary because the buyer is a part of the operation's management team. He or she must understand the establishment's present position and its short- and long-term goals. This knowledge assists the buyer in carrying out purchasing activities according to management's overall plan.

Technical knowledge enables the buyer to do a more efficient job. Textbooks, trade journals, industry associations, and the operation's suppliers are good sources of new information on food marketing, packaging, distribution, and product yields. The buyer's level of technical expertise also depends upon his or her knowledge of the operation's quality, food safety, and cost standards, and of which products meet these standards. A certain amount of purchasing experience might be necessary to develop these skills.

The buyer should also have good interpersonal skills and high ethical standards. Interpersonal skills are critical because the buyer must be a communicator; he or she regularly interacts with department heads, staff members in the purchasing department, and other management staff. The buyer's communication skills are also important when working with suppliers. Ethical standards may be difficult to specify, but certainly honesty and trustworthiness are two important considerations. Ethical standards lead to credibility, an essential element in today's business environment. A buyer frequently faces temptation in the form of opportunities for personal rebates and under-the-table kickbacks. It is management's responsibility to spot-check the purchasing function to keep the buyer honest. Unannounced checks also provide a stimulus for the buyer to avoid compromising the establishment's food safety, quality, and cost control standards.

To perform well, a buyer must accomplish the five functions of purchasing. Although the amount of time devoted to purchasing can vary with the facility's size, all five functions are addressed by a well-planned purchasing control point. First, the buyer is responsible for maintaining adequate inventory levels, in order to reduce or eliminate stockouts which inconvenience production staff and disappoint guests. Second, the buyer should minimize the operation's investment in inventory. There are two reasons for this: excessive inventories promote spoilage and potential contamination, and they tie up funds without earning interest. Third, the buyer must maintain the operation's quality, food safety, and cost standards. Fourth, the buyer must work to maintain the operation's competitive position. And fifth, the buyer must purchase the product, not the deal. He or she should never compromise the establishment's standards for a better price.

The buyer is responsible for conducting negotiations with the operation's suppliers. The negotiations typically cover the as-purchased (AP) price, quantities to be purchased, delivery schedules, and other supplier services. An intimate knowledge of the establishment's standards and product needs is necessary if the buyer is to obtain acceptable products. The buyer must communicate quality, food safety, and cost standards to suppliers. He or she should also keep suppliers informed of ways in which they can improve their services to the operation. Good relationships with suppliers help guarantee that the buyer will get the best value each supplier can offer.

Of course, suppliers cannot always fill orders promptly. Some buyers have circumvented this problem by establishing a reciprocal relationship with competitors. Under such an agreement, when a competitor is temporarily out of a product, the operation supplies it from its own stock until the competitor's order is shipped in. When the operation runs out of a product, the buyer can then call on the competitor and request a temporary loan.

Suppliers. Suppliers are another human component of the purchasing function. The role of suppliers has changed significantly in recent years. In the past, most suppliers distributed certain categories of food products or supplies, such as produce, meats, dairy products, or coffee. Today, however, many suppliers have evolved into full-line or one-stop shopping distributors. This food service distribution concept is known as the **master distributor** concept. Many of the full-line distributors carry from 5,000 to 10,000 different products. One master distributor may be able to satisfy 90 to 100 percent of an operation's purchasing needs. Many businesses currently purchase most of their supplies from a small number of full-line distributors who sell meat, produce, fresh fish, canned foods, frozen foods, cleaning supplies, paper products, flowers, utensils, and kitchen equipment. Larger operations may still buy a few specialty items (for example, exotic fruits and vegetables or dairy products) from specialty suppliers. However, a full-line distributor can usually satisfy all the purchasing needs of a small business.

This one-stop purchasing arrangement increases product consistency and provides purchasing leverage for the facility. It also builds the supplier's trust in the operation and gives management more time for other responsibilities. Furthermore, master distributors often provide services that a specialist cannot offer. These additional services include menu consulting, staff member training programs and seminars, and new product presentations. These advantages make it likely that the master distributor concept will continue to increase in popularity.

One of the disadvantages of the master distributor is that deliveries tend to be weekly rather than daily. This means that planning is more important, both in terms of inventory levels and storage space. For extremely perishable products, a specialty supplier may be the distributor of choice if more frequent deliveries can be obtained.

Regardless of whether a specialty or full-line distributor is used, the establishment should periodically evaluate its suppliers based on the following criteria:

- Food safety policies

- Size and services

- Staff and labor relations

- Purchasing power and financial position

- Products and prices

- Reputation

- Value

A supplier's food safety policies can easily be spot-checked through periodic informal, unannounced visits to the distributor's warehouse or processing plant. The food service operation's representative should check to see if the operation is clean and adequately maintained by taking a walking tour of the facility. The person who receives deliveries can periodically inspect the supplier's delivery vehicles as food is unloaded. Refrigerated and frozen products must be delivered in vehicles equipped with refrigerated storage. Government agencies may be able to provide the food establishment with a general impression of the distributor's facilities based on past inspections. Above all, the supplier must be approved— that is, acceptable to the regulatory authority. Always check with your federal and local officials for guidelines pertaining to approved sources.

The size of the distributing company must be adequate to meet the operation's needs. Supplier services include arranging delivery schedules at the food service operation's convenience, which can help the operation avoid both the overcrowding of storage areas and stockouts. Most suppliers are also willing to carry unusual items as a special service to the operation if these items are needed on a regular basis. Other supplier services include a computer printout of all the products ordered during a given period (such as a week, a month, or a year). This report, called a **velocity report,** gives management a tool to analyze loss, waste, and theft.

A distributing company's sales and delivery personnel must also be evaluated. A supplier should have salespeople who know their products and can help the buyer become familiar with product alternatives that will meet the operation's needs. The supplier's sales representatives can also provide valuable market information. For example, if the distributor learns that a growing region is experiencing heavy rains, its sales representatives should inform the operation's buyer that the price of that region's lettuce will be higher in approximately six weeks. Similarly, the supplier should keep the establishment abreast of market conditions which change with growing seasons. Sales personnel should also keep the establishment informed of promotional discounts offered by processors and manufacturers.

Delivery personnel also represent the supplier. Their appearance and attitude, as well as other labor relations factors such as the supplier's ability to create a team spirit among its staff members, should be considered.

The purchasing power and financial position of the supplier are important. High-volume distributors buy in large quantities at a low cost per unit; thus, a portion of the savings can be passed on to the food service business. A supplier that is on sure financial ground is likely to give the operation good value for its food and non-food product funds.

Naturally, products and prices are a critical evaluation point. Products should meet the establishment's stated specifications. Distributors offering greater product variety are able to serve more types of food service businesses. Suppliers are obligated to charge a fair price. When evaluating prices, however, it is essential to compare like items. In many cases, the edible portion (EP) price is more important than the AP price because the EP price takes into account the product's yield.

The supplier's reputation is built on the company's reliability, consistency, and predictability. The food service operation should select suppliers who stand behind their products and services. It is a good idea to ask for references from the local government agencies and restaurant and hotel associations before choosing suppliers. In one sense, suppliers are partners in the food service business because they have a stake in its success. Buyers and suppliers can work together to satisfy the needs of the operation's target markets.

Value, the final criterion, is an overall assessment of the other six factors. Today, **value-added distributors** offer services beyond those normally expected, including nutritional analysis, quality control testing, idea shows geared toward certain market segments, product education, computer services, and others (see Exhibit 6). Some distributors may require a certain volume of business before offering some of these value-added services. Check with your suppliers to determine their value-added offerings and any restrictions that may apply.

Purchasing and Equipment

Food service businesses purchase a variety of utensils and equipment from suppliers. Utensils are food contact implements or containers. The material content, design, and fabrication of these items should be in accordance with nationally recognized standards and/or tested and listed by nationally recognized organizations. Generally, the materials from which equipment and utensils are constructed must be safe (non-toxic), durable, corrosion-resistant, nonabsorbent, sufficient in weight and thickness to withstand repeated warewashing, finished with a smooth and easily cleanable surface, and resistant to pitting, chipping, crazing, scratching, scoring, distortion, and decomposition.

Most regulatory agencies only allow equipment and utensils which neither contaminate nor impart odors, colors, or tastes to food. For example, only food-grade plastic bags may be purchased for food storage; using utility (non-food-grade) plastic bags can result in the addition of undesirable colors and odors to stored food products. Any equipment or utensils which do not meet these requirements should be eliminated from food service facilities.

Single-service and single-use articles must meet similar standards and must be safe and clean to prevent undesirable additives from entering food. These items

Exhibit 6   Examples of Value-Added Services

Automated Order Entry

Full Test Kitchens

Group Insurance Plans for Independent Small Operators

Market Specialists (chain/national accounts)

Monitoring of Rebates from Manufacturers

On-line Computer Access to Current Product and Pricing Information

On-staff Chefs for Menu Ideas and Recipe Development

On-staff Dietitians for Nutritional Analysis and Special Diets

Operator Newsletters

Placement Services for Personnel

Produce Processing

Product Specialists and Merchandising Ideas

Professionally-Accredited Seminars

Quality Control Testing

"Segmented Idea" Shows

Training for Staff Members

may not be reused. For example, plastic flatware used by guests at an outdoor buffet must be discarded after the buffet.

Equipment and utensils purchased by the operation must also be easy to clean. They must be constructed and repaired with materials that are safe, corrosion resistant, and non-absorbent. Multi-use equipment and utensils must also be smooth, durable, and easily cleanable. (Since single-service articles may not be reused, they need not be easy to clean.) Non-absorbent hardwood (such as hard maple) may be used for baker's tables, salad bowls, and cutting blocks or boards. Wood is not permitted for any other food-contact surfaces. Rubber or plastic materials are permitted if they are easily cleanable and resistant to scoring, decomposition, scratching, and chipping under normal conditions. Rubber or plastic cutting boards are often preferable to wooden boards because they are easier to clean and maintain.

When purchasing cookware, including pots and pans, it is important to consider not only the useful life, but also cleaning and sanitization. Heavy cookware with riveted construction may cost more initially but can last at least ten years if properly maintained. Heavy-gauge stainless steel and aluminum cookware, for example, is designed to withstand the abuses of a commercial kitchen. Avoid purchasing thin-walled aluminum cookware; such items can cause discoloration of sauces or aluminum poisoning when they come into contact with acidic foods. In addition, the bleach in some solutions can wear down the aluminum. All cookware should be hand-washed with pot and pan soap and treated with a sanitizer designed for the purpose.

The important factors in design and fabrication of equipment and utensils are durability and cleanability. In particular, all food-contact surfaces must be designed and fabricated to be smooth; free of breaks, open seams, cracks, chips, pits, and other imperfections; free of sharp internal angles, corners, and crevices; finished to have smooth welds and joints; and accessible for cleaning and inspection. Cast iron is permitted only on grills, griddles, skillets, and other heated surfaces. Materials used as lubricants should not come in contact with food or food-contact surfaces.

Equipment or utensils that do not meet design and fabrication requirements are virtually impossible to keep clean. Violations (such as using dented or chipped equipment and utensils) invite food safety problems. For example, the common practice of lubricating a food mixer with a petroleum-based lubricant may result in the lubricant dripping into and contaminating food.

Glass-stemmed thermometers may not be used to check food temperatures or the temperature of oil in a deep fryer. Soft wood is not permitted for non-food-contact surfaces which are exposed to splashes or food debris and thus require frequent cleaning. Improperly designed and fabricated ventilation hoods may allow possibly contaminated grease or condensation to drip into food. Sinks and drain boards should be self-draining. If a piece of equipment must be taken apart for cleaning, the equipment should be designed to be easily disassembled.

Buyers should be aware that equipment from foreign suppliers (for example, East Indian ovens or Italian pasta machines) may not meet nationally recognized construction codes and specifications. Ask the appropriate government officials to evaluate the equipment based on existing codes.

When purchasing new or used equipment, evaluate it with food safety in mind. Consider asking suppliers for a written guarantee that their equipment is in compliance with relevant codes and standards. Also consider asking suppliers to furnish you with inspection reports on their facilities, or for permission to conduct your own unannounced inspections.

In the United States, The National Sanitation Foundation (NSF) is a non-profit organization that develops standards and criteria for equipment, products, and services in the interest of public health. The NSF seal on equipment and utensils indicates that these items meet most public health standards: the seal only appears on items that have passed a rigorous inspection. NSF is the only organization that develops these types of standards for the food service industry. Other organizations use these standards to test equipment. Three independent organizations test and evaluate food service equipment. Underwriters Laboratories (UL) evaluates electrically powered equipment, while the American Gas Association (AGA) performs similar testing on gas equipment. Environmental Testing Laboratories (ETL) also tests equipment against NSF standards. When applicable, it is a good idea to specify evaluated and tested equipment.

It is important to realize that NSF sets *minimum* standards. Just because an item meets these minimum standards does not guarantee that it is suitable for the intended purpose. For example, equipment designed for home use (non-commercial equipment) may seem a bargain at first glance. However, this equipment is not designed for frequent, large-quantity use. In fact, commercial use of such equipment usually voids the warranty.

One piece of equipment is absolutely essential in virtually all of the control points: a temperature measuring device. This category includes a thermometer, thermocouple, thermistor, or other device. For example, a food thermometer provides an accurate determination of internal product temperature as a product moves through the control points. The recommended accuracy for a product thermometer is $\pm 2°F$ ($\pm 1°C$).

Purchasing and Facilities

A food service operation's facilities help determine the operation's purchasing method. If the facilities are spacious and accommodate many guests, the operation will likely use a formal purchasing method. This method involves relatively large orders. Therefore, competitive buying is used to help control costs. The operation prepares written specifications to communicate product needs to suppliers, and suppliers submit written bids to the operation's buyer. These bids indicate the price they will charge for the desired products if their bid is accepted. Depending on the operation's needs, the buyer may use written negotiations during the formal purchasing process.

In smaller businesses, orders are usually smaller and purchasing procedures tend to be informal. Written specifications, bids, and negotiations are usually not used; the operation provides specifications, suppliers quote prices, and negotiations are conducted either in person or by telephone. While this method is less exact, it is simple and saves time for the small operation. It does, however, result in less operator control.

Purchasing and Change

Perhaps more than any other control point, the purchasing activity is in a constant state of flux. Conditions change from season to season, from week to week, and in some cases, overnight. For example, the availability, prices, and supply levels of products purchased by a food service business often change. Purchasing patterns must be altered when conditions change. However, before a change is implemented, it is important to systematically predict and evaluate its impact on the operation's food safety, quality, and cost standards. As part of this systematic evaluation, the risks must be clarified, analyzed, and reduced, when possible.

In an attempt to minimize uncertainty at the purchasing control point, standards (such as purchase specifications), as well as sensory and temperature checks, should be used to determine product quality and assess the food safety risks. If a system of food safety risk management is in place, it is relatively easy to change a product or update standards. When such a system is not in place, it becomes all the more difficult to control purchasing activities.

Purchasing and Food Safety

Purchasing can be risky if menu planning is haphazard and the objectives of purchasing are not clearly understood. The risks can be reduced if the buyer is armed with knowledge about the operation's:

- Quality, food safety, and cost standards
- Food production methods
- Purchasing procedures
- Suppliers and competitors

Knowledge of quality, food safety, and cost control standards is most important. Jeopardizing the operation's food safety risk management program in order to save a few dollars on the purchase price can be a costly mistake. Similarly, to compromise the establishment's quality standards is to risk losing guests. The buyer must strike a balance between these three types of control, all of which determine the guest experience and the success of the business.

Knowledge of food production methods is also important at the purchasing control point. A buyer must know the yield of a raw ingredient, based on preparation and serving techniques, in order to calculate its EP cost.

The buyer must know purchasing procedures to operate efficiently. A planned, organized system—complete with written product specifications, purchase orders, and product evaluation forms—increases the buyer's control. By carefully reviewing issuing records, the buyer can establish par stocks (minimum quantities) for each item the facility should have on hand. This helps eliminate costly stockouts. An operation cannot negotiate either price or quality when it always buys at the last minute.

Knowledge of suppliers and competitors completes the purchasing success formula. Suppliers can be a valuable source of market information. They can assist the operation in solving yield, food safety, quality, and cost problems. Successful operations are also not afraid to develop reciprocal supply loan relationships with competitors; such relationships are usually beneficial.

Key Terms

convenience foods—Food products purchased in partially or fully prepared forms that enable food service operations to offer new items without buying additional raw ingredients or elaborate equipment. These products reduce in-house requirements, but have a higher purchase price.

cross-utilization—A menu-planning strategy related to rationalization. Its objective: to prepare and serve as many menu items as possible from a limited number of raw ingredients.

first-in, first-out (FIFO) inventory system—A rotation method in which products held in inventory the longest are the first to be issued to production areas; when newly received products enter storage areas, they are placed under or behind products already in storage.

food sample data sheet—A form that standardizes evaluations of products that an operation is considering for purchase; can be used to record purchasing, storing, preparing, and serving information about such products, and also to request nutritional and ingredient analysis information.

inventory—The total supply of items an operation has in stock.

line-up meeting—A five- to ten-minute informal training period with production and/or service staff members before each meal period; gives the chef and the manager an opportunity to explain daily specials, and gives the staff members an opportunity to sample portions of new menu items and to ask questions.

master distributor—A supplier who serves as a full-line or one-stop shopping and delivery service.

purchase order—A form that helps maintain purchasing control; it contains the details of an order placed with a supplier. This standard form is completed by the operation's buyer and sent to the supplier. A copy is retained to facilitate in-house recordkeeping.

rationalization—In menu planning, the creation of a simplified, balanced menu for the sake of guest satisfaction and operational efficiency; frequently results in a limited menu, but the operation can offer several menu items that use the same raw ingredients.

standard purchase specifications—Written guidelines that precisely define the quality, quantity, and other characteristics of the products an establishment buys.

truth-in-menu regulations—Laws requiring accurate menu descriptions of raw ingredients and finished menu items.

value-added distributor—Suppliers who offer services beyond those normally expected, including nutritional analysis, quality control testing, idea shows, product education, computer services, and others.

velocity report—A computer printout provided by suppliers of all the products ordered by a food establishment during a given period (week, month, or year). The report is a management tool for analyzing loss, waste, and theft.

Review Questions

1. What are four important trends affecting menu development?

2. What is the relationship between menu planning and inventory? How do rationalization, diversification, and convenience foods fit into this relationship?

3. The menu planning control point requires considerations for three other major resources besides inventory. What are these resources and their considerations?

4. Why are menu changes implemented? What factors are influential?

5. What are the major truth-in-menu regulations?

6. The purchasing control point is influenced by which factors? What are the functions of this control point?

7. Why are inventory standards important at the purchasing control point?

8. What types of skills are required of a successful buyer?

9. What are the basic guidelines for purchasing equipment? How do facilities influence purchasing procedures?

10. How can a buyer reduce risks at the purchasing control point?

✓ Checklist for Menu Planning ─────────────────

Inventory

_____ The menu achieves the financial objectives, helps create the image, and functions as the plan for the entire operation.

_____ Records are maintained on the menu's sales mix and the popularity of every menu item.

_____ The menu incorporates relevant menu trends.

_____ The menu's effect on the other control points is considered when planning the menu.

_____ Menu items are rationalized and ingredients cross-utilized as much as possible.

_____ High-quality convenience foods are evaluated and used when appropriate.

_____ Menu offerings are based on the expectations of the target markets.

People

_____ The menu communicates the strategy for meeting or exceeding guest expectations.

_____ The appearance, readability, clarity, and pricing strategies of the menu are evaluated regularly.

_____ The skill levels of production staff are evaluated.

_____ The skill levels of service staff are evaluated.

_____ Suppliers are asked for preparation and merchandising suggestions.

_____ Food safety, quality, and cost control standards are maintained.

_____ Servers know the meaning of terms used to describe menu items and their preparation.

Equipment

_____ Equipment is selected based on initial costs, capacity, availability of energy sources, operating costs, maintenance costs, and skill levels of staff members.

_____ Equipment is easy to clean and sanitize.

_____ Equipment design, layout, and installation facilitate both product and-people movement in the kitchen and service areas.

_____ Special functions, banquets, and room service menus are planned realistically, based on the operation's equipment resources.

Facilities

_____ Traffic flow in the kitchen and dining room is evaluated, and the design and layout of the facilities are changed when necessary.

_____ The ambience of the facilities is appropriate for the menu and the expectations of the target markets.

_____ Special functions and banquets are booked with the limitations of the establishment's facilities in mind.

_____ The facilities are maintained in a clean and safe manner.

Truth-in-Menu

_____ Accurate descriptions are used for raw ingredients and finished menu items.

_____ Quality or grade statements are factual.

_____ Sizes, weights, or counts are depicted accurately on the menu.

_____ Frozen or canned items are never billed as fresh.

_____ Preparation techniques are described accurately.

_____ Additional charges for extras are clearly stated on the menu.

_____ Pictures on the menu accurately represent the product served.

_____ Server descriptions are accurate.

_____ Dietary or nutritional claims are precise.

_____ Points of origin are described accurately.

_____ Ingredient and nutritional information is available to those who request it.

Food Safety Risk Management Program

_____ Menu items are considered in light of possible food safety hazards at every control point.

_____ Once the potential hazards are identified, steps are taken to reduce the risks.

✓ Checklist for Purchasing ————————————————

Inventory

_____ Inventory and stock levels are established based on the intended use of the product and the volume of business.

_____ The functions of purchasing are used to guide activities.

_____ Written standard purchase specifications are used and updated periodically as conditions change.

_____ Market conditions are evaluated regularly.

_____ Food sample data sheets are used to select and evaluate products.

_____ Written purchase orders are used to define the details of each order.

_____ All inventory items are obtained from approved and safe sources.

_____ The FIFO inventory system is used by the operations and its suppliers.

People

_____ Purchasing is done by a manager or a key assistant.

_____ The buyer establishes and maintains an adequate supply of food and non-food products.

_____ The buyer minimizes the investment in inventory.

_____ The food safety, quality, and cost standards are defined and maintained while risks are reduced.

_____ The operation's competitive position is maintained.

_____ The buyer purchases the product, not the deal.

_____ The buyer understands the operation's short- and long-term goals.

_____ The buyer possesses managerial, technical, and interpersonal skills.

_____ The buyer is ethical and loyal to the business.

_____ The buyer has an intimate knowledge of the operation and its product needs.

_____ The buyer establishes reciprocal supply loan relationships with the operation's competitors.

_____ The buyer evaluates the master distributor versus the specialty supplier.

_____ The buyer periodically checks the supplier's food safety policies, size, services, staff and labor relations, purchasing power and financial position, products, quality, prices, reputation, and value.

_____ The buyer builds relationships with value-added suppliers.

_____ The buyer uses the supplier as a source of market information.

_____ Staff members in the purchasing department have a formal training program.

Equipment

_____ The materials, design, and fabrication of equipment purchased by the facility meet local, state, and federal health codes.

_____ The operation purchases equipment made of non-toxic materials.

_____ The operation purchases equipment that is easy to clean and maintain.

_____ Single-service items are not washed and re-used.

_____ Food-contact surface are free from cracks, chips, breaks, and difficult-to clean crevices and corners.

_____ Materials used as lubricants do not contaminate food or food-contact surfaces.

_____ When considering equipment manufactured by foreign suppliers, appropriate government officials evaluate it based on existing codes.

_____ Equipment has been tested and evaluated by appropriate government agencies.

_____ Equipment designed for home use is not purchased.

_____ Product thermometers are purchased and used to measure internal product temperature as a product moves through the control points.

_____ Cookware is purchased based on durability and considerations of cleaning and sanitization.

Facilities

_____ The formality or informality of the purchasing arrangement is based on the establishment's facilities.

_____ Facilities are maintained in a clean and safe manner.

Food Safety Risk Management Program

_____ Risks are reduced by knowledge of quality, food safety, and cost standards; food production methods and purchasing procedures; and suppliers and competitors.

_____ Inventory is purchased carefully.

_____ Staff members are trained to maintain standards and reduce risks during purchasing.

_____ Adequate equipment and facilities are present, used, and frequently cleaned, sanitized, and maintained to reduce the risks during purchasing.

Chapter 4 Outline

Competencies

1. Describe inventory controls, standards, and procedures at the receiving control point. (pp. 97–101)

2. Explain the qualifications necessary to perform the receiving function. (pp. 101–104)

3. Describe the elements of proper receiving facilities. (pp. 104–105)

4. Explain the importance of maintaining an optimum inventory. (pp. 105–106)

5. Describe the A-B-C-D scheme of inventory classification, perpetual and physical inventories, and other inventory control measures. (pp. 106–110)

6. Describe the major responsibilities of the storeroom person. (pp. 110–111)

7. Describe the use of thermometers at the storing control point. (p. 111)

8. Describe the three types of storage facilities in a food establishment. (pp. 112–116)

9. Explain what food service managers should know about the issuing control point. (pp. 116–119)

4

The Receiving, Storing, and Issuing Control Points

THE RECEIVING, STORING, AND ISSUING control points of the food safety risk management program are presented together in this chapter because these three activities are interrelated. They are essential to the success of the operation's food safety, quality, and cost control systems. By following the principles of the food safety risk management program at these control points, you will be able to implement and monitor a system to reduce risks.

The Receiving Control Point

The receiving control point follows menu planning and purchasing. The objectives of the receiving function include inspecting deliveries for quality and quantity, checking prices, and deciding whether to accept or reject deliveries. In reality, receiving practices vary: one operation may carefully check each item delivered; another might allow the supplier's truck driver to put the order away. From a control standpoint, the former method is certainly preferable.

The receiving function is critical because at this control point an operation assumes ownership of the products. Careful menu planning and skillful purchasing are wasted if an operation accepts inferior products. Good receiving techniques can maximize the results of the other control points. Risk reduction during receiving requires competent personnel, proper equipment, adequate receiving facilities, established receiving hours, and several types of receiving control forms.

Receiving and Inventory

When inventory items are received at a food establishment, a critical control point must be monitored. The receiver must check inventory quality, cleanliness, and labels very carefully. A temperature check is a good idea for all potentially hazardous foods; improper temperatures should prompt further quality inspection. Refrigerated potentially hazardous foods should generally be received at 41°F (5°C) or less.

Egg products, if liquid, frozen, or dried, should be obtained pasteurized. Shell eggs should be clean and whole and without cracks or checks. Raw eggs should be received in refrigerated equipment that maintains an ambient air temperature of 45°F (7°C). Fluid and dry milk and milk products should also be obtained pasteurized.

Food packages should protect the integrity of the contents, be in good condition upon receipt, and they must be labeled. Raw and frozen molluscan shucked shellfish must be delivered in non-returnable packages labeled with the processor's name, address, and authorized certification number. Shellstock packages must also show the "sell by" or shucked date and location. An operation should retain this source identification for 90 days after the container is empty.

Molluscan shellstock should be received reasonably free of mud, dead shellfish, and shellfish with broken shells. Fish, however, may not be received unless they are commercially and legally caught or harvested or caught recreationally and approved for sale or service by the regulatory authority. Molluscan shellfish that are recreationally caught may not be approved for sale or service.

Before they become inventory items, all delivered products should be verified. This verification is a two-step process. First, the supplier's invoice is checked against the establishment's purchase order and standard purchase specifications. The **invoice** details all the products being delivered to the facility and their corresponding prices. In some cases, it also shows products that are back-ordered or not yet available for delivery. Since the supplier uses the invoices to calculate the amount due, each invoice must be verified for accuracy. The second step entails checking the products against the supplier's invoice. Any products that are priced by weight should be weighed on an accurate scale. Packaged products should be removed from their packing containers, or the weight of the containers should be subtracted from the gross weight. Different cuts of meat which are delivered together must be weighed separately because of varying per-pound prices. Any products purchased on a per-unit basis should be counted before they are accepted. If more than one container of the same product is delivered, a random spot-check may be sufficient to verify the count.

The invoice may need to be modified if some products are spoiled, do not meet the establishment's specifications, or are delivered in the wrong quantities. In such cases, the receiver may fill out a request-for-credit memo stating why the products are unacceptable and asking the supplier to credit the invoice. The supplier should then issue a **credit memo** to adjust the account. A sample request-for-credit memo is shown in Exhibit 1. This form helps to ensure that the food establishment is charged only for the products that conform to its standards. Products that are held for credit for return to the distributor shall be segregated and held in areas away from food, equipment, utensils, linens, and single-service and single-use articles.

Product inspection is essential during receiving. Sensory tests (evaluating a product by its appearance, odor, and feel) are useful in quality inspections. In addition, a temperature check verifies that potentially hazardous foods are not in the temperature danger zone (TDZ). Once products pass the inspection, they should be dated immediately with a marking pen, either on the outer container or the individually wrapped packages. Some operators also mark the price on each product unit, since this helps facilitate physical inventory and helps remind staff members how much food products cost.

A thorough inspection of every product delivery may be a time-consuming task. However, a food service business can only gain from a policy of consistent

Exhibit 1   Request-for-Credit Memo

Request-for-Credit Memo

(prepare in duplicate)   Number: _____

From: _____   To: _____

_____   _____

_____   _____

_____   _____

Credit should be given on the following:

Invoice Number: _____   Invoice Date: _____

Product	Unit	Number	Price/Unit	Total Price

Reason: Total: _____

_____   _____
(delivery person)   (authorizing signature)

inspection. It keeps honest suppliers honest and discourages dishonest suppliers from dealing with the operation. Regular inspections also help reduce risks by preventing the acquisition of unacceptable inventory.

Once the products have been legally accepted, it is time to record the new inventory items and prepare them for storage. Tagging products when they are delivered aids in inventory control later. A sample product storage tag is presented in Exhibit 2. The date on the tag facilitates stock rotation, which is the goal of the FIFO (first-in, first-out) inventory system. Inventory tags with prices also speed up the physical inventory process. In addition, the tagging system provides an audit trail for food products. Initially, one part of the tag is attached to the product, while the other portion is affixed to the invoice. Later, when the product is issued for use, the portion of the tag attached to the product is removed and sent to the operation's accounting office. By matching the product portion of the tag to the invoice portion, the accounting department helps maintain inventory control.

If products are to be used immediately, they are sent directly to kitchen production areas without going through the usual storing and issuing control points. Nevertheless, everything that the facility receives must be recorded on the **daily receiving report**. A sample daily receiving report is shown in Exhibit 3. It lists

Exhibit 2   Storage Tag

Tag Number _____ 1005 _____	Tag Number _____ 1005 _____
Date of Receipt _____ 8/1/00 _____	Date Received _____ 8/1/00 _____
Weight/Cost	Weight _____ 35# _____
35 × $2.85 = $99.75	Price _____ $2.85 _____
(No. of #s) (Price) (Cost)	Cost _____ $99.75 _____
Name of Supplier: _____	Supplier _____ Jacob Meats _____
_____ Jacob Meats _____	Date Issued _____
Date of Issue _____	

Exhibit 3   Daily Receiving Report

Date: _____ 8/1/00 _____   Page __1__ of __2__

Supplier	Invoice No.	Item	Purchase Unit	No. of Purchase Units	Purchase Unit Price	Total Cost	Food Directs	Food Stores	Liquor	Beer	Wine	Soda	Transfer to Storage
1	2	3	4	5	6	7	8	9	10	11	12	13	14
AJAX	10111	Gr. Beef	10#	6	$28.50	$171.00		$171.00					Bill
ABC Liquor	6281	B. Scotch	cs(750)	2	$71.80	$143.00			$143.60				Bill
		H. Chablis	gal	3	$8.50	$25.50					$25.50		Bill
B/E Produce	70666	Lettuce	cs	2	$21.00	$42.00	$42.00						
Totals							$351.00	$475.00	$683.50	—	$102.00		

what was received, the date of the delivery, the name of the supplier, the quantity, the price, and any other relevant comments. The report also provides a record of delivery distribution. The "Food Directs" column indicates the dollar value of products to be sent directly to kitchen production areas. The "Food Stores" column records the dollar value of products to be placed into storage. Generally, the food items placed in storage vastly outnumber the food items sent directly to production.

Storing new inventory items in the proper order can preserve product quality and food safety. The most perishable items—frozen products—should be stored first. Refrigerated meats, fish, poultry, dairy products, and produce should be stored next. The least perishable items—staple foods and non-food supplies—should be stored last. Adhering to this order minimizes product deterioration. At the moment the delivery is accepted, the safety of the food becomes the responsibility of the food establishment. The receiver should strive to keep the time between delivery and storage as short as possible, particularly for frozen and refrigerated food products.

Receiving and People

The number of people working at the receiving control point varies among food service operations. The major determining factors are the size of the operation and its annual sales volume. In a relatively small operation, the manager or the assistant manager is usually in charge of receiving. In larger operations, one full-time or two part-time people typically handle the receiving function. The person in charge of receiving may be called a receiving clerk, steward, or storeroom person. This individual usually reports either to the food controller, the assistant manager, or the food and beverage manager.

Regardless of how many individuals are assigned to the receiving function, the general requirements are the same:

- Good health and personal cleanliness

- Familiarity with the necessary forms, tools, and equipment

- Literacy

- Product knowledge

- Quality and food safety judgment

- Personal integrity, accuracy, and commitment to the interests of the organization

- Ability to coordinate the needs of the operation's departments with the supplies being delivered

Good health and personal cleanliness are important for the receiver, as for all other staff members. Food receivers should wash their hands properly, avoid hand contact with exposed ready-to-eat food, minimize bare hand and arm contact with exposed ready-to-eat food, and use suitable utensils, single-use gloves, and dispensing equipment.

The person in charge of receiving should also be able to effectively use all equipment, facilities, and forms required at this control point. More will be said about these tools in later sections of the chapter.

Because of the volume of written information used at this control point, the operation's receiver must be able to read and write. Among other things, the receiver must be able to check the actual products delivered against the written purchase specifications and purchase orders. A receiver who is illiterate would not see, for example, that the purchase order says "50 ten-ounce prime tenderloin steaks" and could mistakenly accept 40 twelve-ounce choice tenderloin steaks instead.

The receiver should know the quality characteristics outlined in the operation's standard purchase specifications. A knowledge of product grades, weight ranges, and fat trim factors is also necessary. In addition, the receiver must be able to judge the condition of the products and the delivery vehicle.

The receiver should demonstrate both honesty and attention to detail. The receiver's integrity ensures that the establishment's standards, policies, and procedures will not be compromised. He or she must take this important job seriously. Negligence or inaccuracy may cause the business to suffer financial damage. Its reputation may also suffer if hazardous foods are carelessly accepted into the food service system. The receiver must be committed to protecting the interests of the operation.

The receiver must coordinate supply requisitions from all departments with the delivery schedules of suppliers. Ideally, receiving should take place during slow periods in the operation's daily business cycle. This is particularly important when the receiver is also the chef, assistant manager, or manager. The establishment's delivery hours should be posted on the back door as a guide for suppliers. The receiver should be available when deliveries are expected. Staggering food deliveries avoids overloading the storage area facilities. A smoothly run receiving control point is an indication of the receiver's competence and reliability.

Food production experience is essential for the receiver; however, this does not imply that any kitchen staff member in the operation is qualified to perform the receiving function. Only selected and trained staff members should be permitted to receive food and non-food products. A facility that allows the janitor, dishwasher, or busperson to do its receiving is opening the door for trouble; these individuals lack the training to recognize and resolve product problems. A properly trained receiver, on the other hand, knows what to do when there is a problem with product deliveries. The receiver can use his or her clout with the supplier to point out problems to the delivery person and see that they are corrected.

Receiving and Equipment

The receiver must be able to use a variety of equipment. Some equipment is used to gain access to the food for the usual quality and quantity checks. The operation should keep such tools as hammers, pliers, and screwdrivers on hand for the receiver to use in opening crates and boxes. Other equipment serves to verify product quality, quantity, and price. These tools include scales, thermometers, rulers, and calculators.

An accurate scale is crucial to the success of the receiving control point because many products purchased by a food service facility are priced by weight. The receiver should weigh all such products, checking the actual weight against that shown on the invoice. Several types of scales are available for use during receiving. Electronic readout scales are both easy to use and precise. Some of these scales are equipped with a device to stamp the recorded weight directly on the package. Tabletop or counter scales are suitable for checking the weight of lighter products. A large-capacity floor or platform scale is used for bulky or heavy products, which can often be rolled onto the scale with the aid of a handcart. To record the product's net weight, subtract the weight of the cart and packaging material.

Exhibit 4 Measuring Frozen Food Temperatures Without Opening Packages

MEASURING FROZEN FOOD TEMPERATURES

WITHOUT OPENING PACKAGES

Select seven cases of frozen foods. Stack any three of the seven on the floor area of the cold environment for the lot being sampled. Cut sidewall of top case (number three of stack) at either end with a sharp knife as shown in Figures A, B, and C, for different kinds of frozen foods.

Bend the cut tab outward. Insert probe of temperature measurement device at about the center of the first stack of packages and between the first and second layers of packages so that all of the sensing element is in firm contact with package walls. Stack the other four cases on top of the case containing the probe.

Read and record the temperature observed when the needle gives a steady reading. This is generally five minutes, or less for a dial thermometer. Close and tape the cut sidewall area of the case.

For solid pack products (See Figure A) such as frozen spinach, cut sidewall of case at either end (dotted line) and insert probe at approximate center of first stack and between first and second layers of packages so that all of the sensing element is in firm contact with package walls. For poly bags, insert probe in the same direction as the length of the bag and deep enough for firm contact between bags.

Side View, Case of 24
Solid Packed Product

1. Cut case sidewall
2. Bend cut tab
3. Insert probe

Figure A

End View, Case of 24
Fruit, Turned on Side

Figure B

Side View, Case of 6
Frozen 8" Fruit Pies

Figure C

For products such as frozen fruits in paperboard packages with metal ends, turn case on side to give end view above. Cut sidewall of case as shown and follow procedure of *Figure A.*

For products such as frozen 8" fruit pies, with air space between edge of pie and wall of individual carton, cut any side of case as shown and follow procedure of *Figure A.*

Source: National Sanitation Foundation, *Product Temperature Management.*

Some operations attempt to save money by buying inexpensive scales. However, these scales are often inaccurate and, as a result, not useful. An accurate scale is an investment that pays for itself in the long run by allowing the receiver to verify invoices precisely. Scales should be checked for accuracy at least every three months by a qualified expert such as a representative of the government bureau of weights and measures.

Thermometers are also indispensable for proper receiving. In the hands of a knowledgeable receiver, an accurate metal-stemmed pocket probe thermometer is a valuable tool. The temperatures of all perishable products (meats, fish, poultry, produce, and all frozen foods) should be monitored. The internal temperature of refrigerated products must be less than or equal to 41°F (5°C), while frozen foods must be at 0°F (-18°C) or below. If products are delivered at higher temperatures, they must be further evaluated on the basis of appearance, odor, feel, and perhaps taste. Exhibit 4 shows one method of testing the internal product temperatures of frozen foods without opening the packages.

Perishable product inspection at receiving has been made easier by the **time-temperature monitor**. This is a relatively inexpensive device that is attached to boxes or cartons of refrigerated and frozen products just before they leave the processing plant. It measures the combined effects of heat and age by changing color in response to the chemical and physical reactions that take place when a product's temperature exceeds a certain level for an excessive length of time.

Time-temperature monitors benefit a food service business by identifying weaknesses in the distribution system. This new technology allows the operation's receiver to quickly see whether a product has been thawed and then refrozen, making the accept/reject decision faster and more objective. The widespread use of these monitors may also provide a stimulus for suppliers and distributors to maintain correct product temperatures and storage times.

A ruler is useful for checking the size of steaks and roasts and the amount of fat covering them. A calculator allows the receiver to quickly verify the accuracy of the supplier's invoice.

After a delivery is accepted, other equipment is used to prepare and transport items to storage. Marking pens are used to record the product's AP (as-purchased) price directly on the package. This practice prompts other food handlers in the operation to think about the products as being equivalent to money; it also encourages proper food care to reduce contamination and spoilage losses. Marking pens are also used to record the delivery date in order to ensure proper product rotation (FIFO). Dollies and other transportation equipment help the receiver move marked products rapidly into storage, thereby retaining product safety and quality.

Receiving and Facilities

Proper receiving facilities are essential to the maintenance of the establishment's food safety, quality, and cost standards at the receiving control point. Receiving facilities include the inside and outside areas surrounding the loading dock, the back door, and the receiving office.

The condition of the receiving area is critical. Inside floors and walls as well as the receiving dock must be free of debris and food particles; these unclean conditions could contaminate food or food containers before storage. Empty shipping containers and packaging materials should be taken to disposal areas promptly. Some operations put their trash areas near the receiving dock. This practice may create food safety risks and the potential for inventory thefts. Whenever possible, trash containers should be placed in an area that is physically separated from the receiving area.

An operation's outdoor receiving facilities present an image of the establishment to suppliers and competitors. Ideally, receiving docks should be constructed so that deliveries are easy to manage. Adequate ramps, platforms, and truck maneuvering space should be provided. For safety as well as security, the outdoor and indoor receiving areas should be well-lit. The receiving door should also be locked when not in use. Whenever possible, the receiving office should be located between the receiving dock and storage areas. This will minimize the effort and, more important, the time it takes to transport products to storage.

Costs are easier to control when the receiving facilities are equipped with the necessary tools and work surfaces. A work table or desk is essential for record-keeping and administrative responsibilities. Additional table space should be available for opening product containers during inspection of deliveries. Adequate floor space is necessary so that orders do not pile up in the receiving area. Overcrowding in the delivery area results in safety hazards.

Receiving and Change

There is no room for negligence, waste, or error at the receiving control point. Evidence of any of these problems should prompt a thorough evaluation of the receiving function. Management should periodically review receiving practices to identify areas for possible improvement.

Because the control points are all interrelated, receiving should also be re-evaluated when menu planning or purchasing activities change. For example, if a small operation changes its menu and business improves dramatically, the operation's increased sales volume might justify hiring a full-time receiving person and expanding receiving facilities. The operation's orders can only be checked in properly if the receiver has enough time and the proper tools.

Regardless of the size of the business, the more consistent and routine the receiving function becomes, the fewer problems there will be. As with all the other control points, an evaluation of the costs versus the benefits indicates the degree to which more sophisticated controls are required.

Receiving and Food Safety

When food products are delivered to the back door of a food establishment, the risks are transferred from the supplier to the owners and managers of the establishment. A food service operation needs strategies to reduce the risks at this critical control point.

All products must go through a detailed inspection during receiving. Important inspection points include temperature, freshness, wholesomeness, integrity, and case condition. Each product has its own temperature requirements and quality (freshness and wholesomeness) indicators. Freedom from filth, spoilage, or other contamination indicates product integrity. The condition of the cases or containers in which products are delivered indicates how products have been handled before arriving at the food establishment. All food products must also be checked against the establishment's standard purchase specifications.

The receiver must maintain high standards of personal hygiene and cleanliness. Equipment and forms used during receiving enhance cost, food safety, and quality control. The receiver should use these tools at all times. Careful adherence to the receiving standards of the food safety program will help reduce the risks inherent in this control point.

The Storing Control Point

The storing control point serves to protect the operation's food and non-food purchases until they are put to work as income producers. To maximize income, profits, and guest satisfaction, spoilage and contamination must be minimized. The inventory must also be protected from theft and pilferage. Several storage area controls are useful in maintaining a high level of food safety and quality while keeping down costs and risks.

The keys to proper food storage are knowing how items should be stored and having the facilities and equipment to keep the products in optimal condition.

Storing and Inventory

Generally, the larger the inventory dollar value, the more difficult it is to achieve control of the storing function. While too small an inventory can lead to frequent stockouts, an excessively large inventory can cause a number of problems. Most food products, including frozen items, lose volume and quality if stored too long. Pilferage and spoilage losses also tend to increase in direct proportion to the amount of inventory on hand. When staff members see a large quantity of products in stock, they might be tempted to steal, reasoning that no one will notice one less item. Large inventories also encourage waste; staff members are not as likely to conserve food products that are obviously overstocked.

If storage areas are inadequate, excessive inventory might require more labor to handle and rehandle the products. It is more difficult to take inventory in overstocked storage areas, and excessive inventories can tie up the operation's money for long periods of time. They can also enhance the potential for contamination and raise the risks of a foodborne illness outbreak.

In light of these problems, managers may wonder how to achieve an optimum inventory level, avoiding both shortages and overstocking. If sales are properly forecast, purchasing is more accurate and inventory is easier to control. But suppose an establishment finds it necessary to maintain a large inventory, perhaps due to high sales volume and infrequent supplier deliveries. Is a detailed security system necessary for every product in stock? Such a system might require a large storeroom staff and end up costing more than the losses from theft, spoilage, and contamination it is designed to prevent. The dollar value of food products must determine the amount of inventory control necessary to guarantee security.

The value of food products can be compared by price per unit of weight or volume. Relatively few food products have a high dollar value per unit of measure. On the average, less than 20% of the total items in a food service operation's inventory account for over 80% of the total dollar value of the food inventory. The operation's inventory control measures should therefore focus on these high-cost items.

A-B-C-D Inventory Classification. Several techniques for categorizing inventories have been developed. Perhaps the most useful is the **A-B-C-D scheme.** This technique classifies inventory items according to perishability and cost per serving. The categories of the A-B-C-D scheme are presented in Exhibit 5.

Class A inventory items are high in both perishability and cost per serving. Class A items may account for up to 40% of a food service operation's total annual purchases. Class B inventory items are relatively high in cost but low in perishability. These may account for another 20% of a facility's total annual purchases. Class C inventory items are relatively low in cost per serving, but relatively high in

Exhibit 5   The A-B-C-D Classification Scheme for Food Items in Inventory

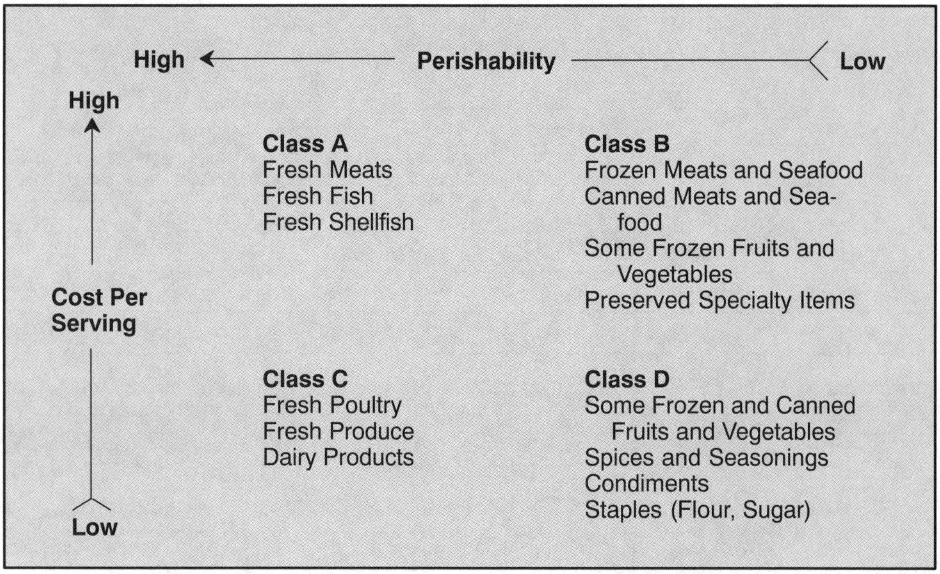

High ←————————— Perishability ——————————< Low

High
↑

Class A
Fresh Meats
Fresh Fish
Fresh Shellfish

Class B
Frozen Meats and Seafood
Canned Meats and Sea-
    food
Some Frozen Fruits and
    Vegetables
Preserved Specialty Items

**Cost Per
Serving**

Class C
Fresh Poultry
Fresh Produce
Dairy Products

Class D
Some Frozen and Canned
    Fruits and Vegetables
Spices and Seasonings
Condiments
Staples (Flour, Sugar)

Low

perishability. Class D inventory items have both the lowest perishability and the lowest cost per serving.

There are many advantages of using the A-B-C-D classification scheme, particularly when the storeroom staff is limited. Analyzing the operation's inventory according to this scheme forces the inventory person to consider both relative perishability and cost per serving. The scheme is also straightforward and easy to use. Inventory control should focus primarily on Class A and Class B items, since these account for the greatest dollar volume of inventory and comprise the products likeliest to be stolen by staff members. Of secondary importance are the Class C items, which should be monitored frequently for contamination and spoilage.

Like most classification schemes, the A-B-C-D system is a simplification of reality. Because relative costs vary from operation to operation, some food items may not be categorized exactly as shown in Exhibit 5. However, regardless of individual variations, a facility's control system should focus primarily on foods high in cost and perishability. Strict accounting for these items should protect more than half of the total dollar value of all food products purchased by the business.

Physical and Perpetual Inventories. Of course, to adapt the A-B-C-D classification scheme to an operation's own needs, management must know exactly what the operation's inventory consists of. There are two widely accepted methods of inventory control: physical inventory and perpetual inventory.

A **physical inventory** is an actual count of what is on the shelves. It must be taken each time an income statement is prepared. A sample physical inventory form is shown in Exhibit 6. The physical inventory must be accurate because it is used to calculate the operation's food costs and **food cost percentage**. The relevant calculations are as follows:

Exhibit 6   Physical Inventory Form

Physical Inventory							
Type of Product: _____				Month _____		Month _____	
Product	**Unit**	**Amount in Storage**	**Purchase Price**	**Total Price**	**Amount in Storage**	**Purchase Price**	**Total Price**
Col. 1	Col. 2	Col. 3	Col. 4	Col. 5	Col. 6	Col. 7	Col. 8
Applesauce	6 #10	4 ⅓	$15.85	$68.63			
Green Beans	6 #10	3 ⅚	18.95	72.58			
Flour	25# bag	3	4.85	14.55			
Rice	50# bag	1	12.50	12.50			
			Total	$486.55			

Gross Food Cost = Beginning Inventory Dollar Value + Purchases − Ending Inventory Value

Net Food Cost = Gross Food Cost + Bar Transfers to the Kitchen − Food Transfers to the Bar − Staff Member Meals − Complimentary Meals

$$\text{Food Cost Percentage} = \frac{\text{Net Food Cost}}{\text{Total Food Sales During the Period}}$$

A physical inventory is also necessary in order to calculate **inventory turnover**—the rate at which inventory is converted to revenue during a given period. An excessively low inventory turnover rate can lead to increased spoilage and contamination as well as tie up cash in inventory. However, if turnover rates are too high, production may be hampered by insufficient inventory. High inventory turnover might also indicate that the business is not taking advantage of quantity discounts. Ideal inventory turnover rates can only be established by tracking past rates and calculating averages. Inventory turnover is calculated as follows:

$$\text{Average Inventory} = \frac{\text{Beginning Inventory Dollar Value} + \text{Ending Inventory Dollar Value}}{2}$$

Exhibit 7   Perpetual Inventory Form

Perpetual Inventory								
Product Name: P.D.Q. Shrimp				**Purchase Unit Size:** 5 lb bag				
Date	**In** Carried Forward	**Out** 15	**Balance**	**Date**	**In** Carried Forward	**Out**	**Balance**	
Col. 1	Col. 2	Col. 3	Col. 4	Col. 1	Col. 2	Col. 3	Col. 4	
5/16		3	12					
5/17		3	9					
5/18	6		15					
5/19		2	13					

The person in charge of inventory control may track turnover in each of the four classes of inventory items. Class A and Class C items should have higher turnover rates than Class B and Class D items. It might also be useful to calculate turnover rates for all categories of potentially hazardous foods, as part of the food safety risk management program. The frequency of deliveries must be considered when establishing inventory control standards.

A **perpetual inventory** is an ongoing record of what is in storage at any given time. As products are added to or removed from storage, the balance figure for each item is adjusted. The actual amount of any item on the shelves should agree exactly with the corresponding balance figure at all times. A perpetual inventory form is presented in Exhibit 7.

Although the perpetual inventory system requires more recordkeeping, it offers several advantages over periodic physical inventories. The perpetual inventory is always up to date, and the close monitoring involved in this system prevents food spoilage from progressing uncontrolled in storage areas. In addition, the perpetual inventory form, if accurate, allows tight control over food products. The perpetual inventory system is used mainly for expensive (Class A and B) menu items such as meat, fish, shellfish, specialty foods, and expensive spices. The perpetual inventory of such costly items lets staff members know that these items are being watched.

Other Inventory Controls. Another important inventory management technique is the rotation of food supplies on a first-in, first-out (FIFO) basis. According to the FIFO system, new stock is stored *behind* old stock so that the older products will always be used first. If products are dated upon receipt, managers can check each storage area during physical inventory to be sure that the FIFO system is being followed. The food production supervisor (usually the chef or assistant manager) should also make a daily FIFO check.

All stored food products, especially those that are potentially hazardous, should be regularly checked for acceptable sensory qualities. Any damaged products or items with abnormal colors, textures, or odors should be discarded. Keeping records on all spoiled food products helps management identify areas for improvement and helps the accounting department maintain accurate inventory values.

Potentially hazardous foods should not be stored in contact with other foods. Cooked foods should be stored above raw foods, and all foods in storage should be dated and wrapped or covered. Remember that foods should never be frozen or refrozen in a food establishment because these freezers are designed to *store* already-frozen foods.

Toxic and poisonous materials—such as cleaners, sanitizers, and pesticides—must be clearly labeled and stored in areas that are physically away from food products. It is a good idea to keep these storage areas locked. These substances should be stored in their original containers, which should not be re-used.

Storing and People

The storing function is a weak link in the control systems of some food service operations. These operations experience large losses due to contamination, spoilage, and deterioration of their food products, usually because no one is in charge of monitoring storage areas. Although a small business may not be able to justify hiring a storeroom person on a full-time basis, responsibility for storage areas must be given to one dependable person (for example, the chef or assistant manager). The establishment's investment in food and non-food products is too great to be treated haphazardly.

The responsibilities of the storeroom person vary with the operation and the dollar value of its inventory. In smaller operations, the storeroom person often has other responsibilities such as receiving, issuing, and/or production. However, these multiple responsibilities need not be a problem if the person follows the proper routines at each control point.

The major responsibilities of the storeroom person are:

- To conduct frequent, careful inspections of product storage areas in the facility

- To prevent waste in the form of spoilage and decreased product quality

- To discard food that is contaminated or spoiled and thus reduce risks

- To reduce financial losses due to theft and pilferage

- To monitor usage rates of each product

- To record inventory dollar amounts using the perpetual inventory and/or physical inventory system

The purpose of a storeroom person's inspections is to ensure that the operation's quality and safety standards are being maintained. Proper care of inventory items also contributes to the cost control program. Waste in the form of spoilage and decreased product quality increases the cost of goods sold and therefore lowers profits. By preserving food properly, the storeroom person makes a major contribution to the operation's bottom-line performance.

Contaminated food must be removed from inventory in order to protect the health of guests and the reputation of the establishment. When in doubt about the safety of an inventory item, it is better to throw it out than to risk an outbreak of foodborne disease. When checking for contamination or spoilage, check the product pull dates on milk and other dairy products.

Unfortunately, theft and pilferage are common in the food service industry. Security is therefore as important in storage areas as it is in the rest of the operation. The establishment of inventory controls can make losses easier to detect.

There are several good reasons for monitoring product usage rates. The information gained in this process can help the purchasing agent to establish par stocks and automatic reorder points, thus minimizing stockouts. The production department can be alerted to surplus products which are not being used up fast enough; these inventory items can then be worked into production before they spoil.

Storing and Equipment

Equipment is an important consideration in each of the three storage areas—dry, refrigerated, and frozen. Ambient storage temperatures in all three of these areas must be monitored with thermometers that are accurate to ±3°F (± 2°C). A thermometer should be placed in the warmest part of each storage area; the warmest part of a refrigerator or freezer is usually near the door. Thermometers should be positioned to be easily readable. A product thermometer with an accuracy of ± 2°F (±1°C) should also be used regularly to monitor the internal product temperatures of potentially hazardous foods in storage.

Many types of storage containers are used to hold food inventory, from pans and pots to plastic containers. When purchasing plastic containers and bags for food storage, buy them from a restaurant supplier and specify food-grade materials. Food products should not be stored in galvanized cans, non-food-grade bags or containers, or cardboard boxes. All containers must be properly labeled with the common name.

The proper storage of equipment and utensils provides protection from food, splashes, and dust in storage areas. Cleaned and sanitized equipment and utensils must be stored in a clean, dry location, in a self-draining position, and covered or inverted at least 6 inches (15.2 cm) above the floor. Utensils should be hung overhead or stored on utensil racks, not in cluttered drawers. Knives and special tools should be stored on trays. The best way to store cutting boards is vertically under counters or in a cutting board rack.

Tableware, including dishes, bowls, platters, and plates of all sizes, can present a unique storage problem. A self-leveling plate dispenser can help prevent breakage and contamination. The spring-loaded dispenser can be loaded with clean, sanitized tableware at the dishwashing machine and wheeled to kitchen areas for service. Some plate dispensers also heat or chill tableware.

Storing and Facilities

Each of the three types of food storage areas—dry, refrigerated, and frozen—has its own standards and requirements.

Dry Storage. Dry storage areas are designed to secure shelf-stable foods that do not require refrigeration. A properly designed dry storage area is clean, orderly, and well-ventilated. Good housekeeping in dry storage areas reduces contamination risks as well as fire hazards.

Dry storage areas should not house motors, compressors, machinery, water and heating pipes, or other utility structures. The walls and floors should be constructed of easy-to-clean materials. Protection from insects and rodents is essential. There should be adequate light for reading product labels. Security measures should include locked doors and proper key control.

All food in the dry storage area must be on shelves at least two inches (5.1 cm) from walls and six inches (15.2 cm) from the floor. This clearance not only facilitates inspection and cleaning, but also aids ventilation, prevents contamination, and eliminates pest harborage areas. All products should be stored at least 18 inches (45.7 cm) away from light bulbs and tubes. Bulbs and tubes should be shielded to protect food supplies from glass fragments in case of breakage.

Many operations use shelving on wheels to facilitate storage area cleaning. Open wire shelving is generally best for all three storage areas because it gives an unobstructed view of the products, permits free air circulation, and is usually more adaptable to changing storage needs. Shelves that are open on both sides and located in the center of the room provide the most efficient use of floor space. This center-aisle (often called "library") arrangement also makes stock rotation easier.

Each type of product in inventory should have its own assigned location in the storeroom. Bulky and heavy items should be placed on lower shelves, and frequently-used items should be placed near the entrance. Whenever a product is opened in storage, it must be kept away from containers that may be contaminated with dirt, wire, splinters, or other debris. The storeroom person must guard the food against physical hazards such as glass fragments and metal chips.

Storage time-temperature combinations are important because they keep food products high in nutrients, at peak flavor and texture, and safe to eat. All food in dry storage areas should be covered, labeled, and dated. Ideal storage temperatures are 50° to 70°F (10° to 21°C). Relative humidity should be about 50 to 60%. A thermometer should be mounted in the dry storage area, and the storeroom person should record the temperature at least twice each day. This and other information may be recorded on a **storage area condition report.** A sample of this form, which is useful for all three types of storage, is presented in Exhibit 8.

Government codes specify dry food storage requirements. The objective in dry storage is to minimize contamination and the proliferation of pathogens. By monitoring storage times and temperatures, an operation protects the quality and safety of its food products and reduces risks.

Refrigerated Storage. Refrigerated storage areas are designed to maintain food products at temperatures of 41°F (5°C) or less. Remember to check government

Exhibit 8   Storage Area Condition Report

AREA

☐ Dry
☐ Refrigerated
☐ Freezer   Date _____

Storage Area	Location	Temperature	Relative Humidity	Time Recorded	Signature of Recorder	Comments

specifications in your area. Refrigerators must have visible thermometers, and temperatures should be checked at least four times per day.

Most operators complain that they lack adequate refrigerated and frozen storage space. While in some cases modification of the facilities may be in order, limited refrigerated and frozen storage space has its advantages. It can force the production supervisor to control food inventories more carefully, to organize the areas more efficiently, and to work to avoid spoilage.

Because refrigerated storage serves to prolong the shelf life of perishable foods, the FIFO system is indispensable. Foods in refrigerated storage must be at least six inches (15.2 cm) off the floor and two inches (5.1 cm) away from walls to allow for air movement and to reduce insect and rodent harborage areas. Doors on refrigeration units should only be opened for a short time and only when necessary. To avoid having to search for an item, it is a good idea to post the contents of each cooling unit on its door. Placing frequently-used foods near the door of the unit also reduces the amount of time the door is open. Food products on shelves must not be jammed against the cooling unit doors when closed. This may damage the door gaskets and thus cause leaks.

Once canned products are opened, they must be removed from their original containers and placed in clean, labeled, dated, covered containers. Perishable or potentially hazardous foods should be refrigerated in pans not more than four inches (10.2 cm) deep.

Leftover food products should be covered to prevent contamination during refrigeration. However, they should not be covered airtight until chilled to 41°F (5°C); placing an airtight cover on food before it is chilled encourages the growth of anaerobic microorganisms during product cooling. Leftover prepared food must be stored above raw ingredients to prevent cross-contamination. Storing warm foods above already-refrigerated foods will allow the heat to dissipate more quickly. Refrigerated leftovers should be labeled with the date they were first stored; potentially hazardous leftovers should be used within 24 hours of storage or thrown out. Any spoiled foods discovered in storage areas should be discarded immediately.

Refrigeration needs have changed with the addition of fresh items to food service menus; these items require more refrigerated storage space. Recently-designed food establishments use a number of refrigeration units to build a refrigeration system. Walk-in refrigerators are used to store large quantities of food in bulk. Some walk-in refrigerators have a thermal curtain made of four-inch (10.2 cm) plastic strips in addition to a door. These curtains conserve energy and prevent accidents because workers can easily enter and exit coolers without having to open or close doors. Reach-in refrigerators are short-term storage units, often placed near cooking stations and stocked with food products needed during the meal period. Refrigerated drawers are an alternative to reach-in refrigerators and are also located near the cooking station. Roll-in refrigerators are specifically designed to accommodate carts. A dual-temperature unit (sometimes called a refrigerator-freezer) can be converted from a freezer to a refrigerator, or vice versa, at the flip of a switch.

Managing food safety is often more critical in refrigerated areas than in dry storage areas. Fortunately, refrigerators are relatively easy to clean and maintain if spills are wiped up promptly. Exterior surfaces should be cleaned daily with a hot water-detergent solution, rinsed, and dried with a clean cloth. The floors of walk-in units should be mopped daily. These floors are easier to maintain if they are made of ceramic quarry tile. On a weekly basis, or more frequently if necessary, the contents of each refrigerator should be transferred to another unit. All shelves should be removed, and the inner walls of the compartment washed, rinsed, and dried. A mild sanitizing solution (180-220 mg/L QUATS) should be applied to the interior surfaces to minimize mold and bacterial growth. Refrigerator shelves should also be washed, rinsed, and dried, and plastic thermal curtains should be cleaned with glass cleaner.

Once a month, the accumulation of dust and grease on the refrigerator's condenser and evaporator units should be cleaned away. Any water condensation should also be removed before the refrigerator is reassembled. The fans and motors inside and outside the refrigerator should be cleaned and checked every three months. Hinges and latches require oiling every six months. All refrigeration units must have thermometers, and they should be checked for accuracy (±3°F/± 2°C) periodically.

Zinc- and chrome-coated wire shelving is usually a problem in high-moisture areas because it tends to rust and is difficult to keep clean. Any rusted shelving should be replaced. Only epoxy-coated or stainless steel open wire shelving on wheels should be used in refrigerators and freezers.

Frozen Storage. The maximum temperature in frozen storage areas is 0°F (-18°C). Like refrigeration units, storage freezers should have visible thermometers which should be checked four times each day. Unsafe temperatures or faulty thermometers should be reported to the food production supervisor immediately. As previously discussed, most freezers in food service operations are designed to keep already-frozen foods frozen—not to freeze foods.

Freezers are available in many forms, including walk-in, reach-in, countertop, and drawer models. Freezers should be defrosted and cleaned at least monthly; follow the same procedure as for cleaning refrigerators, avoiding harsh cleaners and abrasives. The contents should be temporarily transferred to another freezer to prevent thawing. This process is easier if freezer shelves are already on wheels. Condensers, evaporators, and other machinery should be checked monthly.

It is important to guard against loss of quality during freezer storage. Carefully wrapping food products in moisture- and air-resistant wrapping deters dehydration (freezer burn) and other forms of deterioration. The food production supervisor should personally inspect each storage area on a daily basis to be sure the operation's food and beverage assets are being protected.

Some foods freeze better than others. Those that do not freeze well include high-water-content fruits and vegetables such as cucumbers, lettuce, watermelon, and plums. Unblanched vegetables also do not freeze well, and most untreated fruits become mushy when frozen. Dairy products such as yogurt, cream (light and sour), cottage and ricotta cheese, and cream cheese do not freeze well. Some sauces and gravies separate when frozen and thawed. Desserts with dairy products or eggs, such as meringues, custard pies, and puddings, as well as gelatin-based desserts, do not maintain their appearance or consistency when thawed after freezing.

Potentially hazardous foods should never be frozen or thawed and refrozen in the food service operation. All thawing is safer and more efficient under refrigeration: foods thaw under carefully controlled conditions and enable the refrigerator to use less power.

Violations of proper food storage can easily occur in food establishments. Some operations store food products uncovered and unlabeled or in non-food-grade plastic bags. In many establishments, storage areas are not designed to keep food products away from walls and floors. Some storage facilities are not equipped with accurate thermometers. In other operations, no one checks storage temperatures regularly. Such violations, although common, greatly increase the risks of running a food establishment. The operator who avoids such violations will ultimately enjoy greater success.

Storing and Change

A change in storing procedures is necessary when any of the other three control points which precede it are altered. For example, storage area requirements may change drastically if an operation changes from all-scratch preparation methods to the use of convenience foods. More refrigerated and frozen storage areas may be necessary, particularly in an older establishment. Management must consider the resources of the storing control point before making such operational changes.

Storing and Food Safety

Storing is an important activity to monitor in a food establishment for two reasons: food products rarely improve in quality while in storage, and the risk of food contamination is increased by improper storage temperatures or times. All food products must be dated, labeled, and covered before being placed in storage. These controls encourage the use of the FIFO inventory system and minimize the risks of potential contamination. They also help prevent waste which occurs when stored products cannot be identified or when they absorb odors or flavors from other food products.

Temperatures and times must be closely monitored in dry, refrigerated, and frozen storage. Products must also be regularly checked with sensory tests to minimize the chances of serving spoiled products. Staff members at the storing control point should be trained to conduct inspections, prevent waste, identify and dispose of spoiled food products, and reduce risks.

Equipment and facilities must be regularly cleaned, sanitized, and maintained. Written schedules which include detailed staff responsibilities help ensure that these important duties are performed regularly. Such control measures at the storing control point reduce the risks for guests, staff members, and owners of a food establishment.

The Issuing Control Point

The objective of the issuing control point is to ensure proper authorization for the transfer of food products from storage to the production departments of the operation. The issuing function should be designed to guarantee that only authorized staff members order and receive products from the facility's storage areas. A properly designed issuing system also facilitates calculation of the daily food cost. In addition, issuing is an important component of the food safety risk management program: potentially hazardous foods can be exposed to the TDZ at this control point, and additional handling may contaminate food products.

In small operations, formal issuing may be eliminated entirely. In such cases, all purchases are regarded as direct purchases: supplies are charged directly to the department or unit in which they are used. The direct purchase system eliminates the need for a formal requisition. Department staff members simply obtain supplies from a central storage area. These individuals must therefore inform the operation's purchasing agent of shortages or stockouts. Although this system is simple and less time-consuming, it does not provide as much control as a formal system. The informal system also leaves storage areas with no one specifically responsible for them, and thus the operation's issuing control point is at risk.

Issuing and Inventory

A **requisition** is a form for requesting inventory. It is an internal communication tool that shows which department needs which items. A department must provide

Exhibit 9 Food Requisition Form

Food Requisition

Storage Type (check one):   Date: _____

Refrigerated _____   Work Unit: _____

Frozen _____

Dry _____✓_____   Approved for Withdrawal: _____

					Employee Initials	
Item	Purchase Unit	No. of Units	Unit Price	Total Cost	Received By	Withdrawn By
Col. 1	Col. 2	Col. 3	Col. 4	Col. 5	Col. 6	Col. 7
Tomato Paste	CS-6 #10	2 ½	$28.50	$71.25	JC	Ken
Green Beans	CS-6 #10	1 ½	22.75	34.13	JC	Ken
			Total	$596.17		

a written and authorized requisition before being issued any products. Requisition forms may be sequentially numbered and/or color-coded by department for control purposes. A sample food requisition form is shown in Exhibit 9.

Written requisitions provide documentation and, therefore, greater control. Documentation is important whenever a product is transferred from one area of responsibility to another (in this case, from storage to production). A supply of products sufficient for one day or one meal period is usually issued to each department.

The costs of issues should be properly recorded on the requisition form, a process made easier when products are marked with the price during receiving. Costing issues facilitates the calculation of daily food cost and reminds staff members to think of inventory as money. Requisitions must be subtracted from perpetual inventory records to maintain accuracy. Tracking daily issues helps establish usage rates and reorder points.

Issuing should be done on a FIFO basis. This is easier if products are dated before storing. Proper stock rotation minimizes spoilage, contamination, and loss of product quality. The order in which products are assembled for issuing is the reverse of the order in which they are stored. That is, the least perishable items are taken from storage first and the most perishable products last. This minimizes possible contamination and maintains product temperature control.

The food production manager (chef or assistant manager) should be notified if perishable products are nearing the end of their shelf life. Issues should be checked for acceptable odor, feel, and appearance. In addition, a random temperature check should be made with the metal-stemmed product probe thermometer. Remember to always clean and sanitize the metal-stemmed product probe thermometer between changed uses to avoid cross-contamination.

Issuing and People

The person in charge of the storeroom ensures that each order has been properly authorized, removes product storage tags, and fills orders. The storeroom person then costs out each item ordered and totals the costs. He or she sends a copy of the completed requisition to the operation's accounting office along with any storage tags. This system helps prevent theft, pilferage, and unauthorized issues.

While assembling orders, the storeroom person should note any items in short supply and direct this information to the operation's buyer. Accuracy and careful inspection of written requests for inventory items are important during product issuing. In some establishments, the storeroom person also delivers orders to the production departments. Specified issuing times for each department can eliminate confusion and enable the storeroom person to work more efficiently.

Issuing and Equipment

Generally, the same kinds of equipment are used during the receiving and issuing of inventory. Products issued by weight should be weighed before they are released to the production department. A thermometer is used to check internal product temperatures. Calculators are useful in determining the dollar amount of each department's order and the total of all issues for the day. Handcarts and dollies are used to transport products from storage facilities to production areas.

Issuing and Facilities

Storeroom facilities must be attended to if the issuing control system is to remain intact. For maximum security, storeroom facilities should be kept locked with access limited to the storeroom person and the manager. Prohibiting unauthorized access to storage areas helps eliminate theft and pilferage. The facilities used for issuing must be maintained to reduce the risk of product contamination.

Issuing and Change

Issuing, like all of the control points, is affected by changes that occur in the food service system. Existing policies and standards are based on the present system; if a component of the system is modified in the future, it may also be necessary to alter issuing procedures and standards.

Although the requisition form is an important control tool, food establishments with relatively low business volumes are likely to follow an informal set of issuing guidelines. In such operations, production staff members often retrieve food products from an unlocked storage area whenever they need them. However, if the volume of business increases, the operation should implement a formal issuing system. The formal system, complete with storeroom personnel and written requisition forms, will help the operation achieve more control over food safety, cost, and quality—factors that ultimately have a dramatic effect on guest satisfaction.

Issuing and Food Safety

Whenever food products change departments, the responsibility for those products changes departments and risks are increased. Therefore, a written and authorized requisition form is essential at the issuing control point. This tool helps reduce risks because it clearly indicates who receives each food product.

Food products should be checked at issuing with sensory tests. This inspection reduces the risks of a contaminated or spoiled product entering the production control points. Equipment and facilities used during issuing must be regularly cleaned, sanitized, and maintained to prevent cross-contamination and help ensure the safety of finished menu items.

Key Terms

A-B-C-D scheme—A technique for grouping inventory items on a relative basis according to perishability and cost per serving, with Class A items being high in both perishability and cost per serving; Class B items being relatively high in cost, but low in perishability; Class C items being relatively low in cost per serving, but relatively high in perishability; and Class D items having both the lowest perishability and the lowest cost per serving.

credit memo—A form issued by a supplier to adjust an establishment's account. Issued in response to a request-for-credit memo when products are spoiled, do not meet the establishment's specifications, or are delivered in the wrong quantities. Helps ensure that the food establishment is charged only for the products that conform to its standards.

daily receiving report—A record of everything a facility receives; shows what was received, the date of the delivery, the name of the supplier, the quantity, the price, and any other relevant comments. Also provides a record of delivery distribution; the form's "Food Directs" column indicates the dollar value of products to be sent directly to kitchen production areas, and the "Food Stores" column records the dollar value of products to be placed in storage.

food cost percentage—A calculation that expresses food cost as a percentage of sales income.

inventory turnover—The rate at which inventory is converted to revenue during a given period.

invoice—A supplier's statement detailing all the products being delivered to a facility and their corresponding prices; may show products that are back-ordered or not yet available for delivery.

perpetual inventory—An ongoing record of what is in storage at any given time. As products are added to or removed from storage, the balance figure for each item is adjusted.

physical inventory—An actual count of what is in storage, taken each time an income statement is prepared.

requisition—A form for requesting inventory; an internal communication tool that shows which department needs which items. Required before products can be issued.

storage area condition report—A record of the temperatures of food storage areas, taken twice daily. Other information may also be noted.

time-temperature monitor—A device used for perishable product inspection during receiving; it is attached to boxes or cartons of refrigerated and frozen products just before they leave the processing plant. Measures the combined effects of heat and age by changing color when a product's temperature exceeds a certain level for an excessive length of time, allowing an operation's receiver to quickly see whether a product has been thawed and then refrozen.

 Review Questions

1. What inventory controls, standards, and procedures are important at the receiving control point?

2. A staff member performing the receiving function should have what types of qualifications?

3. What equipment items are used at the receiving control point, and why are they important?

4. What are the elements of proper receiving facilities?

5. Why is it important to maintain an optimum inventory?

6. What is the A-B-C-D scheme of inventory classification?

7. How does a perpetual inventory differ from a physical inventory?

8. What are the major responsibilities of the storeroom person?

9. What equipment and facilities considerations are important at the storing control point?

10. What should food service managers know about the issuing control point?

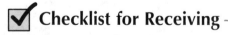 Checklist for Receiving

Inventory

_____ Inventory items are checked for applicable quality, cleanliness, and labeling specifications.

_____ The internal temperatures and sensory-tested qualities of products are evaluated.

_____ Deliveries are verified against the operation's purchase specifications and purchase orders.

_____ The supplier's invoice is checked for accuracy in quality descriptions, quantities, and prices.

_____ All products billed by weight are weighed before the invoice is signed.

_____ Different meat items are weighed separately.

_____ All products billed by count are counted before the invoice is signed.

_____ Products are dated immediately with a marking pen either on the outside container or the individual packages.

_____ Prices may be marked on each product unit.

_____ Where appropriate, product storage tags are used.

_____ All deliveries are recorded on the daily receiving report.

_____ Products are moved to storage in the following order:

  _____ most perishable products (frozen foods)

  _____ moderately perishable products (refrigerated foods)

  _____ least perishable products (dry and non-food items)

_____ A credit memo is requested when products are spoiled, when they do not meet the operation's specifications, or when the wrong amount has been delivered.

People

_____ A member of the management team or a trained staff member performs the receiving function.

_____ The receiver possesses product knowledge, technical skills, and a commitment to the organization.

_____ The receiver judges the quality, quantity, and safety condition of products.

_____ The receiver is in good health and practices good personal hygiene and cleanliness.

_____ The receiver understands how to accurately use all required equipment, facilities, and forms.

_____ The receiver knows what to do when there is a problem with product deliveries.

_____ The receiver is able to read and write, and demonstrates honesty and attention to detail.

_____ The receiver uses the purchasing specifications for all items ordered.

_____ Delivery hours are posted on the receiving door. Delivery times are staggered whenever possible, and do not include mealtime rush periods.

_____ The receiver has been trained to perform his or her duties effectively and efficiently, in cooperation with other departments in the food establishment or hotel.

Equipment

_____ An accurate scale is used during receiving to verify product weights.

_____ Product net weights are recorded and checked against the supplier's invoice.

_____ Metal-stemmed product probe thermometers are used during receiving to check the internal temperatures of refrigerated and frozen products.

_____ Refrigerated products are at 41°F (5°C) or less and frozen products are at 0°F (-18°C) or less when delivered.

_____ Tools for opening containers and boxes are available and used properly.

_____ The date of the delivery and the AP price are recorded directly on product packages with a marking pen.

_____ Other tools (including rulers, calculators, transport trucks, dollies, and other equipment to move products) are readily available and used properly.

Facilities

_____ The loading dock and receiving areas are cleaned daily and maintained regularly.

_____ The supplier's truck is periodically inspected for contamination.

_____ Debris or food particles are not allowed to accumulate in receiving areas.

_____ Garbage and trash areas are physically separated from the receiving area, if possible.

_____ The receiving area is well-lit and equipped with the necessary tools and work tables.

Food Safety Risk Management Program

_____ Potentially hazardous foods are carefully inspected during receiving.

_____ If acceptable, products are moved to storage as quickly as possible.

_____ Food handlers are trained to maintain standards and reduce risks during receiving.

_____ Adequate equipment and facilities are present, used, and cleaned, sanitized, and maintained frequently to reduce the risks during receiving.

✓ Checklist for Storing ——————————————

Inventory

_____ Food products are stored on shelves at least six inches (15.2 cm) off the floor and two inches (5.1 cm) away from the walls.

_____ Storage temperatures and relative humidities are maintained as follows:

  _____ Dry storage: 50° to 70°F (10° to 21°C); 50 to 60% relative humidity

  _____ Refrigerated storage: 41°F (5°C) or less; 80 to 90% relative humidity

  _____ Freezer storage: 0°F (-18°C) or less

_____ New inventory is placed behind old inventory as part of the FIFO system.

_____ Bulky and heavy items are stored on lower shelves.

_____ High-use items are stored near the entrance.

_____ A specific place is assigned to each type of item in inventory.

_____ Storage time-temperature combinations are closely monitored.

_____ Refrigerated leftovers are marked with the date they are first stored.

_____ Perishable and potentially hazardous leftovers are stored refrigerated in pans no more than four inches (10.2 cm) deep, and served or discarded within 24 hours.

_____ Inventory items are stored so as to prevent cross-contamination.

_____ Packaged food is not stored in contact with water or undrained ice.

_____ Toxic chemicals (cleaners, sanitizers, and pesticides) are stored away from food products, in physically separate, locked areas.

_____ All damaged products and those with abnormal odors or colors are discarded.

_____ Records of all spoiled food are maintained. Problem areas are identified and deficiencies are corrected.

_____ The A-B-C-D inventory classification is used where applicable.

_____ Perpetual and/or physical inventory systems are used to control inventory.

_____ Inventory turnover is calculated and monitored.

_____ Sensory tests (such as smell, appearance, and feel) are used during storing to monitor product quality.

_____ Potentially hazardous foods are not stored in contact with other foods.

_____ Cooked foods are stored above raw foods.

_____ All foods in storage are dated and wrapped or covered.

_____ Food service freezers are used to store already-frozen foods, not to freeze or re-freeze them.

People

_____ Storage area staff members are aware of standards for reducing inventory contamination, spoilage, and quality losses.

_____ Storage area staff members realize that inventory represents an investment that does not earn interest.

_____ A specific person is in charge of accurate and careful inspection of storage areas on a daily basis.

_____ Storage area staff members control the quality, food safety, and costs of inventory.

_____ Storage area staff members monitor the usage rates of inventory items.

_____ Storage area staff members help establish par stocks and reorder points to minimize stockouts and spoilage.

_____ The controller and storage area staff members record inventory dollar amounts.

_____ Storage area staff members are trained to maintain the operation's standards.

Equipment

_____ All storage areas have thermometers accurate to ±3°F (± 2°C).

_____ Storage area temperatures are checked several times each day.

_____ Internal product temperatures are measured with metal-stemmed product probe thermometers accurate to ± 2°F (±1°C).

_____ Cleaned and sanitized equipment and utensils are stored in a clean and dry location, in a self-draining position, and covered or inverted.

_____ Cleaned and sanitized equipment and utensils are stored at least six inches (15.2 cm) off the floor and protected from splash and dust.

_____ Equipment and utensils are not stored under exposed sewer or water lines.

_____ Equipment, utensils, or single-service items are not stored in toilet rooms or vestibules.

_____ Only food-grade containers and bags are used to store food products.

_____ Utensils are stored on utensil racks or hung overhead, not in cluttered drawers.

_____ Knives and special tools are stored on trays.

_____ Cutting boards are stored vertically under counters in a cutting board rack.

_____ Self-leveling dispensers are used to store tableware, including dishes, bowls, platters, and plates.

Facilities

_____ Storage areas are kept clean, orderly, and well-ventilated.

_____ Dry storage areas do not house motors, machinery, water and heating pipes, and other utility structures.

_____ Walls and floors are constructed of easy-to-clean materials.

_____ Insect and rodent controls are checked regularly in all storage areas.

_____ Key and lock controls are used to maintain security in storage areas.

_____ Storage areas have adequate lighting, and bulbs and tubes are shielded for protection.

_____ The door of each refrigerator and freezer is marked with the contents of the unit.

_____ Refrigeration and frozen storage units are not overloaded with inventory.

_____ Stainless steel or epoxy-coated open wire shelving on wheels is used in walk-in refrigerators and freezers and in dry storage areas.

_____   A system of regular cleaning and maintenance is followed.

_____   A storage area temperature-recording form is used.

Food Safety Risk Management Program

_____   Potentially hazardous foods are stored carefully and safely.

_____   Food handlers are trained to maintain standards and reduce risks during storing.

_____   Adequate facilities and equipment are present, used, and are frequently cleaned, sanitized, and maintained to reduce the risks during storing.

☑ Checklist for Issuing

Inventory

_____   Requisition forms are sequentially numbered or color-coded to facilitate recordkeeping.

_____   Each department is issued sufficient product quantities to last for one meal period or one day.

_____   Proper stock rotation (the FIFO system) is used to minimize contamination, spoilage, and product quality loss.

_____   Issues are costed accurately so that the total value of requisitions can be calculated on a daily basis.

_____   Sensory tests (such as odor, feel, appearance) are used to check inventory during issuing.

_____   Temperatures are checked with a cleaned and sanitized metal-stemmed product probe thermometer.

People

_____   The issuer releases products only with a written requisition.

_____   The issuer checks to see that the requisition is properly authorized.

_____   The issuer costs the items and extends the figures on the requisition.

_____   The issuer removes storage tags from products and attaches them to the requisition.

_____   The issuer removes products from storage in the following order:

      _____   least perishable products (dry and non-food items)

      _____   moderately perishable products (refrigerated foods)

_____ most perishable products (frozen foods)

_____ The issuer has been trained to maintain the operation's standards.

Equipment

_____ Products issued by weight are weighed before release to the production department.

_____ Calculators, handcarts, and other tools are used when necessary.

_____ A metal-stemmed product probe thermometer is used to check the internal product temperature during issuing.

Facilities

_____ Storeroom facilities are locked when unattended.

_____ Storeroom facilities are only accessible to authorized staff members.

_____ Facilities used for issuing are cleaned and maintained regularly to reduce the risk of product contamination.

Food Safety Risk Management Program

_____ Potentially hazardous foods are issued carefully and safely.

_____ Food handlers are trained to maintain standards and reduce risks during issuing.

_____ Adequate facilities and equipment are present, used, and are frequently cleaned, sanitized, and maintained to reduce the risks during issuing.

Chapter 5 Outline

The Preparing Control Point
    Preparing and Inventory
    Preparing and People
    Preparing and Equipment
    Preparing and Facilities
    Preparing and Change
    Preparing and Food Safety
The Cooking Control Point
    Cooking and Inventory
    Cooking and People
    Cooking and Equipment
    Cooking and Facilities
    Cooking and Change
    Cooking and Food Safety
The Holding Control Point
    Holding and Inventory
    Holding and People
    Holding and Equipment
    Holding and Facilities
    Holding and Change
    Holding and Food Safety

Competencies

1. List the special food safety concerns, the riskiest food products, and measures for reducing risks at the preparing control point. (pp. 129–133)

2. Describe personal hygiene standards for preparation staff, and explain the role of the master food production planning worksheet. (p. 134)

3. Identify the equipment used at the preparing control point, and describe its proper care and installation. (pp. 134–142)

4. Outline the three objectives of cooking, and identify measures for reducing risks at this control point. (pp. 142–144)

5. Describe the use and care of equipment used to heat food. (pp. 144–149)

6. Describe the use and care of miscellaneous food service equipment. (p. 149)

7. Describe measures for protecting inventory at the holding control point. (pp. 149–150)

8. Describe equipment used at the holding control point. (pp. 150–157)

5

The Preparing, Cooking, and Holding Control Points

THIS CHAPTER DISCUSSES the preparing, cooking, and holding control points of the food safety risk management program. Collectively, these three activities are known as **production.** The emphasis on each of the control points varies with the food service operation's menu. Certain menu items might not pass through all three control points. For example, some foods are served raw and chilled. Convenience foods undergo little preparation in the kitchen. And cooked-to-order menu items are seldom held for more than a few minutes before service. Regardless of the menu, the three production control points are critical to an operation's food safety risk management program.

The Preparing Control Point

The preparing control point includes all activities performed on foods before they are cooked or served raw. Preparation is a critical food safety control point for several reasons. First, when food products are removed from storage and unwrapped, they are unavoidably exposed to many potential sources of contamination. Second, the preparing function takes place at room temperature and therefore in the temperature danger zone (TDZ) of 41°F (5°C) to 140°F (60°C). Third, since people handle the food products at this control point, coughs, sneezes, and direct contact can introduce additional contamination. Finally, some foods—such as salads, fresh fruits and vegetables, unbaked frozen desserts, and dairy products—move directly from preparation to service. The safe handling of these products is especially important because there is no opportunity to destroy harmful microorganisms with heat.

The preparing function in a food service operation is also crucial to quality and cost control. Preparation begins the process of converting raw ingredients to finished menu items. Food preparation mistakes may be irreversible and costly. If an operation serves poorly prepared items, its guests will not be satisfied. Discarding such items adds to the operation's food cost.

It is difficult to prescribe hard and fast rules for the preparing control point because there are many different types of food service businesses, each with different menus, procedures, and objectives. Therefore, the following sections present general principles that are applicable to most operations.

Preparing and Inventory

Preparation and cooking alter foods physically and/or chemically. The objective of these activities is to enhance food quality while protecting the safety of the food and controlling waste. Preparing and cooking must be done properly to ensure safe products and maximum yields.

Some inventory items are riskier than others during the preparing control point. These items include:

- Potentially hazardous foods

- Foods that possess natural contaminants (such as soil-grown vegetables and fresh fish)

- Foods that are handled a great deal and thus susceptible to cross-contamination

- Foods that have multiple preparation steps

- Foods that are exposed to kitchen temperatures (TDZ) for long periods of time

- Foods that have gone through a number of temperature changes

- Foods that are prepared in large quantities

All of these foods must be handled very carefully. Staff members should be aware of the risks and know the procedures for reducing risks when handling these foods.

Government codes address potentially hazardous foods that will not receive further cooking. The ingredients must be chilled. Potentially hazardous foods that are reconstituted or fortified during preparing must be held at 41°F (5°C) or below. Raw fruits and vegetables must be washed in potable water before preparation.

All ingredients should be assembled in the work area before preparation begins. This pre-preparation, known as *mise en place* ("put in place"), reduces errors and speeds up the actual preparation process. In addition, *mise en place* reduces the food handling time and exposure to the TDZ.

Preparation activities include washing, peeling, trimming, dicing, chopping, and cutting. When cutting boards can no longer be effectively cleaned and sanitized, they should be discarded.

Some food establishments butcher their own meats from wholesale cuts. In-house meat-cutting procedures must focus on food safety, since these products are potentially hazardous foods. The skill levels of preparation personnel, the establishment's menu, and the facilities should be considered when deciding whether to butcher meats in-house.

Thawing. Frozen food products may be cooked directly from the frozen state or thawed during preparing and prior to cooking. But frozen food thawing is potentially hazardous if food products are exposed to the temperature danger zone. Remember, the TDZ may be different in your locality. The defrosting method selected should minimize contact with the TDZ. *Never thaw frozen foods at room temperature.* The risks are too great.

Some frozen foods undergo a process known as *slacking* that allows the temperature of the food to gradually increase from –10°F (–23°C) to 25°F (–4°C).

Slacking is done in preparation for deep-fat frying or to facilitate even-heat penetration during the cooking of previously block-frozen food such as spinach.

Thawing under refrigeration at temperatures of 41°F (5°C) or less is recommended, since it minimizes contact with the TDZ. This method also minimizes product quality loss and exposure to contamination. It works well for frozen fruit, poultry, fish, shellfish, and large cuts of meat. There is an added advantage to thawing under refrigeration: frozen food placed in a refrigerator to thaw will draw heat from the other refrigerated products. This heat exchange saves energy by reducing the amount of time the refrigerator's cooling equipment has to run. Today's food establishments are often designed with back-to-back walk-in freezer and refrigerator combinations. This design allows the (outer) refrigerator to serve as a buffer zone between the heat of the kitchen and the freezer, thus reducing the amount of cold air lost from the freezer.

Thawing completely submerged in cold running water (70°F [21°C] or less) is also acceptable. The running water's velocity must be sufficient to agitate and float off loose particles in the overflow, and the water must not run so long that the temperature of the thawed ready-to-eat food rises above 41°F (5°C). Items thawed in this manner must be protected from water damage by being tightly wrapped or placed in watertight containers. This method works well with frozen fruit. Some jurisdictions do not recommend thawing potentially hazardous foods under cold running water.

With some food products, thawing as part of the cooking process can save time and still be safe. Small cuts of meat, poultry, fish, and frozen vegetables are usually defrosted and cooked simultaneously. Thawing may take place for ready-to-eat food by any of the approved procedures if it is prepared for immediate service in response to an individual consumer's order. Breaded vegetables, fish, and shellfish are actually better when they are cooked directly from the frozen state.

Microwave oven thawing may be used for some food products, although there are limitations. Microwave thawing is acceptable only when it is part of the cooking process or when the thawed food products are transferred to conventional cooking equipment for immediate cooking with no interruptions in the transfer process. Bread and rolls are toughened when heated in a microwave oven, and large pieces of meat may not fit into the oven's chamber.

It is important to remember that since foods are not pure water they are not frozen at 32°F (0°C) as water is. Foods freeze and thaw at temperatures between 25°F (–4°C) and 32°F (0°C). Frozen foods have several opportunities to defrost during handling, transportation, and storing. If the food is thawed and then refrozen, large ice crystals will form and will reduce the product's quality.

Standard Recipes. A **standard recipe** is a written procedure for the production of a given food item. It lists the exact quantity of each ingredient to be used, the sequential order in which ingredients are put together, cooking times and temperatures, and the equipment necessary to produce the finished product. Standard recipes are essential if an operation is to achieve consistency in product quality, food safety, and cost. A sample standard recipe form is illustrated in Exhibit 1.

Standard recipes allow the operator to precisely determine the cost per portion, or **standard recipe cost,** of finished menu items. This information is necessary

Exhibit 1   Sample Standard Recipe

<table>
<tr>
<td colspan="2" align="center">Fish Fillet Amandine</td>
<td colspan="2">IX. MAIN DISHES—FISH 2
Baking Temperature: 450°F
Baking Time: 14-15 min</td>
</tr>
<tr>
<td>Yield: _____
Size: _____</td>
<td></td>
<td>Yield: 60
Size: 6 oz</td>
<td></td>
</tr>
<tr>
<th>Amount</th>
<th>Ingredients</th>
<th>Amount</th>
<th>Procedure</th>
</tr>
<tr>
<td>_____</td>
<td>Fish fillets, fresh or frozen 6 oz portion</td>
<td>22$\frac{1}{2}$ lb</td>
<td>1. Defrost fillets if frozen fish is used.
2. Arrange defrosted or fresh fillets in single layers on greased sheet pans.</td>
</tr>
<tr>
<td>_____</td>
<td>Almonds, toasted, chopped or slivered</td>
<td>1 lb</td>
<td>3. To toast almonds:
   a. Spread on sheet pans.
   b. Place in 350°F oven until lightly toasted.
     Approximate time: 15 min.</td>
</tr>
<tr>
<td>_____</td>
<td>Margarine or butter, softened</td>
<td>2 lb 8 oz</td>
<td>4. Add almonds, lemon juice, lemon peel, salt, and pepper to softened margarine or butter.</td>
</tr>
<tr>
<td>_____
_____
_____</td>
<td>Lemon juice
Lemon peel, grated
Salt</td>
<td>$\frac{1}{2}$ cup
2$\frac{3}{4}$ oz
4 tbsp</td>
<td>5. Mix thoroughly.
6. Spread margarine mixture on fillets as uniformly as possible.
    Amount per fillet: #60 scoop</td>
</tr>
<tr>
<td>_____
_____</td>
<td>Pepper, white
Weight: margarine-almond mixture</td>
<td>1 tbsp
4 lb</td>
<td>7. Bake at 450°F for approx. 15 min or until fish flakes when tested with fork.
8. Sprinkle lightly with chopped parsley or sprigs of parsley when served.</td>
</tr>
</table>

for pricing menu items accurately. A **product cost analysis form** is used to calculate the cost per portion. A sample of this form is shown in Exhibit 2. The standard recipe cost is calculated by adding the costs of all ingredients in a recipe (total product cost) and dividing by the yield (number of servings).

For these calculations to be accurate, the operation must have and use **standard portion sizes.** Standard portion sizes help the operation deliver its products consistently without cheating itself or its guests. To help maintain consistent portion sizes, an operation should:

- Follow standard recipes exactly to obtain intended yields

- Use scales and other measuring devices during preparation, cooking, and portioning for service

- Purchase pre-portioned goods when available and portion as many items as possible during preparation

Standard recipes should be changed as necessary to compensate for changing resources or other operational changes. The production manager or staff members may be able to improve standard recipes. New recipes copied from magazines or

Exhibit 2   Sample Product Cost Analysis Form

A. **Name of Menu Item** *Fish Fillet Amandine*

B. **Portion Size** *6 oz Fish/#60 Scoop Sauce*

C. **Number of Portions** *60*

Ingredient	Amount	Cost/Unit	Total Cost
1	2	3	4
Fish Fillets	22 lb 8 oz	$4.85/lb	$109.13
Almonds	1 lb	4.26/lb	4.26
Butter/Margarine	2 lb 8 oz	1.35/lb	3.38
Lemon Juice	1/2 cup	1.90/16 oz (2 cups)	.48
Lemon Peel	3 lemons	.75/each	2.25
Salt	TT	-	-
Pepper	TT	-	-
		Total	$119.50

$119.50	÷	60	=	$1.99
Total Cost (col. 4)		Number Portions (C)		Standard Portion Cost

supplied by other establishments should be adapted to the needs of the operation, its staff members, and its guests.

Convenience Foods. Some food service managers have a hard time deciding whether to use convenience foods. These products are delivered to the facility in a ready-to-cook or ready-to-eat form and therefore require less in-house labor to prepare for service. Convenience foods give kitchen staff more time for other work. For example, an executive chef who uses natural convenience food bases can devote more time to management responsibilities.

Convenience products offer several advantages to a food service operation. First, they are characterized by a consistency that is often difficult to achieve in products prepared on-site. Second, because convenience foods produce a specific yield, they have an easy-to-calculate portion cost and make it easier to control portions. Many convenience foods come pre-portioned or with a certain number of portions in the case or container. Third, convenience products can reduce waste by making it easier to use only the amount needed; for example, the chef need not prepare an entire pot of stock for a recipe that only calls for two cups. Fourth, convenience foods facilitate menu expansion. Combining high-quality convenience products with signature ingredients is a relatively easy way to add new items to the menu.

Convenience foods can reduce *or* increase handling and storage costs, depending on the existing facilities and the type of storage each product requires. Therefore, each product must be judged individually. Management should also evaluate the quality of each product carefully. Convenience foods should be of equal or higher quality than similar products prepared on-site.

Preparing and People

Regulatory standards regarding personal hygiene apply to every staff member in a food establishment. Because these standards are especially important for food handlers, we will review them here briefly.

All production staff members should wear uniforms and preferably change into them when they report for work. Street clothes or uniforms worn outside the establishment can introduce contamination at the preparing control point. Preparation staff members must also wear hair restraints such as caps, chef's hats, or hair nets. Hair in food not only is distasteful to guests, but also is a source of pathogenic organisms.

Smoking must be prohibited in food preparation areas because food can be contaminated by tobacco, ashes, or saliva. Staff members should also not eat in food preparation areas. Given that the cook or chef must periodically taste food products, sampling procedures must maintain food safety. Utensils used for tasting should never be re-introduced to food products, and no one should use his or her fingers to sample food.

Handwashing is critical before, during, and after food preparation activities. Production staff members may wear single-use gloves for only one task, such as working with ready-to-eat food or with raw animal food. The gloves must be discarded when damaged or soiled, or when interruptions occur in the task or operation. Single-use gloves are not designed to be used in place of proper handwashing or other food safety procedures.

Finally, the operation should not allow unauthorized people in the food preparation area. In addition to bringing in contaminants, they present a security risk.

It is important that food preparation staff members do their work accurately. Accuracy reduces waste and losses resulting from improper ingredient handling, weighing, and measuring. It also ensures a high-quality end product. Some operations have an ingredient room adjacent to the storeroom. Personnel in the ingredient room carefully measure and weigh raw ingredients before issuing them to the kitchen. This arrangement reduces waste and helps ensure that the proper quantities are used in recipe preparation.

The preparation function in large operations is easier to control with a **master food production planning worksheet.** A sample is presented in Exhibit 3. The worksheet provides a format for planning both people and product utilization for each meal or special function. The worksheet informs production staff members exactly what and how much to prepare: it lists each menu item, the standard portion size, and the forecasted number of portions. The form provides a guide for requisitioning and issuing raw materials. It also has a place for both the number of portions served and the number of portions left over. Because the worksheet serves as an overall food plan for a meal or special function, it can also be used to schedule production staff members.

Preparing and Equipment

A variety of equipment is used at the preparing control point. Because most preparation equipment is in direct contact with food, it is important to clean, sanitize, and maintain these items properly in order to avoid cross-contamination.

Exhibit 3 Master Food Production Planning Worksheet

Day Tuesday					Master Food Production Planning Worksheet				Local Weather Forecast: Cloudy & mild	
Date 8/1/00									Special Plans: Party of 15 — steaks	

Items	Standard Portion Size	Forecasted Portions			Adjusted Forecast	Requisitioning Guide Data		Remarks	Number of Portions Left Over	Actual Number Served
		Guests	Officers	Total Forecast		Raw Materials Requested	State of Preparation			
Appetizers										
Shrimp Cocktail	5 ea	48	—	48	51	12 lbs of 21-25 count	R T C		—	53
Fruit Cup	5 oz	18	1	19	20	See Recipe for 20 Portions			—	19
Marinated Herring	2½ oz	15	1	16	16	2½ lbs	R T E		—	14
Half Grapefruit	½ ea	8	—	8	8	4 Grapefruit			—	9
Soup	6 oz	30	3	33	36	Prepare 2 Gallons			5	32
Entrees										
Sirloin Steak	14 oz	28	—	28	29	29 Sirloin Steaks (Btchr.)	R T C		—	28
Prime Ribs	9 oz	61	1	62	64	3 Ribs of Beef	R T C	Use Re-heat if necessary	out at 10:45 p.m.	62
Lobster	1½ lb	26	—	26	28	28 Lobsters (check stock)				26
Ragout of Lamb	4 oz	24	2	26	26	12 lbs lamb fore (¾" pcs.)		Recipe No. E.402	1 +	25
Half Chicken	½ ea	34	2	36	38	38 halves (check stock)			—	39
Vegetables & Salads										
Whipped Potatoes	3 oz	55	1	56	58	13 lbs	A P		2-3	56
Baked Potatoes	1 ea	112	3	115	120	120 Idahos			out at 11:10 p.m.	120
Asparagus Spears	3 ea	108	—	108	113	8 No. 2 cans			2	110
Half Tomato	½ ea	48	4	52	54	27 Tomatoes			2	52
Tossed Salad	2½ oz	105	3	108	112	See Recipe No. S.302			—	114
Hearts of Lettuce	¼ hd	63	2	65	67	18 heads			—	69
Desserts										
Brownie w/ice cream	1 sq./1½ oz	21	2	23	26	1 pan brownies			—	24
Fresh Fruits	3 oz	10	—	10	11	See Recipe No. D.113			—	10
Ice Cream	2½ oz	35	3	38	40	Check stock			—	43
Apple Pie	⅟₇ cut	21	—	21	21	3 Pies			out at 10:50 p.m.	21
Devils Food Cake	⅛ cut	8	—	8	8	1 cake			1	7
Total No. of Persons		173	5	178	185					180

Abbreviations: A P – as purchased; R T C – ready-to-cook; R T E – ready-to-eat.

Food mixers are used to incorporate solids into liquids, liquids into solids, liquids into liquids, and gases into liquids and solids. Several attachments are available that grind, grate, whip, beat, knead, slice, emulsify, chop, and mix. Food mixers are highly versatile and are available in both countertop and floor models. Mixer capacities range from 5 quarts (4.7 liters) to 100 gallons (378.5 liters).

Food mixers are easy to clean. The bowl and beaters can be cleaned, rinsed, and sanitized in the pot and pan station. The exterior of the mixer should be wiped after each use with a hot water-detergent solution, rinsed, and dried with a soft cloth. Lubricating movable parts once each month keeps the mixer in good working condition. Use a food-grade lubricant, as it might come into contact with unprotected food.

Food processors, slicers, choppers, blenders, and grinders save time and reduce the number of monotonous kitchen tasks. The heavy-duty construction of a quantity kitchen food processor makes it highly versatile. This specialized equipment should be cleaned and maintained according to the manufacturer's recommendations. If not properly cleaned and maintained, such equipment can spread contamination through countless batches of food, much of which will not be cooked or heated before service.

Kitchenware—including knives, scoops, funnels, whips, spoons, spatulas, sifters, strainers, sieves, ladles, graters, slicers, peelers, forks, and other hand tools—must be cleaned and sanitized, either manually or mechanically, after each changed use. Sanitized kitchenware should be stored to prevent contamination. In-use kitchenware of any kind (including single-use gloves) must be handled carefully to avoid cross-contamination.

Kitchenware can sometimes be used and set aside for short periods of time. It should be placed flat on a clean food preparation surface. However, if a substantial amount of time elapses, kitchenware should be cleaned and sanitized before re-using, especially if it is being used to prepare potentially hazardous foods. Never place kitchenware in the space between preparation tables, between the wall and preparation tables, or in your pocket.

Work tables should be cleaned frequently—at least every time a change in use occurs. It is important to remove food and utensils from the surface before cleaning work tables with a hot water-detergent solution. Cleaning should be followed by sanitizing with a chlorine (100 mg/L) solution. Drawers under work tables are more useful if they are cleaned out once a week. It is even more efficient to eliminate all storage drawers from the kitchen and store utensils on stainless steel open wire shelving.

Cutting boards and blocks, like work tables, must be cleaned and sanitized after each changed use. Many government health departments do not allow wooden cutting boards because they are difficult to keep clean, particularly as they become scored with use. These regulatory agencies specify cutting boards made of rubber or plastic materials that meet established standards. Rubber or plastic boards are not as easily scored as wooden boards. Once boards are scored to the point where they can no longer be cleaned and sanitized, they should be thrown out.

Cutting boards and blocks should be washed by hand in a hot water–detergent solution, as mechanical dishwashers can warp them. Boards are sanitized by dipping them in a dilute chlorine bleach (50 mg/L) solution. They should then be rinsed and allowed to air dry.

Equipment Installation. Preparation equipment, if properly installed and used, can raise productivity and efficiency at this control point. Equipment must be installed and located to prevent the contamination of food and food-contact surfaces. Installation must also allow for easy cleaning and sanitizing of equipment and adjacent surfaces. Equipment, whether fixed or mobile, may not be installed under exposed or unprotected sewer lines or any other potential sources of contamination, such as stairs. This requirement may be extended to include water lines, if condensation is a problem.

Mobile equipment—equipment on wheels or casters—is easier to clean and sanitize. Mobile equipment costs more than fixed equipment and has additional parts that might need maintenance. Utility connections should be flexible or fitted with quick-disconnects.

Fixed equipment should allow for easy cleaning and sanitizing of adjacent areas; otherwise, there should be no more than one thirty-second of an inch (.8 mm) of space between the equipment and walls or ceilings. Floor-mounted equipment with legs should be at least six inches (15.2 cm) from the floor. The base of equipment without legs should be sealed as illustrated in Exhibit 4. Heavy equipment

Exhibit 4   Floor- and Pedestal-Mounted Equipment Installations

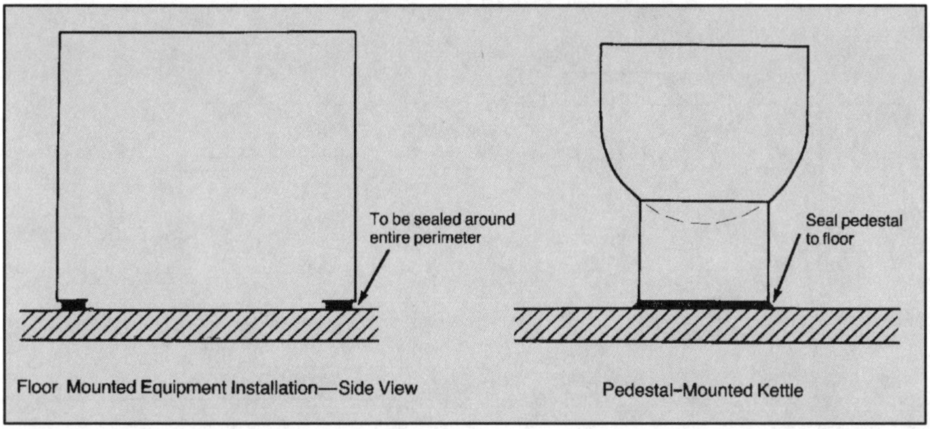

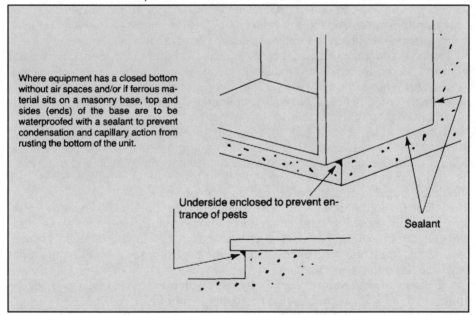

To be sealed around
entire perimeter

Seal pedestal
to floor

Floor Mounted Equipment Installation—Side View

Pedestal-Mounted Kettle

Source: National Sanitation Foundation, *Sanitation Aspects of Food Service Facility Plan Preparation and Review.*

Exhibit 5   Solid Masonry Base Installation—Side View

Where equipment has a closed bottom
without air spaces and/or if ferrous material sits on a masonry base, top and
sides (ends) of the base are to be
waterproofed with a sealant to prevent
condensation and capillary action from
rusting the bottom of the unit.

Underside enclosed to prevent entrance of pests

Sealant

Source: National Sanitation Foundation, *Sanitation Aspects of Food Service Facility Plan Preparation and Review.*

may be installed on a masonry base, which eliminates the need for cleaning below the equipment. Such equipment should be installed as illustrated in Exhibit 5. All openings to hollow spaces beneath the equipment and between the masonry base

Exhibit 6   Installation of Cantilevered Equipment

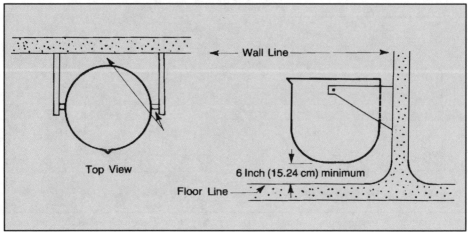

Source: National Sanitation Foundation, *Sanitation Aspects of Food Service Facility Plan Preparation and Review.*

and equipment must be sealed to prevent the entrance of insects or rodents. Once heavy equipment is sealed to a masonry base, it is extremely expensive to remove, so installations should be carefully considered in advance.

Some equipment is **cantilevered**—that is, wall-mounted with a horizontal support. For example, some models of steam-jacketed kettles are cantilevered. These items should be installed so that debris and liquid waste do not collect between the equipment and the wall or under the equipment. A proper installation of cantilevered equipment is illustrated in Exhibit 6.

Table-mounted equipment with legs should have a minimum clearance of four inches (10.2 cm) between the bottom of the equipment and the table. Portable equipment on a countertop must be easily movable by one person and must have quick-disconnects or flexible utility lines. Fixed counter equipment without legs should be sealed to the counter around the entire base.

All aisles and working spaces between equipment and walls must be unobstructed. They should be large enough to allow personnel to perform their duties without contaminating food or food-contact surfaces. Equipment can be a source of food contamination, so in all installations the prevention of potential contamination is an important consideration.

Equipment needed for preparation is based on the menu. If a menu change is anticipated, additional preparation or cooking equipment may have to be purchased. If a new menu item will require a specialized piece of equipment, the cost of adding the equipment must be weighed against the profits the new item is expected to generate. Other factors such as operating skills required, risk management, monthly utility charges, and maintenance of the establishment's quality standards also must be considered.

It is a good idea to submit an **equipment schedule** (Exhibit 7) and **equipment installation information** (Exhibit 8) to appropriate government officials

Exhibit 7   Equipment Schedule

Item No.[1]	Quantity	List of Equipment	Description & Model Nos.[2,3,4]

Source: National Sanitation Foundation, *Sanitation Aspects of Food Service Facility Plan Preparation and Review.*

Footnotes:

[1]Key to Floor Plan.
[2]Indicate Custom Fabricated (C.F.).
[3]Indicate Listings (UL, NSF, AGA), etc.
[4]If narrative description is required, use back of this sheet.

before purchasing or installing equipment. Health authorities can use these two documents to identify potential food safety hazards. This may help the operation avoid unwise equipment purchases that add to the food safety risks of running a food service establishment.

Preparing and Facilities

Preparation facilities vary in size and layout with the type of operation and its menu. However, every kitchen is divided into a series of work centers for preparing related products. In small kitchens, the arrangement of equipment in a single room serves to divide work centers, while in larger kitchens some work centers are in separate rooms. For example, in a large operation the *garde-manger*—a cold food preparation department responsible for such dishes as aspic, pâté, mousse,

Exhibit 8   Equipment Installation Information

Item No.	Accessories	Plumbing								Remarks	Electrical									Installation Information
		Water[1]			Waste			Faucets												
		Cold	140° F	180° F	Size	Type	Height	Type	By											

Source: National Sanitation Foundation, *Sanitation Aspects of Food Service Facility Plan Preparation and Review.*

Footnotes:

[1]If water at other temperatures is required, indicate as a remark and supply information separately.

salads and dressings, and sauces—may be located in a chilled pantry room; in a small establishment the *garde-manger* may consist of an area of the kitchen with chilled preparation surfaces. (The term *garde-manger* is also applied to a chef who specializes in the production of cold dishes.)

The layout of facilities is especially important in smaller operations, where every inch of space must be used efficiently. Careful planning can help management get the most out of an operation's facilities. For example, suppose management is considering the preparation of fresh fruits and vegetables. One important planning consideration might be the location of preparation activities: will all preparation take place in one area, or will items be washed, peeled, and trimmed in one area and cut and weighed in another? Management must also decide which staff members will perform which preparing functions. These decisions, in turn, will influence the layout of preparation facilities.

Preparation facilities should be designed to move products from the issuing control point to the cooking control point quickly and easily. Minimum handling also reduces food safety risks. Adequate equipment, work tables, lighting, and ventilation are necessary for efficient preparation. Concentrating food preparation in a few areas may raise staff productivity.

Preparation facilities should comply with regulatory agency requirements. Facilities should be designed to minimize contamination risks and physical hazards, and should be cleaned and sanitized regularly.

Preparing and Change

Changes occur daily in the food service industry as a result of evolving guest demands and modifications in the food processing, manufacturing, and distribution systems. Many of these changes force food service managers to re-evaluate their preparing functions. Preparation activities that were once part of every food service business are often no longer necessary; for example, many operations now purchase cleaned, peeled, and trimmed fresh vegetables and ready-to-serve salads. Likewise, most operations now buy pre-portioned meat products, and some purchase fully cooked, ready-to-slice roasts for sandwiches and other menu items. The availability of high-quality frozen convenience doughs and bread products allows many establishments to offer freshly prepared bakery items with relatively limited equipment and facilities. The availability of several high-quality natural food bases has virtually eliminated the need for a simmering stockpot. These convenience products reduce waste, spoilage, and food safety risks.

Because the preparing control point is subject to frequent changes, flexible equipment is a good investment for most operations. Multi-use equipment (discussed later in the chapter) enhances menu flexibility and efficient use of kitchen space.

Preparing and Food Safety

Standards at the preparing control point, the initial production activity, are necessary to reduce risks throughout production. The standard recipe is one of the most important controls. Standard recipes allow the operation to prepare a specific quantity of each food item and to produce finished products of consistent quality. Some standard recipes can be modified to reduce risks; for example, the pH of a finished product can be lowered by adding high-acid ingredients, or the amount of a potentially hazardous ingredient can be decreased. Standard recipes should only be modified, however, if the changes do not negatively affect the quality of the menu item or guest satisfaction.

Raw products served uncooked must be carefully washed and handled during preparation. Sensory tests should be used repeatedly to evaluate the quality of all food products. Preparation staff members can help reduce risks by adhering to rules of personal cleanliness and hygiene, including frequent handwashing, using single-use gloves for handling food, and wearing clean uniforms and proper hair restraints. Safe food-tasting procedures are essential. Equipment and facilities must be properly cleaned, sanitized, and maintained. All of these strategies are designed to reduce risks during preparation.

The Cooking Control Point

The heat added to food during cooking causes a number of physical and chemical changes to food products. The cooking control point should be designed to achieve three objectives: to destroy harmful microorganisms; to increase the digestibility of food; and to alter its form, flavor, color, texture, and appearance.

Cooking can destroy or inactivate some pathogens. The success of inactivation or destruction depends on the temperature, time, cooking method, characteristics of the food product, and type and quantity of organisms present. Toxins and organisms that form spores are generally heat-stable. For example, spores of *Clostridium perfringens* are not destroyed by normal cooking procedures. The toxin of *Staphylococcus aureus* is also stable at normal cooking temperatures.

Cooking is necessary to increase the digestibility of many food products. Heat makes many proteins, fats, and carbohydrates easier to digest. Unfortunately, cooking can also reduce the nutritional value of food products by destroying some of the vitamins they contain. In general, shorter cooking times minimize vitamin loss.

Cooking alters the form, flavor, color, texture, and appearance of food products. These chemical and physical changes increase the palatability of food products. Strict time-temperature controls, combined with standardized production techniques, can enhance food quality and, therefore, guest satisfaction.

Cooking and Inventory

Cooking involves combining the appropriate amounts of ingredients according to standard recipes and heating at the proper temperature for a designated period of time. The product resulting from the cooking process often bears little resemblance to the raw ingredients from which it was produced.

One of the primary objectives of guidelines for food preparation is the prevention of cross-contamination. Equipment and kitchenware must be cleaned and sanitized after each changed use. For example, if a food slicer is used to slice raw boneless beef loins into eight-ounce New York strip steaks, it must be cleaned and sanitized before it is used to slice any item other than raw beef loins. Food-contact surfaces on equipment must also be cleaned and sanitized if an interruption in operations has occurred. For example, suppose a slicer is used to slice cooked boneless prime rib for a banquet. After all of the prime rib is sliced and plated, it is placed in a food warmer and held at 130°F (54°C) or above. Forty minutes later, when the prime rib is served, the banquet workers discover that they still need 23 orders of prime rib. The slicer must be cleaned and sanitized before additional prime rib can be portioned. Any kitchenware used to handle the prime rib must also be cleaned and sanitized before re-use.

Potentially hazardous foods must be heated to a minimum internal temperature of 145°F (63°C) for 15 seconds during cooking. The exceptions to this rule are pork and game animals, comminuted fish and meats, injected meats, and eggs (155°F [68°C] for 15 seconds); field-dressed wild game animals, poultry, stuffed fish, stuffed meat, stuffed pasta, stuffed poultry, or stuffing containing fish, meat, or poultry (165°F [74°C] or above for at least 15 seconds); and beef roasts.

Beef roasts should be cooked in a preheated oven. Table A, below, shows the oven parameters required to destroy pathogens on the surface of beef roasts and corned beef. The minimum holding times required at specified temperatures are shown in Table B.

Table A

	Oven Temperature	
	Roast Weight	
Oven Type	Less than 4.5 kg (10 lbs)	4.5 kg (10 lbs) or more
Still Dry	177°C (350°F) or more	121°C (250°F) or more
Convection	163°C (325°F) or more	121°C (250°F) or more
High Humidity[1]	121°C (250°F) or less	121°C (250°F) or less

[1]Relative humidity greater than 90% for at least 1 hour as measured in the cooking chamber or exit of the oven; or in a moisture-impermeable bag that provides 100% humidity.

Table B

Temperature °C (°F)	Time[1]	Temperature °C (°F)	Time[1]	Temperature °C (°F)	Time[1]
54 (130)	112 minutes	58 (136)	28 minutes	61 (142)	8 minutes
56 (132)	56 minutes	59 (138)	18 minutes	62 (144)	5 minutes
57 (134)	36 minutes	60 (140)	12 minutes	63 (145)	4 minutes

[1]Holding time may include postoven heat rise.

Raw animal foods cooked in a microwave oven must reach temperatures of at least 165°F (74°C) in all parts of the food and be allowed to remain covered for two minutes after they are cooked to obtain temperature equilibrium. Microwave ovens might cook some foods unevenly. For example, microwaves heat and cook the outside layers of thick foods (such as roasts), while the interior is cooked by conduction, a slower heating process.

Food establishments can still serve steak tartare, sushi, and soft-cooked eggs. However, establishments must provide consumers with information stating that food safety requires that these foods be cooked thoroughly. Alternatively, the establishment may be granted a variance by reason of its having an approved HACCP plan in place. A variance requires the adoption of a HACCP plan that is approved *in advance* by the regulatory authority.

Food products should never be reheated on a steam table. This equipment is not designed to produce sufficient internal temperatures in food products. Generally, reheated potentially hazardous foods should reach a temperature of 165°F (74°C) for 15 seconds.

Food is exposed to many sources of contamination during the cooking process. Some products must be manipulated and formed by hand, which heightens the risks. The dangers inherent in the cooking control point can be reduced by following regulatory codes to the letter.

Cooking and People

Staff members at the cooking control point are responsible for cooked-to-order appetizers, entrées, side dishes, and desserts. The number of people involved in the cooking control point depends on the extent of the menu and the operation's volume of business.

Accuracy is essential at the cooking control point. Cooks and chefs are expected to follow the operation's production standards. The master food production planning worksheet outlines what to requisition and cook for each meal period. Standard recipes should be followed exactly.

Personal hygiene and cleanliness standards are especially important for staff members who cook. These standards reduce the opportunities for product contamination both before and after cooking.

In some food establishments, production and service personnel have an antagonistic relationship. This creates an atmosphere of hostility, which is not conducive to achieving the goals of the operation. Management must care enough to take an active role in improving the situation by encouraging production and service staff to work together cooperatively. Some managers have servers and kitchen staff members trade jobs one day each week or month. This strategy helps each person appreciate the complexities of the other person's job and may lead to better cooperation.

Cooking and Equipment

Cooking equipment is an investment; it must be regularly cleaned and maintained to prolong its useful life, minimize repair and energy costs, reduce risks, and protect food products. For these reasons, the discussion that follows includes requirements for cleaning and sanitizing. Equipment manufacturers' instructions should be followed if they are available. Information on equipment cleaning procedures is also available from several manufacturers of cleaning and sanitizing compounds.

Equipment Used to Add Heat to Food. A quantity production kitchen uses several types of equipment to add heat to food. Broilers, fryers, griddles, grills, ovens, ranges, steam-powered equipment, tilting braising pans, food warmers, coffee urns, and toasters add heat to food by conduction (heat transfer through direct contact), convection (heat transfer through circulating air or fluid), radiation (heat transfer through wave energy), or a combination of these.

Broilers cook food with dry heat generated from an intense heat source. Broilers are fast and versatile, and a variety of models and designs are available. An overhead fired broiler cooks food from the top. The rate of cooking is controlled by raising and lowering the grate that holds the food. A salamander is a small overhead fired broiler used to glaze or finish food products immediately before service. A ceramic overhead broiler uses a series of ceramic plates to distribute heat evenly. An infrared overhead broiler offers the advantage of fast temperature recovery and is well suited to high-volume food service operations.

Char-broilers cook food on a grate from a heat source located below the food. Char-broilers may be powered by gas or electricity or may burn wood or charcoal. Char-broilers using mesquite or hardwood fuels have been used to prepare fresh fish and seafood. However, this relatively slow broiler uses energy inefficiently and results in a great deal of product shrinkage. Many fast-food chains use conveyorized broilers because they cook rapidly. Rotisserie broilers cook food while it is displayed to guests; the food rotates on a shaft or skewer while cooking. The meat used in the popular Greek sandwich called a *gyro* is usually cooked on, and then sliced from, a rotisserie broiler.

In general, a broiler should be cleaned and sanitized according to the manufacturer's instructions. The grease drip pans should be emptied, washed, and dried daily. The grates and drip shield should be washed and dried at least once each day or at the end of each shift. The broiler chamber and the exterior of the broiler should be cleaned with hot water and detergent and wiped dry with a clean cloth. It is also a good practice to degrease the broiler and clean the burners at least once a month. Representatives of the local public utility should periodically recalibrate the controls on broilers and all cooking equipment.

Fryers cook food products by convection in hot fat or oil. Fryers are either gas-powered or electric. Most fryers are very energy-efficient because they have automatic temperature controls. Pressure fryers decrease smoke and other vapors while reducing the amount of oil foods absorb. Pressure fryers are extremely energy-efficient and cook more quickly and evenly than regular fryers.

Most frying oil is chemically modified to extend its useful life. Only high-quality oil should be used for frying, as poor quality fat or oil may become rancid quickly. Rancidity reactions occur more rapidly in the presence of heavy metals, salt, moisture, and loose food particles. Therefore, foods to be fried should be as free as possible from moisture and crumbs and should never be salted directly over the frying oil. Filtering oil daily removes most of the food particles in the frying medium and thus helps prevent rancidity. It is important to keep the fryer covered when it is not being used.

Certain recommended cleaning techniques apply to most fryers. First, the outer surface of fryers should be wiped every day with a clean, moist cloth. Fryers should be emptied and cleaned at least once each week. If the operation does a great deal of frying, daily cleaning may be necessary. The following procedure should be used to clean fryers:

1. Remove the frying oil and filter or discard it, depending on its condition.

2. Fill the frying chamber with water and a cleaning compound, and boil this solution for 10 to 15 minutes.

3. Drain the solution from the fryer.

4. Clean the inside of the fryer with a specially designed fryer brush to remove any remaining food particles.

5. Rinse the fryer with a vinegar and water solution, followed by a clean water rinse.

6. Dry the fryer.

7. Fill the clean fryer either with the filtered frying oil or with fresh oil.

8. Cover the fryer until its next use.

Grease filters used to strain frying oil are single-service articles and should never be re-used. Filtering equipment should be handled in the same way as food-contact equipment. It should be stored covered.

A griddle cooks food on a metal surface heated from below by either gas or electricity. (The term "grill" is frequently used incorrectly to refer to a griddle; a grill is actually a broiler.) The surface temperature of a griddle is controlled by an automatic thermostat. A grooved griddle is used to cook steaks and hamburgers. Its grooves or ribs create a pattern on the surface of food similar to markings from broiler grates. Griddles are not very energy-efficient because of their large exposed heating surface. Dirty griddles use more energy than clean ones.

Griddles must be cleaned in two ways. Each time a griddle is used, excess food should be scraped off with a sharp-edged metal scraper. The griddle should also be cleaned thoroughly once each day. Rub the hot surface of the griddle with a liquid frying compound or unsalted shortening to soften burned-on food particles. A griddle pad or brick can be used to remove cooked-on food. Then wash the griddle surface with a solution of detergent in hot water. The surface of the griddle should then be rinsed, dried, and rubbed with the liquid frying compound or shortening to protect the cooking surface.

Other parts of the griddle should also be cleaned daily. A small amount of water can be carefully poured on the back of the griddle's cooking surface to steam off cooked-on food. (Be careful to avoid steam burns.) The drip pans should be removed, emptied, washed, and dried. Clean, rinse, and dry the exterior of the griddle as well.

An oven is simply a heated chamber for cooking food. A conventional or deck oven cooks food by a combination of conduction, convection, and radiation. Conventional ovens powered by gas or electricity are often used for baking and roasting.

Convection ovens use a fan to force hot air into direct contact with the food. As a result, convection ovens cook food much faster than conventional ovens at the same temperature. Products cooked in a convection oven also exhibit less shrinkage, retain more moisture, and develop better crust color than foods prepared in a conventional oven, provided that both temperature and time are strictly controlled. It is best to follow the manufacturer's time and temperature combinations.

Microwave ovens convert alternating electric current to electromagnetic energy. Microwaves cause the water molecules in food to vibrate rapidly. This vibration generates heat, which cooks the food. Metal dishes and utensils are generally not used in microwave ovens because they reflect microwaves. Follow the manufacturer's operating and cleaning instructions for microwave ovens.

Combination ovens combine the best features of convection ovens and steamers. They are capable of providing pressureless steam, convection heat, or both in a compact unit that takes up relatively little floor space. Combination ovens are frequently electrically powered, although gas models are available. Controls are electro-mechanical or solid state, and some models are capable of automated cooking. In areas with hard water (water with a high mineral content), combination ovens may need to be equipped with a water treatment system.

Careful cleaning of all ovens is important. All oven spills should be wiped up promptly. Conventional or convection ovens should be cooled before daily cleaning. Remove baked-on spills with a scraper. Brush the deck and wipe the chamber with a detergent-water solution. Never pour water directly on the oven; this can warp the deck if it is hot. Do not use caustic (highly alkaline) solutions on the oven's interior or exterior because they will damage the finish. Oven burners should be cleaned monthly. Controls should be calibrated periodically by a public utility representative.

Convection oven racks can be removed, washed, rinsed, and dried. These ovens should be cleaned at least monthly, or more often if they are used heavily. Each month, the fan in a convection oven should also be disassembled and cleaned. Microwave ovens can be washed inside and out with a detergent-water solution as needed. Remove bits of food from inside drains when cleaning combination ovens.

Along with ovens, ranges are the most frequently used type of cooking equipment in a food service kitchen. Ranges provide heated surfaces for cooking food in pots and pans. Ranges generally use energy inefficiently because a large amount of the cooking surface is exposed. Open-top ranges cook food directly over open burners. These ranges are well suited to menus with many cooked-to-order items because they heat up almost instantly. Hot-top ranges have a smooth surface made from a large metal plate or a series of concentric rings. The center ring is the hottest part of the surface. Placement of the pots and pans in relation to the center ring determines the amount of heat applied to food. Hot-top ranges require more preheating time than open-top ranges. Some ranges are designed with a combination of cooking surfaces.

All spills on ranges should be wiped up immediately. On an open-top range, grates, burner bowls, and spillover trays should be cleaned daily. Each month, the range should be degreased and the gas burners unclogged with a stiff wire brush. The surface of a hot-top range should be cleaned when slightly warm. A blunt scraper is used to remove stubborn food spills. After it has cooled, the top section can be removed, washed, and dried. All soil under rings and plates must be removed. The exterior surfaces of all ranges should be washed, dried, and wiped with a soft cloth daily.

Steam-powered equipment is becoming popular in quantity production kitchens because it is so energy-efficient. A steam-jacketed kettle consists of a stainless steel kettle within a larger kettle. Steam in the enclosed space between the two kettles cooks food very rapidly. This item is often used to cook liquid foods such as soups and sauces. Steam-jacketed kettles are available with capacities ranging from 1 quart (.95 liter) to 200 gallons (757 liters) or more. They are powered by electricity, gas, or pressurized steam from another source.

Steam-jacketed kettles should be cleaned after each use. Presoaking may be necessary if food is crusted on the inside of the kettle. Scrub the inside of the kettle with a clean soft-bristle brush. Then rinse the kettle and remove and clean the drain valve. The draw-off line and strainer should also be cleaned. The outside of the kettle should be washed with a hot water-detergent solution, rinsed, and wiped dry. The steam trap should be checked weekly, and mineral scale should be removed from the boiler at least every six months. In areas with hard water, the boiler may need to be descaled more frequently.

Compartment steamers cook foods by exposing them directly to steam. These devices are also rapid and energy-efficient, and preserve much of a product's original nutrients, texture, taste, appearance, and color. Compartment steamers cook at a constant temperature, so time must be carefully controlled to avoid overcooking. Compartment steamers may operate with steam pressure ranging from 0 to 15 pounds per square inch.

Compartment steamers are basically self-cleaning except for their interior racks, which can be cleaned in a mechanical dishwasher. The interior of a compartment steamer should be wiped dry after each use, and any food debris should be removed. In addition, the water line should be drained once each week. The boiler should be descaled once every six months, or more frequently in hard-water areas.

A tilting braising pan is a highly versatile unit. It can be used to fry, braise, simmer, or reheat a variety of food products. Food cooked in a tilting braising pan exhibits little shrinkage and retains its moisture. A tilting braising pan may be powered by gas or electricity. This equipment is also labor-efficient because it cooks a large volume of food with one person operating it.

A tilting braising pan should be cleaned after each use. Fill the pan with a detergent-water solution and close the cover to steam off food debris. Use a clean non-abrasive brush to remove remaining food particles, tilt the pan to remove the water, and rinse and dry the unit. Grease on the outside surfaces can be removed easily with an ammonia-water solution. However, this solution should never be poured on hot surfaces because toxic ammonia gas will be released. The tilting mechanism of the braising pan should be lubricated at least once each month.

Coffee urns should be cleaned after each use; accumulated oils and deposits can spoil even the most expensive coffee. After each brew, empty the leftover coffee out of the urn and discard the coffee grounds. Rinse the basket with clean cold water. Never use soap or detergent in a coffee urn. The inside of the urn should be rinsed with fresh water and then cleaned with an urn brush and a chemical specifically formulated for cleaning coffee makers. After cleaning, the cleaner should be thoroughly rinsed out by filling the urn with fresh water and emptying it twice. Leave one or two gallons of fresh water in the urn until it is used again, but discard this water before brewing. The exterior of the urn, including gauges and faucets, should be wiped down daily.

Toasters must be cleaned daily. Like all electric appliances, toasters should be unplugged before cleaning. Crumbs on the moving parts and in the collection tray can be removed with a soft brush. Trays and some moving parts are removable in some models. The outside of a toaster can be cleaned with a mild detergent–hot water solution, rinsed, and wiped dry.

Miscellaneous Food Service Equipment. Equipment not used for cooking is common in food service kitchens and must be cleaned regularly to minimize contamination risks.

Ice used as a food or cooling medium should be made from drinking water. Ice machines may not be used for chilled storage of other food products. It is important to store the scoop on a clean surface or in the ice, with the handle extended out of the ice. The scoop should be washed in a hot water–detergent solution, rinsed, sanitized, and air-dried daily. The exterior of the ice machine should be similarly cleaned on a daily basis. Once a month, all ice should be removed from the ice machine, the machine should be shut down, and the inside of the machine should be washed, rinsed, sanitized, and dried. Evaporator and condenser motors should be checked, and any necessary maintenance performed at that time. Follow the manufacturer's recommendations for cleaning and descaling the interior of the unit. While the machine is shut down, check and replace the water filter if necessary.

Can openers must be cleaned daily. It is important to scrub the blade to remove accumulations of food that may dull the blade. A dull can opener blade can cause dangerous metal splinters to drop into food. The outside of the can opener should also be washed, rinsed, and dried.

Exhaust hoods are designed to remove grease, heat, moisture, and odors from the kitchen. The outside of all hoods should be cleaned and polished weekly. Inside filters should be removed for steam-cleaning at least once a week, and more often if the hoods are located near heavily used fryers. This may be done in-house or by a contract service. Gutters or pans that catch grease can be cleaned, rinsed, and dried while the filters are out.

Cooking and Facilities

Careful planning of production facilities reduces food safety hazards and risks while creating a more efficient operation. Facilities planning begins with the menu, because it determines what is to be cooked and therefore the types of facilities needed. The number of meals to be served also has an impact on the facilities design. The kind and amount of food prepared determines the allocation of work areas and storage space.

Distances between work stations are an important consideration. There must be ample space in the kitchen to avoid traffic jams of people and products. On the other hand, large distances between work areas may not result in the most efficient use of space. An operation must try to reach a balance in order to maximize return on the investment in facilities. Management must review regulatory codes and ordinances before making any decisions about facilities design. These codes cover lighting, ventilation, food safety, and construction requirements.

Energy usage is another important consideration in facilities design. Well-planned facilities equipped with energy-efficient equipment can reduce energy bills and result in substantial savings. Proposed menu changes provide a good opportunity for considering how the facilities and equipment can be made more cost-effective. One strategy is to install flexible equipment such as the combination oven.

Equipment and facilities do not last forever, but cleaning and preventive maintenance will prolong their useful life. Ease of cleaning and maintenance are important considerations in selecting wall, floor, and ceiling materials for the food production work centers.

Cooking and Change

Change affects the cooking control point in much the same way that it affects the other basic operating activities: standards for cooking may need to be re-evaluated if conditions change. For example, if the operation begins to use more convenience food products, cooking procedures will change. The addition of ethnic food items to the menu is another example of change at the cooking control point. Production staff members may require special training to prepare the new items. Steam equipment is often used to cook ethnic foods, and some menu items may require specialty equipment such as woks, Chinese barbecue ranges, taco ranges, and semi-automatic pasta cookers. Managers should evaluate the effects of a change on the operation's control points and on its overall food safety risk management program *before* the change is implemented. The regulatory agency must be notified prior to the installation of new equipment.

Cooking and Food Safety

At the cooking control point, food products are exposed to physical and chemical changes that can increase risks. Standard recipes must be closely followed, especially time and temperature combinations. Cooking times and internal product temperatures are designed to produce a satisfactory finished menu item and to destroy or inactivate pathogens.

Proper training of staff members at the cooking control point is the best way to reduce risks. Training should include the use of standard recipes, time-temperature combinations, sensory tests, personal cleanliness and hygiene, safe food handling, and the proper use of equipment and facilities.

It is critical to regularly clean, sanitize, and maintain all equipment, facilities, and utensils used at the cooking control point, including the metal-stemmed product probe thermometer. This important piece of equipment must be cleaned and sanitized after each changed use.

The Holding Control Point

In many establishments, it is not feasible to cook all foods to order during rush periods or for large groups. Some menu items are prepared in advance and held for later service. Thus, for many food service operations, holding is a critical control point. Some menu items are held hot, some cold. To maintain product quality and minimize microbiological hazards, the holding time must be as short as possible and strict temperature controls must be observed. Holding is also critical for products removed from storage but not served; these should be promptly returned to storage for later use.

Ideally, food should be served immediately after cooking, thus avoiding the holding step altogether. However, since most operations do not always have this option, the resources under the holding control point must be standardized using the food safety risk management program.

Holding and Inventory

Product holding aims to maintain the safety and quality of food items until they are needed for service. Hot foods must not be allowed to cool between production and service. Hot food can be held safely with hot-holding equipment designed to operate at temperatures in excess of 140°F (60°C). Different hot foods have their own holding temperature requirements. Entrées and meat dishes are generally held at 140°F (60°C). Sauces, gravies, and thick soups are usually held between 140°F (60°C) and 180°F (82°C). Thin soups and hot beverages should be held in the range of 180°F (82°C) to 190°F (88°C).

When batches of food are held for service, there is often food left over. Cooked potentially hazardous foods should be cooled from 140°F (60°C) to 70°F (21°C) within two hours, and from 70°F (21°C) to 41°F (5°C) or below within four hours. If prepared from ingredients at ambient (kitchen) temperature, such as canned tuna, potentially hazardous foods should be cooled to 41°F (5°C) or below within four hours. Highly perishable potentially hazardous leftovers—like puddings, hollandaise sauce, and custards—should be discarded after holding.

Other leftover foods should be quick-chilled to 41°F (5°C) or less in pans that are no more than four inches (10.2 cm) deep. The size of the pan is important because it affects the **heat transfer rate**—in this case, the rate at which heat leaves the food. Large masses of food—such as soup in a stockpot—cool very slowly. Leftovers that must be stored in containers, such as soups and sauces, should be divided into small batches and chilled in shallow pans. Large pieces of food, like roasts, can be chilled quickly by cutting them into smaller or thinner pieces. Removing meat from the bone speeds the cooling process.

Slow cooling negatively affects the quality, nutritional value, and safety of food products. Leftovers should be chilled to 70°F (21°C) or less within two hours and to 41°F (5°C) or less within four hours. Placing products in a freezer or refrigeration unit with forced air circulation for 30 minutes will lower the temperature quickly. If containers of leftovers can be sealed, they can be submerged in ice water or exposed to cold running water for quick-chilling. Liquid foods can be quick-chilled by agitating them in containers exposed to ice or ice water. In some liquid foods, ice may be added as an ingredient to hasten cooling.

Leftovers should be covered, labeled, and dated before refrigeration. Airtight containers can create favorable conditions for the growth of anaerobic microbes during cooling, so covers should be loose-fitting or left slightly ajar until the product temperature is below 41°F (5°C). Remember, the temperature danger zone may be different in your area. Leftover food products should never be refrozen.

Improper food cooling is a major cause of foodborne illness. To manage the risks, always cool foods properly. Remember that acidic foods such as chili and tomato sauce contain volatile organic acids which may negatively affect the equipment and the refrigeration process.

When potentially hazardous foods are reheated for hot holding, all parts of the food must reach a minimum internal temperature of 165°F (74°C) for 15 seconds.

Sensory tests are frequently used during holding. While they are important, it is even more important to regularly check the temperature of food products and holding equipment. This combination will help lower risks.

Holding and People

Food production staff members should be aware of the potential for contamination and quality deterioration in menu items held for later service. Ideally, products would be prepared, cooked, and served immediately. However, limited resources (people, equipment, and facilities) make it difficult for food service operations to approximate this ideal flow. Peaks and valleys in guest demand for menu items also make holding necessary.

Time-temperature control during holding is essential to maintain the safety and quality of food products. Foods held hot must maintain internal temperatures of 140°F (60°C) or higher. Internal temperatures should be checked frequently with a metal-stemmed product probe thermometer. The critical temperatures chart presented in Exhibit 9 can be used to train and remind food service staff members of the temperatures required for safe hot and cold food holding. This chart includes temperatures that are significant for some of the other control points as well.

Staff members responsible for product holding must practice good personal hygiene. Once products are cooked and pathogens killed or inactivated, food can be recontaminated by staff members who do not maintain high standards of personal cleanliness.

Holding and Equipment

The amount of hot-holding equipment an operation needs depends on peak demand for the equipment. Generally, production staff should restock hot-holding equipment every 15 to 30 minutes in order to maintain product quality. Small batch production methods help to minimize excess holding. Hot-holding equipment is designed to facilitate rapid service with minimum effort. It is not, however, designed to heat food. Food products must be heated to proper temperatures before being placed in hot-holding equipment.

A variety of equipment is used to maintain the temperatures of ready-to-serve foods. Steam tables and bains-marie use steam and hot water, respectively, to keep food in containers hot. There are ovens that cook meats at low temperatures and then hold them with little additional cooking or shrinkage.

Warming drawers are typically used to hold bread and rolls near the food pickup point so that servers can plate these items immediately before service. Infrared warmers are usually mounted above the food pickup counter to keep plated foods hot; warming lamps serve the same purpose. Other equipment includes heated cabinets and pass-through holding units—units with doors on

Exhibit 9   Critical Temperatures for Food Service

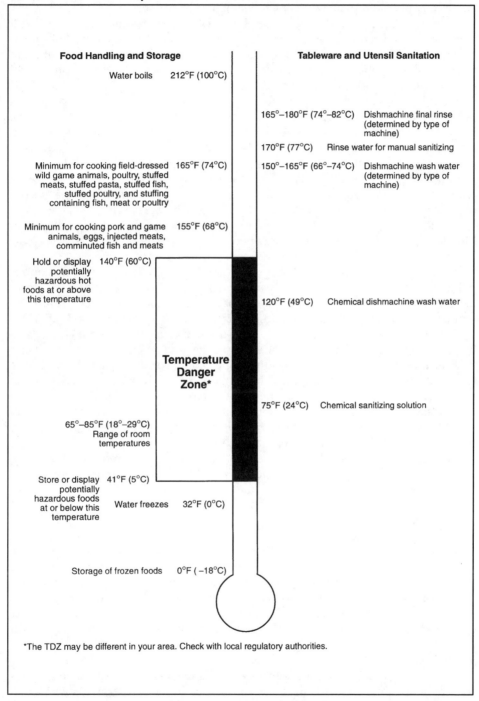

Food Handling and Storage

Water boils   212°F (100°C)

Minimum for cooking field-dressed   165°F (74°C)
wild game animals, poultry, stuffed
meats, stuffed pasta, stuffed fish,
stuffed poultry, and stuffing
containing fish, meat or poultry

Minimum for cooking pork and game   155°F (68°C)
animals, eggs, injected meats,
comminuted fish and meats

Hold or display   140°F (60°C)
potentially
hazardous hot
foods at or above
this temperature

**Temperature
Danger
Zone***

65°–85°F (18°–29°C)
Range of room
temperatures

Store or display   41°F (5°C)
potentially
hazardous foods
at or below this   Water freezes   32°F (0°C)
temperature

Storage of frozen foods   0°F (−18°C)

Tableware and Utensil Sanitation

165°–180°F (74°–82°C)   Dishmachine final rinse
(determined by type of
machine)

170°F (77°C)   Rinse water for manual sanitizing

150°–165°F (66°–74°C)   Dishmachine wash water
(determined by type of
machine)

120°F (49°C)   Chemical dishmachine wash water

75°F (24°C)   Chemical sanitizing solution

*The TDZ may be different in your area. Check with local regulatory authorities.

two sides, situated between preparation and service areas. Some operations use electrically powered plate warmers to heat plates before service.

Hot-holding equipment should be able to withstand the rigors of intense rush periods. If mobile equipment is purchased, the necessary utility connections must be available. Mobile units should be loaded from the bottom up to prevent them from becoming top-heavy and unstable. Heated cabinets should be purchased with insulation to reduce energy costs.

Cold-holding is designed to facilitate rapid server pickup. Pass-through refrigerators hold food between preparation and service areas. Countertop units with glass doors can be used to display food during holding. Refrigerators, freezers, and mobile refrigeration units are also used to maintain cold food products at proper storage temperatures. The temperature of refrigerated foods should not exceed 41°F (5°C). Some food items, such as frozen desserts, require lower temperatures. Frozen menu items should not exceed 0°F (–18°C). Appetizers, salads, cold meats and seafood, and desserts are often held cold before service.

Cold-holding equipment is more versatile if the temperature is adjustable. Mobile equipment allows staff members to move equipment as necessary. Cold-holding equipment should be insulated to maximize energy usage.

The one piece of equipment that is absolutely essential at the holding control point is a metal-stemmed product probe thermometer. The best model for monitoring the internal temperatures of most products is the dial face, metal probe thermometer (see Exhibit 10). It is accurate to ± 2°F (±1°C), has a range from 0° to 220°F (–18° to 104°C), and is easy to use. To measure temperatures, insert a clean, sanitized thermometer into the geometric center of the food product. The thermometer may take time to stabilize, so the reading should only be taken when the indicated temperature is no longer changing. The manufacturer's instructions may provide other recommendations. Thermometers should be cleaned and sanitized after each use so that they do not become a source of food contamination. Thermometers should also be calibrated periodically by either the ice point method, the boiling point method, or the screening method (see Exhibit 11).

Alternatives to probe thermometers include battery-powered or rechargeable electronic digital testing thermometers. These products are more appropriate when measuring the temperatures of small portions or thin inventory items such as fish fillets or hamburger. Like probe thermometers, they should be cleaned and sanitized after each changed use.

Holding equipment must also be equipped with temperature sensing devices accurate to ±3°F (± 2°C). Equipment thermometers should indicate the temperature in the coolest part of hot-holding equipment and the warmest part of cold-holding equipment. Temperature readings can be checked against a portable thermometer.

A variety of containers are designed to hold cooked food for service. Containers must be made of food-grade materials and be cleaned and sanitized after each changed use. Galvanized containers should not be used for holding food products, particularly those high in organic acids such as tomato products and lemon juice.

Portioning equipment and utensils must be used carefully to prevent cross-contamination. In a kitchen where there is an interruption in service, such as in a

Exhibit 10   Information for Selecting Product Temperatures

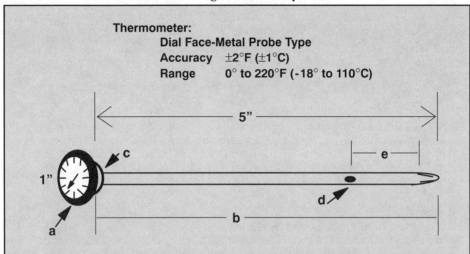

Thermometer:
Dial Face-Metal Probe Type
Accuracy   ±2°F (±1°C)
Range   0° to 220°F (-18° to 110°C)

A.   Dial face diameter should be a minimum of 1 inch (25.4 mm) with 2°F (1°C) increments. A range of 0° to 220°F (-17.8 to 104.4°C) is satisfactory for most applications. More specific ranges may be desirable in some instances. If the thermometer is not to be used as a "pocket" instrument, a larger dial face is desirable to improve readability.

B.   For most evaluations, a minimum stem length of 5 inches (127 mm) is sufficient. Some applications require a longer stem.

C.   Some instruments are available with a "calibration nut," immediately behind the dial, for adjusting the indicating needle during calibration.

D.   The immersion point on most product thermometers is about 2 inches (5 cm) up the stem. The immersion point varies for different makes, so be sure to read the manufacturer's instructions for specifics.

E.   In practice, the temperature on the dial is an approximate average of temperatures being sensed between the immersion point and immediately behind the tip.

Warning: Glass, liquid-filled instruments are **not permitted** for taking temperatures directly in food product because of the danger of breakage and mercury poisoning.

Source: National Sanitation Foundation, *Product Temperature Management.*

kitchen preparing cooked-to-order items for a hotel dining room, kitchenware must be stored in a safe and sanitary way. Plastic gloves used to portion foods during holding should not be re-used because they are single-use items.

Proper use of equipment and utensils is also important when food is portioned at the holding control point. Scoops and ladles must be used properly to ensure standard portion sizes. Scalloped dishes, vegetables, and pot pies are

Exhibit 11   Field Checking (Calibration) of Thermometers

In general, the calibration shift of a thermometer will be consistent throughout its range, except when the instrument has been physically damaged, in which case it should be discarded. There are three ways to check the calibration of a thermometer.

Ice Point Method
This is the best method for checking the accuracy of any thermometer except maximum-registering thermometers. Fill an insulated container, such as a wide mouth "thermos" bottle, with a mixture of potable crushed ice and water. The container must have crushed ice throughout to provide an environment of 32°F (0°C), so you may have to pack more ice into the container during the process. When the mixture of ice and water has stabilized (after four to five minutes), insert the thermometer to the appropriate immersion depth. Be sure to hold the stem of the instrument away from the bottom and sides of the container (preferably one inch) to avoid error. The ice point method permits calibration to within 0.1°F.

Boiling Point Method
This method, accurate to within 1°F (0.6°C) of the true temperature, is not as accurate as the ice point method. But it is the only method that can be used with maximum-registering thermometers. It is also useful to verify suspicion of a damaged instrument.

Place a container of potable water on a heating element. After the water in the container has reached a complete "rolling" boil, insert the instrument to the appropriate immersion depth. Immerse maximum-registering thermometers completely. Be sure there is at least a 2-inch clearance between the stem or sensing element and the bottom and sides of the container.

In the boiling point method, you must take into account your elevation above sea level. Use this rule of thumb: for each 550 feet above sea level, the boiling point of water is lowered 1°F (0.6°C). For example, if you are at an elevation of 5000 feet, the boiling point of water is approximately 203°F (95°C) (5000/550 = 9.09, and 212°F − 9.09°F = 203°F).

Screening (checking)
The screening method, accurate to within 1°F to 2°F, can be effective for field purposes. To check fixed units, thermostats, and recording thermometers, place a portable or testing thermometer near the sensing element of the fixed unit (within 1/4 to 1/2 inch). Allow the testing thermometer to reach equilibrium, and then compare readings.
ALWAYS KNOW THE CHARACTERISTICS OF THE THERMOMETERS YOU ARE USING!

Source: National Sanitation Foundation, *Product Temperature Management.*

frequently held (and served) in individual casseroles. Such practices aid the operation's cost control program and help ensure guest satisfaction.

Holding and Facilities

The facilities resource considerations during the holding control point mirror the considerations under the other two production control points: preparing and cooking. Facilities must be designed, installed, cleaned, and maintained to meet the minimum standards described in regulatory codes. It is essential to check with local regulatory agencies to determine additional requirements.

Holding and Change

Product holding requirements change with the menu and often with the day of the week and the meal period. For example, a hotel with multiple food service outlets has a variety of hot- and cold-holding needs. In the hotel coffee shop, fruits may be prepared for breakfast and held refrigerated, while hot breakfast items are probably cooked to order and served immediately. Lunch and dinner in the main dining room may involve a combination of menu items held hot, held cold, and cooked to order. For large banquets, all salads, entrées, side dishes, and desserts are held either hot or cold, depending on the nature of the product. Room service products are held hot or cold during transportation to guestrooms. Managers must constantly re-evaluate food product holding requirements based on changing needs.

Holding and Food Safety

Holding is the most critical of the production control points because the opportunity to expose potentially hazardous foods to the temperature danger zone is greatest. Excessive holding times raise risks and also lower product quality. Internal product temperatures, as well as holding times, must be closely monitored. It is also important to clean and sanitize probe thermometers after each changed use to avoid cross-contaminating food products.

Personal cleanliness and hygiene is also important at the holding control point. Leftover foods must be handled carefully and chilled quickly, if appropriate. Potentially hazardous leftovers should be used within 24 hours or discarded.

Equipment, utensils, and facilities used for holding food products must be regularly cleaned, sanitized, and maintained. Staff members trained to follow proper procedures and maintain standards are the key to monitoring the food safety risk management program, and thus reducing risks, at the holding control point.

🔑 Key Terms

cantilevered—Food production equipment that is wall-mounted with a horizontal support.

equipment installation information—Details about food production equipment that should be submitted to health officials (with an equipment schedule) to identify potential food safety hazards.

equipment schedule—A list of planned food production equipment; submitted to health officials before purchase or installation to identify potential sanitation hazards.

garde-manger—In a large operation, a cold food preparation department responsible for such dishes as aspic, pâté, mousse, salads and dressings, and sauces; in a small establishment, an area of the kitchen with chilled preparation surfaces; also, a chef who specializes in the production of cold dishes.

heat transfer rate—The rate at which heat leaves cooked food; pan size is an important factor.

master food production planning worksheet—An overall plan for a meal or special function that helps control the preparation function in large operations. It provides a format for planning staff and product utilization for each meal or special function; it also shows production personnel exactly what and how much to prepare—each menu item, the standard portion size, and the forecasted number of portions.

mise en place—Literally, "put in place." In the production area, *mise en place* refers to the assembly of raw ingredients for menu items. *Mise en place* reduces errors, speeds up the actual preparation process, and reduces food handling time and exposure to the temperature danger zone (TDZ).

production—A combination of the preparing, cooking, and holding control points.

product cost analysis form—A document used to calculate the cost per portion of standard recipes.

standard portion sizes—Consistent serving sizes, made possible by (1) following standard recipes exactly to obtain intended yields; (2) using scales and other measuring devices during preparation, cooking, and portioning; (3) purchasing pre-portioned foods when available; and (4) portioning as many items as possible during preparation.

standard recipe—A written procedure for the production of a given food item; lists the exact quantity of each ingredient to be used, the sequential order in which ingredients are put together, cooking times and temperatures, and the equipment necessary to produce the finished product. Essential for consistency in product quality, food safety, and cost.

standard recipe cost—The cost per portion of finished menu items—information necessary for pricing menu items accurately. Calculated by adding the costs of all ingredients in a recipe (total product cost) and dividing by the yield (number of servings).

Review Questions

1. What are the special food safety concerns, the riskiest food products, and measures for reducing risks at the preparing control point?

2. What are the roles of standard recipes and convenience foods at each production control point?

3. Why are personal hygiene standards at the production control points important?

4. How is the master food production planning worksheet used?

5. What types of equipment are used at the preparing control point? What are the proper care and installation procedures for this equipment?

6. What are the three objectives of cooking, and how are risks reduced at the cooking control point?

7. What are the special use and care procedures for equipment used to add heat to food?

8. What items are included in the miscellaneous food service equipment category?

9. How is inventory protected at the holding control point?

10. What types of equipment does the holding control point require?

 Checklist for Preparing

Inventory

_____ Products are protected from food safety risks, quality deterioration, and waste.

_____ Standard (written) recipes are used to maintain consistency in quality, food safety, and cost.

_____ Standard portion sizes are used to maintain consistency.

_____ A product cost analysis form is used and updated when market prices change.

_____ The on-site versus convenience decision is evaluated regularly.

_____ The following are treated as high-risk inventory items:

      _____ potentially hazardous foods

      _____ foods that possess natural contaminants

      _____ foods that are handled a great deal and could be cross-contaminated

      _____ foods that have multiple preparation steps

      _____ foods that are exposed to kitchen temperatures (TDZ) for long periods of time

      _____ foods that have gone through a number of temperature changes

      _____ foods that are prepared in large quantities

_____ Sensory tests are used to evaluate inventory items.

_____ All necessary ingredients and equipment are gathered before beginning preparation.

_____ Standard recipes are revised, if possible, to make them less risky.

People

_____   Rules of personal hygiene and cleanliness are strictly enforced.

_____   Handwashing takes place before, during, and after preparation activities.

_____   All food service staff members wear clean outer clothing.

_____   Effective hair restraints are used to prevent contamination of food and food-contact surfaces.

_____   Staff members consume food only in designated staff dining areas.

_____   Staff members use tobacco only in designated areas.

_____   Staff members handle soiled tableware in a way that minimizes contamination of their hands.

_____   Preparation staff members accurately weigh and measure ingredients.

_____   A master food production planning worksheet is used.

_____   Preparation staff members are trained to maintain the establishment's standards.

Equipment

_____   Equipment is installed and operated properly to prevent contamination of all surfaces.

_____   Whenever possible, mobile equipment is purchased to facilitate cleaning.

_____   Equipment is installed away from potential sources of contamination.

_____   All openings to hollow spaces beneath and between equipment are sealed.

_____   Aisles and working spaces between equipment and walls are unobstructed.

_____   The list of proposed equipment purchases and equipment installation plans are submitted to health department officials before purchasing or installing equipment.

_____   Kitchenware is cleaned and sanitized after each changed use.

_____   In-use preparation equipment and utensils are handled and stored properly to reduce risks.

Facilities

_____   Facilities are designed to efficiently move products from issuing to preparation areas.

_____ Preparation areas have adequate equipment, work tables, lighting, and ventilation.

_____ Essential equipment is added and unnecessary equipment is removed.

_____ Preparation facilities comply with regulatory requirements.

_____ The layout of facilities is designed to reduce contamination risks and facilitate the use of equipment.

_____ Facilities are cleaned, sanitized, and maintained regularly.

Food Safety Risk Management Program

_____ Inventory is handled carefully and prepared safely.

_____ Food service staff members are trained to maintain standards and reduce the risks during preparing.

_____ Adequate facilities and equipment are present and used, and they are cleaned, sanitized, and maintained frequently to reduce the risks during preparing.

☑ Checklist for Cooking

Inventory

_____ Food is cooked with as little manual contact as possible, and the correct utensils are used to handle food.

_____ Surfaces are cleaned and sanitized before use to avoid cross-contamination of food products.

_____ Potentially hazardous foods are cooked to a minimum internal temperature of 145°F (63°C) for 15 seconds *except:*

  _____ Field-dressed wild game animals, poultry, stuffed fish, stuffed meats, stuffed pasta, stuffed poultry, and stuffing containing fish, meat, or poultry are cooked to a minimum of 165°F (74°C).

  _____ Pork and game animals, comminuted meats and fish, injected meats, and eggs are cooked to a minimum of 155°F (68°C) for 15 seconds.

  _____ All products are cooked 25°F (14°C) higher in a microwave oven and allowed to stand covered for 2 minutes after cooking.

_____ Potentially hazardous foods are reheated to an internal temperature of 165°F (74°C) for 15 seconds.

_____ Internal temperatures are monitored with metal-stemmed product probe thermometers accurate to ± 2°F (±1°C).

_____ Potentially hazardous foods are thawed safely.

_____ Sensory tests are used in combination with temperature checks.

People

_____ All staff members practice good personal hygiene and cleanliness.

_____ Staff members work accurately.

_____ Standard recipes are used to maintain consistency in quality, food safety, and costs.

_____ Ingredient amounts, cooking times, and cooking temperatures are followed precisely.

_____ Finished products are safely sampled.

_____ Production staff members work closely and in cooperation with service staff members.

_____ Production staff members are trained to maintain the operation's standards.

Equipment

_____ Staff members treat equipment as an investment that must be regularly cleaned and maintained.

_____ The manufacturer's instructions for cleaning, sanitizing, maintaining, and operating equipment are followed.

_____ Supervisors inspect equipment daily to determine that the establishment's standards for cleaning, sanitizing, maintenance, and operation of the equipment are being followed.

_____ Staff members are trained to clean and sanitize equipment as soon as they finish using it.

_____ A cleaning schedule is developed, including instructions for cleaning and maintenance for each piece of equipment and work area.

_____ Equipment is selected on the basis of initial costs, availability of energy sources, operating costs, maintenance costs, and personnel skill levels.

Facilities

_____ Facility requirements are based on the menu.

_____ Distances between work stations are designed for efficient movement of people and products.

_____ Cleaning and preventive maintenance are high priorities.

_____ Walls, ceilings, floors, and equipment are easy to clean and maintain.

_____ When possible, flexible equipment is installed in facilities.

Food Safety Risk Management Program

_____ Inventory is handled carefully and cooked safely.

_____ Staff members are trained to maintain standards and reduce risks during cooking.

_____ Adequate equipment and facilities are present and used, and they are cleaned, sanitized, and maintained regularly to reduce the risks during cooking.

✓ Checklist for Holding ───────────────────────

Inventory

_____ When leftovers remain after the meal period, they are cooled quickly and safely in small batches; leftover egg- and cream-based potentially hazardous foods are discarded immediately after the meal period.

_____ Leftovers are cooled to 70°F (21°C) or less within two hours and 41°F (5°C) or less within four hours.

_____ Leftovers are covered, labeled, and dated before refrigerating.

_____ Leftovers are not refrozen.

_____ Sensory tests are used in combination with temperature checks.

People

_____ Staff members are aware of the potential for quality deterioration and food safety risks during holding.

_____ Staff members maintain strict time-temperature controls.

_____ Staff members monitor internal temperatures of products and keep them at 140°F (60°C) or above.

_____ Staff members are aware of the critical temperatures for food holding.

_____ Staff members are trained to maintain the operation's standards.

_____ Staff members practice good personal hygiene and cleanliness.

Equipment

_____ The quantity of hot-holding equipment available is based on peak demand estimates.

_____ Small batch production is used whenever possible.

_____ Food holding equipment is used correctly and carefully.

_____ A metal-stemmed product probe thermometer is used to monitor internal product temperatures.

_____ The thermometer is cleaned and sanitized after each use.

_____ The temperature is read after inserting the thermometer into the geometric center of the food product.

_____ The thermometer is given time to stabilize.

_____ The manufacturer's instructions are reviewed and followed.

_____ Holding equipment has built-in thermometers accurate to ±3°F (± 2°C).

_____ Containers made out of food-grade materials are used to hold food and are cleaned and sanitized after each changed use.

_____ Portion equipment and utensils are used carefully to prevent cross-contamination.

Facilities

_____ Facilities are designed, installed, cleaned, and maintained to meet regulatory standards.

Food Safety Risk Management Program

_____ Inventory is handled carefully and held safely.

_____ Staff members are trained to maintain standards and reduce risks during holding.

_____ Adequate equipment and facilities are present and used, and they are cleaned, sanitized, and maintained frequently to reduce the risks during holding.

Chapter 6 Outline

Traditional Table Service
    Serving and Inventory
    Serving and People
    Serving and Equipment
    Serving and Facilities
Other Types of Food Service
    Temporary Food Service
    Banquet and Buffet Service
    Off-Premises Catering
    Room Service
    Mobile Food Service
    Serving and Change
    Serving and Food Safety

Competencies

1. Describe control measures for self-service food bars. (pp. 167–169)

2. Explain procedures for protecting food inventory at the serving control point. (pp. 169–171)

3. List food safety standards for food servers, and outline server responsibilities. (pp. 171–173)

4. Describe the proper use and care of equipment at the serving control point, and describe dining room inspection procedures. (pp. 173–175)

5. Explain special food safety requirements for temporary food establishments. (pp. 175–176)

6. Describe banquet and buffet service, and outline control procedures for each. (pp. 176–177)

7. Describe standards for off-premises catering and room service. (pp. 177–178)

8. Explain the food safety requirements for mobile food service operations. (pp. 179–180)

The Serving Control Point

WHEN ASKED TO RANK the internal attributes which influence their selection of a restaurant, respondents in a survey of over 1,500 fast-food and full-service restaurant guests placed "service" second only to "good quality food." Almost half of the respondents said that service was "most important" or "very important" when selecting a restaurant. A majority of respondents also said that if they had a negative service experience at one restaurant in a chain, it would affect their decision to visit another restaurant within the same chain. As these results indicate, service is an essential component of the guest's overall hospitality experience. Service that meets or exceeds guest expectations generates repeat business and increases revenues.

Like the other control points in the food safety risk management program, serving requires food safety, quality, and cost controls. Quality is especially important at this control point—both in the products served and the service itself. Many factors affect the quality of service in a food service operation. They include the communication and cooperation between kitchen and dining room staff members, the flow of products, the menu, the design and layout of the kitchen and dining room, and the style of service. Service standards vary greatly among operations. However, no matter what type of service an operation offers, management is responsible for standardizing ordering procedures and abbreviations, serving procedures, food safety practices, staff requirements, and risk reduction. Food safety risk management is an essential component of the service strategy.

Food service assumes many forms today, and each type of service requires slightly different standards. For example, outdoor food service is limited by unique food safety considerations. Catering service calls for specialized transportation equipment that can protect food safety. This chapter presents standards for traditional table service and its variations, followed by a brief discussion of other types of service.

Traditional Table Service

There are several variations of traditional table service. Most operations, with the exception of fast-food restaurants, offer one or more of these types of service. **Plate service** is a basic service style in which fully cooked menu items are individually portioned, plated (put on plates) in the kitchen, and carried to each guest directly. **Cart service** is used for menu items prepared by the server beside the guest's table in the dining room; menu items are cooked, and sometimes flambéed, in front of the guest. **Family-style service** requires food to be placed on large platters or in large bowls, which are taken to the tables by servers. Guests pass the food around their table and serve themselves. Self-service salad, soup, and dessert bars are popular variations of family-style service. In **platter service,** servers bring platters of fully cooked food to the dining room, present them to the guest for approval, and then serve the food.

Each service style has slightly different food safety considerations. In plate service, foods are heated to proper serving temperatures in the kitchen and delivered to the guest quickly to maintain their proper temperature and quality. Cart service eliminates the transportation of cooked menu items from the kitchen to the dining room, but it requires servers to be certain that products cooked at tableside reach adequate internal temperatures. In addition, the ventilation system should be capable of removing heat, odors, and smoke from the dining room. For example, Japanese-style food establishments feature cooking performed at guest tables equipped with drop-in stainless steel or nickel-plated top griddles. Local health officials may require a ventilation hood above the griddle to remove cooling vapors and products of combustion. In addition, makeup air capacity needs to be carefully considered. It is always a good idea to check with health officials before installing this equipment. Servers should be especially careful when preparing and presenting flambéed items.

Platter service, like plate service, aids food safety because food products cooked in the kitchen are likelier to reach adequate internal temperatures. However, as with plate service, product temperatures are difficult to maintain as the items are carried from the kitchen to the dining room. The temperature of hot food items continues to drop as the server presents the platter for approval and transfers the food from the platter to the plates. Whether food is plated in the kitchen or the dining room, serving techniques must maintain food safety.

Family-style service is appropriate for banquets because it facilitates the delivery of menu items to large groups of people. However, product temperatures are often difficult to maintain as food is passed around the table. Food may also be contaminated if a guest coughs or sneezes while passing a bowl or platter of food. Leftover portions of food may not be served again, except that packaged non-potentially hazardous food that is still packaged and is still in sound condition may be re-served. The size of the serving container and the amount of food placed at each table should be carefully considered to reduce waste. After use at a table, the serving containers and utensils must be washed, rinsed, and sanitized before the containers are refilled.

Self-service food bars also present food safety problems. Many food service operators are discovering that salad bars can present high risks. Some fast-food chains have opted for pre-packaged salads to avoid these risks. Salad bars, if not properly maintained, can be perceived as messy and unsafe. Some outbreaks of foodborne illness have been traced to salad bars.

However, certain procedures can help control the salad bar and reduce risks. The condition and temperature of the food and the salad bar should be checked every 10 to 15 minutes. Spills should be wiped up and utensils replaced when necessary. To ensure freshness and quality, foods should be placed in relatively small containers, replaced frequently, displayed on crushed ice or in cold inserts, and be protected by properly designed sneeze guards (food shields). These safety devices should extend the length and width of the bar and be positioned 10 to 12 inches (25.4 to 30.5 cm) above the food. Display stands for unwrapped food must be effectively shielded to intercept the direct line between the average guest's mouth and the food being displayed.

Soup and dessert bars call for similar procedures. Equipment should be able to maintain product temperatures. Covers, but not food shields, are required for self-service soup containers. The covers do not have to be hinged or self-closing. It is a good idea to display small amounts and replace them frequently. Constant supervision of all types of food bars is crucial to risk reduction and should be part of every server's responsibilities.

Serving and Inventory

Inventory items prepared by the production department are delivered to guests during service. Regulatory codes specify requirements for safe food display and service. These regulations apply not only to food served from the kitchen but also to items set up for guest self-service at soup and salad bars, buffet tables, sandwich bars, and dessert bars. These guidelines can help the operation control its investment in inventory and reduce its risks at the serving control point.

Potentially hazardous foods must be kept out of the Temperature Danger Zone (41°F [5°C] to 140°F [60°C]) at the serving control point. Hot food should be served on heated plates, and cold food should be served on chilled plates. This practice helps to keep product temperatures outside the TDZ and enhances product quality.

Foods on display must be protected from contamination through the use of packaging; counter, service line, or salad bar food guards; display cases; or other effective means. Molluscan shellfish life-support system display tanks may be used to store and display shellfish offered for human consumption if there is an approved HACCP plan and additional controls.

When second portions and refills are offered, clean tableware, including single-service articles, must be used. Utensils or effective dispensing methods that protect food from contamination are required in self-service. Self-service buffets and salad bars should be monitored by a staff member trained in safe operating procedures. This is an excellent procedure in all control points.

Once served, potentially hazardous foods must be discarded and not re-served. Food dispensing utensils must be available for each container displayed at a consumer self-service buffet or salad bar.

Milk and milk products served as beverages should be served in unopened, commercially filled packages of one pint (.47 liter) or less or drawn from a commercial milk dispenser into a cleaned and sanitized glass. Dairy or non-dairy coffee creamers should be individually packaged, drawn from a refrigerated dispenser, or poured from a covered pitcher. If stored at the sidestand, milk or cream must be refrigerated. Individually portioned coffee creamer that has been ultra-high-temperature pasteurized, aseptically filled, and hermetically sealed is the only liquid dairy or non-dairy coffee cream exempted from refrigeration requirements. It is exempt because it has a shelf life of 120 days at room temperature.

Dressings, seasonings, and condiments (flavor enhancers such as chutney, mustard, and relish) on tables or self-service stands must be presented in covered containers, dispensers, or single-serving packages. Catsup and other sauces may be served in their original containers or in pour-type dispensers. Generally, the refilling of original containers is prohibited. Sugar on tables should be in either individual packets or pour-type dispensers.

Ice for guest consumption should be handled with ice-dispensing utensils (scoops or tongs) or dispensed by an automatic ice machine. Guests should serve themselves only from automatic dispensers. Ice-dispensing utensils should be stored in a clean and safe manner between uses.

Dispensing utensils or gloves should be used for all food serving. In-use dispensing utensils can be stored in the food with the handles extended, or under running water, or clean and dry. Production staff or servers should never dispense food with their hands unless wearing single-use gloves; likewise, guests should use utensils and not their hands for serving themselves.

Leftover food returned to the kitchen must not be re-served. For example, crocks of cheese and ramekins of butter should be served only once. The exception to this rule is packaged, non-potentially hazardous food in sound condition. Self-service guests should not re-use tableware when they return to the service area for additional food; however, they may re-use beverage glasses and cups. Unpackaged food on display should be protected from guest contamination by easily cleanable sneeze guards.

Servers should be trained to recognize acceptable quality because they perform the final quality control check of menu items before the items are served. Food quality can be judged by appearance, texture and consistency, temperature, and flavor.

Appearance is an important aspect of product quality. Guests evaluate food appearance based on color, spacing, neatness, and garnish. The appearance of foods should always match the pictures of the items on the menu.

Color is an important quality consideration. For example, bright yellow, artificial-looking chicken gravy is unappealing to most guests. Golden-brown bakery products, on the other hand, appeal to the eye. Casseroles are attractive when they are evenly browned. Fruits, vegetables, seafood, meats, and poultry products should have natural colors.

The size and shape of foods also contribute to their appearance. Broken, misshapen, or ragged vegetables can destroy the appearance of an entire plate of food. Food items should not be crowded on the plate or hanging over the edge. The neatness of the food presentation also makes a statement about the establishment's standards. Liquid foods should not spill or run over the edges of tableware. If two foods with sauces are to be served at the same time, one should be served in a side dish. Similarly, if a menu item is served with a thin sauce, it should be served in a side dish.

Garnishes are artistic touches that complete the image a plate of food presents. Some garnishes (such as parsley, spiced apple rings, and orange wedges) are so commonly used that guests ignore them. Some upscale establishments use a variety of in-season fresh fruit garnishes that are relatively inexpensive to buy and prepare. Melon wedges, strawberries, kiwi fruit, and mango slices are interesting garnish alternatives. Other operations use edible flowers (such as pansies) as garnishes.

The texture and consistency of food products are also important components of quality. Dried-out bakery products, broken breadsticks and crackers, wilted salads, lumpy gravies and puddings, and runny custards are examples of poor food quality. Some operations display photographs of standard food presentations in the pickup area of the kitchen so servers and production staff can easily compare them with finished items before service.

Product temperature contributes to the overall quality of food products. Internal product temperatures should be checked with a probe thermometer. As previously noted, hot foods should be served on heated tableware and cold foods should be served on chilled tableware. When assembling orders, the server should gather room temperature products first, then chilled foods, and finally hot foods.

Food flavor—a combination of taste and odor—is probably the most important quality indicator. Servers should sample menu items regularly at staff meetings so they will be able to describe menu items from experience and answer guest questions accurately.

Serving and People

The term "server" may be used to refer to any person directly involved in the service of food or beverages. The image and size of the establishment generally determine whether other positions are included in the serving function. A host may greet and seat guests and supervise dining room staff. In some large or formal dining rooms, a maître d'hôtel may supervise service and be assisted by a captain. Buspersons assist servers by clearing and setting up tables. A cashier is frequently assigned the responsibility of handling all guest payments. In some establishments, certain positions are combined. For example, one staff member serves as cashier and host. Servers sometimes clear and set up tables.

Servers, like all food service staff members, must practice good personal hygiene and cleanliness. Standards of personal hygiene should be adapted to the individual operation and presented to all staff members during orientation and training.

Proper handwashing is extremely important. Servers should wash their hands before starting work and frequently throughout the shift. It is also important that they wash their hands immediately after any of the following activities: touching hair or skin, sneezing, coughing, using a handkerchief, smoking, visiting the restroom, handling raw food products, or handling soiled containers or tableware.

In addition to proper handwashing, the following standards apply to all servers:

- Do not smoke, chew gum, or eat in the dining room or kitchen.

- Never serve food that has left the plate or fallen to the floor.

- Replace dropped tableware with clean items.

- Avoid touching food with your hands. Use recommended utensils, and store the utensils in a sanitary manner when not in use.

- Do not touch parts of tableware which come into contact with food or with the guest's mouth.

- Never carry a service towel or napkin over your shoulder or under your arm.

- Be certain the bottom of tableware is clean before placing it on the table. Remove all soiled tableware and return it to the dirty dish station to prevent its re-use.

- Keep the tops, bottoms, and sides of serving trays clean to prevent unnecessary soiling of uniforms, tableware, and tablecloths.

- Maintain a clean and professional appearance.

- Work carefully, keeping standards of cleanliness in mind.

Guests expect their dining experiences to be both safe and pleasant. If servers violate the standards of personal hygiene or cleanliness with unsanitary practices, disease agents may be transmitted to guests. In addition, physical foodborne contaminants, such as hair or glass fragments, can result in an unpleasant dining experience or a guest injury.

When placing orders in the kitchen, the server's timing is critical to the rapid flow of products to the dining room. Properly timed orders are plated and served almost simultaneously, thus maintaining product temperatures and reducing food safety risks. In some operations, an **expediter** acts as a communication link between the kitchen staff and servers. Servers give their orders to the expediter, who calls the orders to the appropriate kitchen stations. The expediter must know cooking times, coordinate them to sequentially deliver cooked foods for pickup, and provide leadership during hectic rush periods. He or she should be a member of the management team.

Once orders are prepared, they must be served promptly. Cooked food held hot under infrared units or heat lamps may lose some of its quality. In order to deliver cooked menu items to guests as soon as the food is ready, some operations follow a procedure known as the **flying food show.** Under this procedure, the first server to arrive at the pickup point delivers whichever menu items are ready for service. This procedure can only be implemented if order tickets show which table and guest is to receive each order.

In some operations, servers are responsible for some production and portioning. Servers might be responsible for portioning beverages, soups, or desserts, adding dressings to salads, garnishing plates, and obtaining food accompaniments such as sauces. In all cases, servers must follow the establishment's food safety and portioning standards. Servers should also load serving trays carefully to reduce the likelihood of accidents.

Once food is served, servers should return frequently to the table to remove dirty dishes, refill water glasses, and empty ashtrays. After guests leave, the table should be cleared and reset with clean items. Whoever performs this duty—a server or a busperson—should wash his or her hands after handling soiled tableware and before resetting the table with clean items. After the table is reset, the server should make sure that the chairs are clean and properly arranged for the next guest.

Servers need not wash their hands every time they handle money. Although money is often thought of as "dirty," currency does not support enough microorganisms to be a source of contamination. However, guests generally do not like to see servers handle money and then serve food.

Serving and Equipment

Servers work with a variety of equipment. Serving equipment must be cleaned, sanitized, stored, and handled in a manner that prevents subsequent contamination.

Dishes, cups, glasses, and flatware should only be handled in places that will not come into contact with food or with the guest's mouth. Knives, forks, and spoons that are not pre-wrapped should be presented so that only handles are touched by staff members (and by customers if self-service is provided). Single-service articles that are intended for food-contact or lip-contact should be furnished for customers when self-service is provided. These items should be distributed from an approved dispenser or with the original, individual wrappers intact. Dishes should be held with four fingers on the bottom and the thumb on the edge, not touching the food. Cups and flatware should be touched only on the handles. Glasses should be grasped at the base and placed on the table without touching the rim. Ice placed in glasses and bread and rolls placed in bread baskets should only be handled with scoops or tongs designed for these purposes.

Pre-set tableware must be wrapped, covered, or inverted. Pre-setting should not be a substitute for proper utensil storage. Extra settings of tableware should be removed from the table when guests are seated. This not only helps protect the quality of tableware, but also prevents needless washing, rinsing, and sanitizing of clean tableware. Sneeze guards and proper serving utensils are required on self-service food bars in the dining room.

In some operations, a busperson clears soiled tableware and resets tables. In other operations, servers perform these duties. In both cases, care must be taken when clean and sanitized tableware is handled after touching soiled tableware. After handling soiled tableware or wiping cloths, staff members should wash their hands before touching cleaned and sanitized tableware. This minimizes the potential for cross-contamination.

Two or more servers often share a **sidestand,** which holds supplies of tableware, ice, condiments, dairy products, and some beverages for easy access. Two food safety considerations are important at the sidestand. First, all equipment and food products must be stored to minimize contamination. No soiled napkins, tableware, or equipment should be placed on the sidestand. These items can contaminate clean food and utensils. Second, the temperatures of food products stored on the sidestand must be kept out of the TDZ. This is particularly important for dairy products (such as butter and coffee cream) and any other potentially hazardous foods. These items must be refrigerated. It is helpful to stock the sidestand with enough cups, saucers, bread and butter plates, serving trays, tray stands, and other necessary items to last through a whole shift. Supplies should be stocked in a neat, orderly, and convenient way before customers arrive. A busperson may help keep the station neat, clean, and stocked.

Tables and chairs should be dusted or wiped to remove food debris before the establishment opens each day. Servers should inspect them frequently throughout their shifts for cleanliness and proper setup. Floors should be checked for spilled food. If the dining room has windows, the ledges should be dusted at least once each day.

Equipment placed on tables must be kept clean. This is often a part of the server's side work. Sugar dispensers and salt and pepper shakers should be wiped clean at least once a day. If glass dispensers or shakers are used, they should be periodically emptied, washed, rinsed, dried, and refilled. The volume of business affects the amount of sugar, salt, and pepper used at each table and, therefore, the frequency of refilling. Some operations now use disposable dispensers and shakers to reduce the labor costs associated with maintaining these items.

If syrup or condiments such as catsup, mustard, and steak sauce are placed on tables, the exterior of the containers should be cleaned regularly. They can be wiped with a damp cloth to remove fingerprints and drips. Original condiment containers designed for dispensing (like catsup bottles) should not be washed and refilled. Wide-mouth condiment or syrup bottles can easily become contaminated and should not be used in the dining room. Individual packages or portions may be the most safe.

Napkins are usually folded before service. They should be stored so as to prevent soiling. Paper napkins should be discarded from tables after service, even if they look clean. Cloth napkins must be properly laundered after each use and should never be used to wipe flatware, glasses, cups, or ashtrays. Ashtrays should be clean and stocked with matches. Servers should check their trays before beginning work. The bottom, top, and sides of a tray should be free from grease, food, and other debris.

One item frequently neglected during side work is flatware. Soiled, spotted eating utensils are both unsightly and pose food safety risks. Soiled flatware may require soaking before it is washed in the dish machine. After washing, it should be checked to ensure that soil and spots have been removed.

Plate and platter covers allow servers to carry more orders on each tray. They also help maintain a menu item's serving temperature if the item is placed on a heated or chilled plate in the kitchen. Covers also help guard against contamination during transportation from the kitchen to the guest. Plate and platter covers must be regularly cleaned and sanitized and stored in such a manner as to prevent contamination before their next use.

Take-out service requires additional equipment to hold packaged foods hot or cold. Some holding units have clear covers or doors to display the selection of hot and cold menu items to guests. Equipment selection is based on the menu items offered for take-out. Holding equipment should be able to maintain the proper temperatures and relative humidities. It should be cleaned and sanitized regularly.

Care should be exercised in handling all equipment used for serving. Waste and breakage can harm the establishment's competitive position. Each time a server carelessly soils linen, wastes supplies, or throws away or breaks tableware, the operation's costs increase. If fragments of glass find their way into guests' food or beverage products, the operation's revenues decrease. The net effect of such carelessness is generally poor bottom-line results.

Serving and Facilities

The cleaning, repair, and maintenance of the operation's facilities are essential at all control points. These activities are particularly important at the serving control point because the dining room environment directly affects guest satisfaction. A clean and pleasant dining room enhances the operation's image and makes a positive first impression on guests.

The dining room supervisor should inspect the facilities with all the lights turned on before service begins. This daily inspection is part of the overall preparation for service. The supervisor should check floors, walls, and ceilings to see if maintenance or repairs are necessary. In addition, tables, chairs, and booths should be inspected for cleanliness. Menus should be inspected to ensure that daily specials are attached. Dirty or damaged menus should be removed from circulation. The inspection should include food displays and sidestands. Equipment should be functioning properly to maintain product temperatures.

After the inspection, the dining room supervisor should adjust the lighting levels to create the proper ambiance. The ventilation system should be designed so that the dining room does not become stuffy or smoky while guests are dining.

While wood is sometimes used to create a cozy dining atmosphere, untreated wood is subject to decay caused by bacteria and fungi. This process is accelerated by alternating periods of moisture and dryness. Wood for holding and displaying fresh fruits, fresh vegetables, and nuts in the shell may be treated with a preservative approved for such use.

One additional consideration is important for the serving facilities: animals. Although there are some exceptions, specifically with support animals for disabled guests or staff members, animals are not generally allowed in food establishments.

Other Types of Food Service

Temporary Food Service

Temporary food establishments are granted a license to serve food for a limited period of time (usually no more that 14 consecutive days), often at fairs, sporting events, and concerts. Some food service and lodging establishments also set up temporary service facilities for special outdoor events such as luaus, barbecues, and weddings.

Temporary food service requirements in your area may be very restrictive. Potentially hazardous foods may be served from such units provided that the food requires a limited amount of preparation and cooking (as, for example, frankfurters and hamburgers). Other potentially hazardous foods are strictly prohibited. Some potentially hazardous foods, such as ice cream and potato salad, may be served in individual portions if they are prepared under safe conditions and are not stored in the TDZ before sale.

All the general food handling requirements previously discussed apply to temporary units. Ice should be dispensed by staff members using proper utensils. Equipment in a temporary unit should be installed so that it is easy to clean. If there are no facilities for cleaning and sanitizing tableware, the operation should provide only single-service tableware. Potable water in adequate quantities is necessary for food preparation, equipment and utensil cleaning, and handwashing. Food should not be stored in contact with water or undrained ice. Waste and sewage must be disposed of according to applicable laws. Handwashing facilities are required in a temporary food service unit.

Floors should be constructed of materials that are easy to clean. Ceilings may be constructed of canvas, wood, or other material that adequately protects food preparation areas. Walls, ceilings, and doors should prevent the entry of insects. Counter service areas should have tight-fitting solid or screened windows or doors which are kept closed when not in use. Check with your health authorities for additional regulations.

Banquet and Buffet Service

Many food service and lodging operations provide some form of banquet service. The nature of the banquet function may vary from a simple coffee break with fresh fruits and specialty pastries to a formal dinner with multiple courses. In any case, menu items should be chosen with ease and speed of service in mind, since all guests should be served at about the same time.

Banquet service can be highly profitable if planned carefully. From a control standpoint, banquet service has two advantages: both the menu and the number of people to be served are established well in advance of service. This information facilitates planning and allocation of the operation's resources. Many operations use a part-time staff to supplement their regular production and service staff during banquet service.

On the other hand, an inadequately planned banquet can be a disaster. The pressures inherent in the food service business are greater when large numbers of people must be served in a relatively short period of time. Under these circumstances, mistakes can happen easily. The problems are compounded when proper time-temperature controls are not in place.

Because banquets are served so quickly, station setup is important. Equipment requirements vary with the type of banquet and the menu. General service standards apply, although they may be simplified to facilitate serving large numbers of people.

In banquet service, time-temperature control is critical. It is virtually impossible to prepare dozens, hundreds, or thousands of individual plates as service progresses. Therefore, foods are usually pre-plated for large banquets and held hot or cold in holding cabinets. Refrigerated mobile storage units must maintain internal product temperatures of 41°F (5°C) or less. Mobile hot storage cabinets must maintain a minimum internal product temperature of 140°F (60°C). Recall that the temperature danger zone may be defined differently in your area. Check with health authorities.

Buffet service is popular in many food service and lodging establishments. Some use buffet service in combination with banquet service, serving, for example, appetizers buffet-style during the cocktail hour, and the rest of the meal banquet-style. Other special functions use buffet service exclusively. By attractively arranging a seemingly endless array of food products, establishments using this service exceed the expectations of guests, who enjoy being able to choose whatever they like in unlimited quantities. Buffet service also provides the opportunity to create food displays and showpieces.

Some buffets feature a carver who slices meats or poultry at the buffet table in the dining room. Servers sometimes portion some or all of the food products and assist guests. At most buffets, servers deliver beverages, bread and butter, and desserts directly to guest tables. Other buffets are completely self-serve.

Time-temperature control in buffet service is very important. Whenever large quantities of food are displayed, special equipment is necessary to keep product temperatures outside the TDZ. For cold products, ice is usually an acceptable means of maintaining chilled temperatures. However, food products must not be directly exposed to ice or melted water; food must be held in bowls and containers. Small containers that are refilled frequently not only enhance the attractiveness of the buffet table, but also help to maintain proper temperatures.

Hot buffet food can be held at or above 140°F (60°C) in a number of ways. Chafing dishes powered by electricity or canned heat are usually used to hold hot foods on a buffet table. Large roasts, hams, and turkeys to be carved in the dining room should be displayed under infrared heat lamps. Care should be taken to control time-temperature combinations, particularly when buffets are set up outdoors.

Adequate space for display tables and guest tables is an important facilities consideration for buffets and banquets. Crowded, hot, smoke-filled rooms make for an unpleasant dining experience. Adequate space also allows for more efficient movement of inventory and people.

Outdoor service presents unique concerns. The most important consideration is that food be protected from dust and contamination. The operation may need to use special coverings for food and beverage products to protect them between production and service. Outdoor food preparation may involve other special regulations enforced by health department officials. It is a good idea to check with authorities for laws governing outdoor cooking and dining areas before planning such functions.

Off-Premises Catering

In an effort to use resources more efficiently and to generate increased revenue, many food service and lodging businesses offer catering services off the premises. Some fast-food operations have also added catering services to strengthen their bottom lines. Some companies contract their catering services to specific locations such as airports.

Special holding equipment and transportation vehicles are necessary for off-premises catering. This equipment is designed to consistently maintain specified product temperatures. Because improper transportation of food products heightens the food safety risks, special attention must be given to this aspect of off-premises catering in order to protect the health of guests. Operations that cater off-premises should consider transportation as an additional control point.

General serving standards apply to catering service. Time-temperature combinations, personal hygiene and cleanliness, and clean, sanitized, properly maintained equipment and facilities are important.

Room Service

Room service varies greatly from one lodging property to the next, but there are some basic procedures common to most properties. Most room service orders are called in to the room service operator, who relays the order to the kitchen and the room server. Operators should be well informed about menu item ingredients and production techniques. While the order is being produced, the server covers a rolling table or service tray with a clean cloth or napkin. The server then assembles all tableware, cold beverages, condiments, and spices, followed by other cold food items. When these items have been placed on the table or tray, the server adds coffee or other hot beverages. When cooking is completed, the hot food is plated and covered, placed on the tray, table, or in a food warmer, and delivered to the guest.

Hot foods should be left in warmers for the guest's self-service unless he or she indicates otherwise. Before leaving, the server should ask the guest when the tray or table should be removed. Dirty dishes should be collected from rooms and hallways as soon as possible.

Transportation is a critical control point in room service and is important to product quality and safety. Hot food should be hot; cold food should be cold. Both should be tasty and delivered promptly. Time and temperature are the most important elements, because as product holding times increase, so does the likelihood of contamination. Some properties offer **split service**—that is, servers deliver courses separately. Split service helps maintain food quality and safety; each course can be portioned and served when it is ready, eliminating short-term holding in the kitchen.

For most room service operations, breakfast is the easiest meal to sell and the most difficult to deliver properly. Many breakfast combinations featuring eggs simply do not maintain product temperatures during transportation. It is also difficult to deliver toast to guestrooms at proper temperatures. A limited menu consisting of products that will survive the trip from the kitchen to the guestroom may be a good alternative. Specialty pastries, for example, may be offered instead of toast on room service menus. Scrambled eggs may be preferable to eggs Benedict because hollandaise sauce is highly perishable.

Room service is undergoing dramatic changes at some hotel properties. Because it is a costly amenity in a time when labor is short and maintenance and overhead costs are high, some hotels are opting for lower-cost alternatives. Many properties in the economy and all-suite segments have added food to guestroom mini-bars, placed microwave ovens in guestroom kitchens, added pizza delivery service, and entered joint agreements with nearby fast-food restaurants to avoid in-house food service. Regardless of which room service option a property chooses, it should be controlled by the food safety risk management program.

Mobile Food Service

Mobile food units are those that do not necessarily operate in a fixed location. Examples of mobile units are pushcarts, catering trucks designed to sell food at a number of locations, and ice cream and snack food trucks. Generally, the serving standards already discussed apply to mobile food service units. Some areas do not allow the sale of potentially hazardous foods from mobile units. It is a good idea to check with regulatory authorities when applying for a permit or license.

Mobile units should have a source of potable water. The water system has to be under pressure and of sufficient capacity to furnish enough cold and hot water for handwashing, equipment and utensil cleaning, and food preparation. Any liquid waste resulting from the operation of the mobile unit must be stored in a tank that is at least 15% larger in capacity than the water supply tank. Connections to the water supply tank must be of a different size or type than the connections to the waste tank.

Mobile units must operate from a **commissary** and report daily for cleaning, servicing, and restocking. The commissary must operate according to all requirements for food service operations. The commissary must have a servicing area for the mobile units. Servicing includes the emptying of liquid waste safely. Overhead protection is required in the various areas where mobile units are supplied, cleaned, and serviced.

If a mobile food unit sells only prepared food packaged in individual servings, requirements for water and sewage systems do not apply. Cleaning and sanitizing equipment is not necessary in a mobile unit if the necessary equipment is provided and used at the unit's commissary. Frankfurters may be prepared in mobile units. Only single-service articles may be provided to the unit's guests.

Serving and Change

Changes in any of the control points before serving can necessitate changes at the serving control point. An addition to the menu changes the information that servers need to adequately answer guest questions. A new menu item may also require servers to learn new serving techniques.

Self-service options—such as a salad bar—change the work that servers perform. They also present special food safety concerns, including protecting food products from contamination and exposure to the TDZ. Likewise, service styles other than traditional table service—such as banquet service, room service, and catering—have their own special food safety considerations. For example, a manager must decide if the operation has sufficient staff to offer room service and which menu items can be served safely. Managers must consider the food safety impact on the serving control point when planning other changes in the operation.

Serving and Food Safety

Serving is a critical control point because food products must be delivered from the kitchen to the guest, which increases the risks. Serving all hot foods on heated plates and cold foods on chilled plates helps maintain proper product temperatures and enhances guest satisfaction. Servers, like other staff members, should adhere closely to rules of personal cleanliness and hygiene. They must also handle all food products carefully.

All equipment, utensils, and facilities used at the serving control point must be regularly cleaned, sanitized, and maintained. In addition to contributing to the establishment's image, these items help the operation control risks. The food safety risk management program during serving helps ensure product safety, risk reduction, and guest satisfaction.

Key Terms

cart service—A variation of table service used by servers for preparing menu items beside the guest's table in the dining room. Menu items are cooked, sometimes flambéed, in front of the guest.

commissary—A centralized serving area for mobile food service units.

expediter—A staff member who acts as a communication link between kitchen personnel and servers. Servers give their orders to the expediter, who calls the orders to the appropriate kitchen stations. An expediter must know cooking times, coordinate them to sequentially deliver cooked foods for pickup, and provide leadership during hectic rush periods. An expediter should be a member of the management team.

family-style service—A table service style in which food is placed on large platters or in large bowls which are taken to the tables by servers. Guests pass the food around their table and serve themselves.

flying food show—A procedure for delivering cooked menu items to guests as soon as the food is ready. The first server to arrive at the pickup point delivers the menu items that are ready for service; can only be implemented if order tickets show which guest at which table is to receive each order.

mobile food unit—A moving food service operation; does not necessarily operate in a fixed location. Examples are pushcarts, catering trucks designed to sell food in a number of locations, and ice cream and snack food trucks.

plate service—A table service style in which fully cooked menu items are individually portioned, plated (put on plates) in the kitchen, and carried to each guest directly.

platter service—A table service style in which servers carry platters of fully cooked food to the dining room, present them to the guest for approval, and then serve the food.

sidestand—A service stand that holds supplies of tableware, ice, condiments, dairy products, and some beverages for easy access.

split service—A food service method in which servers deliver courses separately; it helps maintain food quality and safety because each course can be portioned and served when it is ready, eliminating short-term holding in the kitchen.

temporary food establishment—A food establishment that operates at a fixed location for not more than 14 consecutive days in conjunction with a single event or celebration.

Review Questions

1. What are the basic types of table service and what special food safety considerations does each type entail?

2. What kinds of control measures are effective for salad bars and other self-service food bars?

3. How is food inventory protected at the serving control point?

4. What food safety procedures and personal hygiene habits are food servers required to practice?

5. How should dishes, cups, glasses, and flatware be handled? What other procedures are required for the use and care of equipment at the serving control point?

6. Why are dining room inspections necessary? What does the supervisor/inspector look for?

7. What are the special food safety requirements for temporary food establishments?

8. What control procedures are important for banquet and buffet service?

9. Off-premises catering and room service present what types of food safety and quality risks?

10. What are mobile food units? What food safety and serving standards do they require?

Checklist for Serving

Inventory

_____   Potentially hazardous foods are not exposed to the TDZ during display and service.

_____   Ice is dispensed with ice-dispensing utensils or automatic ice machines; guests should use only automatic dispensing machines.

_____   Only single-serving packages or approved self-service containers are used for condiments, seasonings, and dressings.

_____   Dispensing utensils are stored safely before and during service.

_____   Only those foods that are not potentially hazardous and are still packaged and in sound condition are re-served.

_____ Food on display is protected from contamination and contact with the temperature danger zone.

_____ Self-service guests do not re-use tableware (except beverage cups and glasses).

_____ Servers know acceptable quality levels defined in terms of appearance, texture, color, temperature, and flavor, and check all menu items before serving the guest.

People

_____ Servers understand the operation's quality, cost, and food safety standards.

_____ Staffing decisions are based on the menu, personnel skill levels, hours of service, the size of the operation and its sales volume, and guest expectations.

_____ Servers prepare themselves and their stations for service before the shift begins.

_____ Servers restock their stations and complete closing duties before leaving.

_____ Servers adhere to standards of personal hygiene and cleanliness.

_____ Dining room supervisors conduct a staff member line-up meeting and inspection of the facilities immediately before the meal period begins.

_____ Servers place orders with the kitchen using standard ordering procedures.

_____ Servers load their trays carefully.

_____ If an expediter is used, that individual is a selected and trained member of the management team.

_____ Servers and managers check food bars regularly for cleanliness and orderliness.

Equipment

_____ Staff members regularly clean and sanitize equipment and utensils used in the service of food and beverage products.

_____ Clean and sanitized utensils and equipment are stored in a way that prevents recontamination.

_____ Tableware is handled so as to prevent contamination.

_____ Stations and sidestands are kept stocked with adequate supplies of tableware and other necessities.

_____ Food products at stations and sidestands are kept out of the temperature danger zone.

_____ Tables, chairs, floors, and windows are cleaned and maintained regularly.

_____ Condiment and spice containers are cleaned regularly.

_____ Staff members are careful when handling all equipment used in service.

_____ Plate and platter covers are used to protect menu items and help maintain product temperatures as they are transported from the kitchen to the guest.

_____ Take-out operations are evaluated carefully before implementation.

Facilities

_____ Facilities are routinely cleaned, maintained, and repaired.

_____ Restrooms are inspected and cleaned regularly.

_____ Facilities are kept clean, dry, and odor-free.

_____ Adequate lighting levels are maintained.

_____ The supervisor conducts a facility inspection immediately before the meal period.

_____ Menus are inspected and all dirty or damaged menus are removed from circulation.

_____ Pets are not allowed in the facilities.

Food Safety Risk Management Program

_____ Potentially hazardous foods are served carefully and safely.

_____ Food servers are trained to maintain standards and reduce risks during serving.

_____ Adequate facilities and equipment are present and used, and are cleaned, sanitized, and maintained frequently to reduce the risks during serving.

Temporary Food Establishments

_____ Regulations regarding potentially hazardous foods are observed.

_____ Ice is stored in single-use wet strength paper or plastic bags and proper dispensing utensils are used.

_____ Equipment is installed, cleaned, sanitized, and maintained properly.

_____ Only single-service articles are used if no facilities are available for tableware cleaning and sanitizing.

_____ Potable water is available for food preparation, handwashing, and equipment and utensil cleaning.

_____ Food is not stored in contact with undrained ice or water.

_____ Sewage and waste are disposed of according to law.

_____ Handwashing facilities are available.

_____ Walls, ceilings, floors, and doors prevent the entry of pests.

Banquet and Buffet Service

_____ Correct time-temperature controls are observed.

_____ Station setup is checked before service begins.

_____ Menu items are chosen with ease, safety, and speed of service in mind.

_____ The necessary equipment and utensils to maintain product temperatures are available.

_____ Adequate spacing is provided for display tables and guest tables.

Off-Premises Catering

_____ A sufficient quantity of special equipment and transportation vehicles is available.

_____ Product time-temperature controls are closely monitored.

_____ Food is protected during storage and transportation.

Room Service

_____ Product quality and time-temperature controls are assessed.

_____ The menu is limited to those items that the operation can successfully prepare and deliver to the guestrooms.

_____ Soiled tableware, linen, and equipment are removed from the guestrooms or hallways promptly.

_____ Room service is evaluated regularly and changed if necessary.

Mobile Food Service

_____ Local health department requirements are investigated and followed.

_____ Equipment is cleaned, sanitized, and maintained regularly.

_____ Only those food products permitted by the local health authority are prepared and served.

_____ Only single-service articles are provided to guests.

_____ The water and waste retention systems conform to local health codes.

_____ Mobile food units report daily to the commissary for cleaning, servicing, and restocking of food and beverage inventory.

_____ The commissary is operated under the requirements of the local health authorities.

Chapter 7 Outline

Cleaning, Maintenance, and Inventory
    Cleaning Agents
    Sanitizers
    Proper Handling of Cleaners and
      Sanitizers
Cleaning, Maintenance, and People
Cleaning, Maintenance, and Equipment
    Manual Systems
    Mechanical Systems
Pest Control
    Insects
    Rodents
    Control Measures
Cleaning, Maintenance, and Change
Cleaning, Maintenance, and Food Safety

Competencies

1. Identify the types of soil found in food service operations, and define cleaning and sanitizing. (p. 187)

2. Describe types and uses of cleaning agents. (pp. 187–188)

3. Identify and describe the uses of five types of sanitizers. (pp. 188–190)

4. Describe guidelines for using cleaners and sanitizers. (pp. 190–192)

5. Briefly explain manual cleaning and sanitizing procedures. (pp. 192–195)

6. Briefly explain mechanical cleaning and sanitizing procedures. (pp. 195–201)

7. Summarize the physical and behavioral characteristics of flies and cockroaches, and describe their preferred environments. (pp. 201–203)

8. Summarize the physical and behavioral characteristics of rats and mice, and describe their preferred environments. (pp. 203–204)

9. Identify guidelines for a food service pest control program, including basic environmental and chemical control. (pp. 204–206)

7

The Cleaning and Maintenance Control Point

ALTHOUGH THE CLEANING AND MAINTENANCE function is listed last in the sequence of control points within the food safety risk management program, it is the cornerstone. Success at this control point is crucial to an operation's overall program. This chapter focuses on the first three of the four resources under a manager's control at the cleaning and maintenance control point: inventory, people, and equipment.

Cleaning, Maintenance, and Inventory

Many cleaning and sanitizing agents are toxic chemicals. However, they are essential for the normal operation of a food service business. Cleaners and sanitizers are used to maintain safe facilities, equipment, and utensils by removing soil and killing harmful pathogens.

Throughout this chapter, the term "soil" refers to a substance which is in the wrong place. For example, cooking oil is necessary for the proper operation of a fryer, but cooking oil on tableware is considered soil. Organic soil consists of food products. Organic soil is produced by cooking equipment and is deposited on ceilings, walls, and exhaust hoods. Food production equipment, utensils, and tableware are also subject to organic soiling in the course of normal use.

Inorganic soil includes airborne and bonded dust. Airborne dust is freefloating, while bonded dust adheres to surfaces. Chemical deposits, which include detergent residues and mineral scale, are also considered inorganic soil. These deposits may build up on tableware, utensils, and equipment.

Cleaning is the removal of soil. The cleaning process can prevent the accumulation of food residues and the growth of microorganisms, thereby reducing **spoilage.** Sanitizing is the destruction of pathogens that survive the cleaning process. Sanitizing is necessary because items that look clean are not necessarily sanitized. Likewise, cleaning is necessary because it is nearly impossible to sanitize a soiled item.

Cleaning Agents

There are many types of cleaning agents used in a food establishment. Any of these products may be called a "detergent." However, this term usually refers to synthetic detergents, which are more alkaline than soaps. Soap is an alkaline salt of organic acid. Cleaning agents dissolve or disperse soils and hold them in suspension (usually in water).

Soaps are used primarily for handwashing because they do not irritate the skin as detergents do. There has been some concern that bar soap may be a fomite (an inanimate object capable of transmitting infectious microorganisms). However, bar soap is not likely to support the growth of microorganisms. The major disadvantage of soap as a cleaning agent is that it produces a residue (soap scum) when combined with hard water.

Detergents are relatively unaffected by hard water and are therefore used for most cleaning purposes other than handwashing. They are especially effective in removing fats and oils. Some detergents soften water, and some have a germicidal effect. (Such detergents do not replace sanitizing, however.) Important factors to consider when selecting a detergent include the surface to be cleaned, the type of soil, and the cleaning process.

Dishwashing detergents must be measured carefully to ensure the best results. Dishwashing machines usually use powdered detergents and are often equipped with automatic dispensing devices. Liquid detergents are usually used for manual dishwashing. Some highly alkaline detergents may irritate skin and should be used with rubber gloves.

Abrasive cleaners are used to scour off rust, grease, and heavy soil. Because they contain abrasive substances, they can permanently scratch stainless steel and porcelain surfaces. Therefore, staff members should use them with caution and only after proper training.

Acid cleaners vary in strength. Weak citric acid is used to wipe stainless steel. Hydrochloric acid (muriatic or plumber's acid) is used to remove hard water mineral deposits. Acid cleaners must be used with extreme caution and only by trained staff. Drain cleaners, many of which are acid-based, must also be used carefully to avoid skin irritation and food contamination.

Degreasers are highly alkaline and are usually skin irritants. Degreasers may be alkali-, chlorine-, or hydrocarbon solvent–based. Some are water-soluble or used as vapors. Degreasers in the form of vapors are used in cleaning kitchen exhaust ducts. Solvent cleaners are produced from emulsifiers and hydrocarbons. These heavy-duty degreasers are used to remove grease from exterior surfaces, driveways, and vehicles.

Metal cleaners and polishes are oils or oil emulsions that remove both soil and oxidation from pots and pans. If not rinsed away thoroughly, they may leave behind a white film which contaminates food and equipment.

Deodorizers are used to remove unpleasant, lingering odors in restrooms. They may leave a residue on surfaces if used improperly. Deodorizers should never be used in place of proper cleaning.

Sanitizers

Sanitizers are chemical compounds that destroy pathogens. There are five types of sanitizers in general use: chlorine-based sanitizers, iodine-based sanitizers, quaternary ammonium compounds, acid-anionic surfactants, and phenolic sanitizers.

The type of sanitizer an operation uses for a particular application depends on the method of warewashing (manual or mechanical) and the type of item being sanitized.

Chlorine-based sanitizers are inexpensive and popular. These sanitizers are active against all microorganisms and spores if used in a concentration of 25 mg/L (milligrams/liter) at pH 10 or less and a temperature of 120°F (49°C); 50 mg/L at pH 10 or less and a temperature of 100°F (38°C); or 100 mg/L at pH 10 or less and a temperature of 55°F (13°C) with an exposure of at least seven seconds. Higher concentrations do not increase effectiveness. (The concentration of chlorine sanitizers can be easily determined with a field test kit.) Chlorine compounds are unaffected by hard water and do not leave a residue. However, they do possess a characteristic chlorine odor and have a relatively short shelf life. Other disadvantages include decreased effectiveness as the pH increases above 8.0, possible skin irritation, corrosion of some metals, and rapid break-up from some solutions. Chlorine sanitizers are usually applied for one minute or more at temperatures of 75°F (24°C) or above.

Iodine-based sanitizers (iodophors) are stable (do not deteriorate easily), have a long shelf life, and will destroy most bacterial cells (but not spores). Iodophors are effective in hard water and are non-corrosive. They do not leave a residue or irritate skin. Because iodophors have a brown or amber color, their concentration is easily measured visually. Iodophors work somewhat slowly at a pH of 5.0 or above (for example, when used with an alkaline detergent). They may also stain some surfaces. Iodophors are more expensive than some other sanitizers. They should be applied in a concentration of 12.5 to 25 mg/L for one minute or more at temperatures of 75° to 120°F (24° to 49°C) and a pH of 5.0 or less. They should not be used at temperatures above 120°F (49°C).

Quaternary ammonium compounds (QUATS) are stable, have a long shelf life, and are active against most microorganisms. They work best within a pH range of 9 to 10 and leave behind a film that controls bacterial growth. QUATS are non-corrosive and non-irritating and both eliminate and prevent odors. However, QUATS destroy some microorganisms slowly and are incompatible with common detergents. They are also expensive. Their residue makes these sanitizers impractical for many uses (such as cleaning tableware); however, the residue is desirable on some surfaces (such as refrigerator interiors) to control bacterial activity. QUATS are usually applied in concentrations of 180 to 220 mg/L for one minute or longer at temperatures of 75°F (24°C) and above.

Acid-anionic surfactants are stable, have a long shelf life, and are active against most microorganisms. They are odorless, non-staining, and effective in hard water. They have a low toxicity when left as a residual antibacterial film. Acid-anionic surfactants are only effective at relatively low pHs (1.9 to 3.0). They are corrosive to metal surfaces other than stainless steel and aluminum and do not destroy most bacterial spores. Acid-anionic surfactants should be applied in concentrations of 100 to 200 mg/L for at least one minute at temperatures of 75° to 110°F (24° to 43°C).

Phenolic sanitizers work well at pH levels between 6 and 7. They become more stable when combined with synthetic anionics. Phenolic compounds act as deodorizers but have limited applications. They should not be used to sanitize food-handling equipment.

Proper Handling of Cleaners and Sanitizers

The chemistry of cleaner and sanitizer formulation is an exact science. It is a dangerous practice to mix cleaning or sanitizing compounds in-house. It would be wrong, for example, to assume that, because bleach is an effective sanitizer and ammonia is a good cleaner, the two combined might be an inexpensive all-purpose cleaner. These two chemicals produce a deadly gas when combined. Similarly, if QUATS are mixed with chlorine compounds, the mixture releases a great deal of heat. *Never mix your own cleaners or sanitizers.*

It is also important to follow the manufacturer's recommendations for the proper mixture and application of cleaners and sanitizers. Improper concentrations are ineffective if too low and wasteful, sometimes harmful, if too high. Staff members should be trained to measure and use cleaners and sanitizers carefully. Managers must ensure that these procedures are followed even at the busiest times.

Because many cleaners and sanitizers are toxic chemicals, these substances must be clearly labeled and stored in a locked area used for no other purpose. Toxic chemicals should never be stored with food products. They should be stored in their original containers. Only those chemicals necessary for maintaining the operation's environment should be stored on the premises. Whenever possible, toxic substances should have distinctive colors and packaging so they will not be confused with food products. Recall that chemicals to be used in dilute solution (for example, detergents and sanitizers) may be safely stored in their original containers on shelves above or below work areas. Chemicals used without dilution (such as oven cleaners and silver polishes) should not be stored in work areas.

Some examples will illustrate the importance of these safety precautions. One operation used liquid chlorine bleach as a kitchen sanitizer. One of the staff members transferred some bleach from its large original container into a smaller, empty vinegar bottle. The next morning, the breakfast cook used the bleach in the vinegar bottle to mix a solution for poaching eggs. In another incident, the kitchen manager of a food service commissary encountered some strange-tasting soup in her operation. In the course of questioning the cook about each item in the standard recipe, the manager discovered that the cook had used soap flakes (stored in an unmarked container) in place of salt.

The objective of safe chemical storage is to prevent food and equipment contamination and to protect staff members and guests. Following regulatory codes can help managers significantly reduce the risks that toxic chemicals pose.

Cleaning, Maintenance, and People

The success of the operation's food safety risk management program depends greatly on people. The success of the cleaning and maintenance control point is particularly dependent on the operation's systematic approach to this resource.

In some cases, outside personnel are brought in to help with cleaning and maintenance. Outside contractors may be employed for monthly, quarterly, or semi-annual heavy cleaning and maintenance jobs. They may strip and reseal floors or clean exhaust hoods and ventilation ducts in the kitchen. In most establishments, an outside contractor regularly provides pest control services.

Routine cleaning is usually the responsibility of in-house staff. All staff members should understand the proper procedures for cleaning and maintaining the equipment and facilities in their work areas. Each person in the operation is responsible, to some extent, for the cleaning and maintenance function. When production or service staff members are not busy with other duties, they should be cleaning.

To be successful, the operation's cleaning program must be formalized. Written cleaning procedures are important. Management should establish written cleaning procedures for each area and piece of equipment in the operation. Each procedure should briefly describe the task, list the steps in the task, and indicate the materials and tools necessary.

It is a good idea to post cleaning procedures near the equipment they pertain to so staff members can refer to them easily. Written procedures are also useful for on-the-job training and for management evaluation of the cleaning program. Each manager should monitor cleaning procedures in his or her department. This follow-up demonstrates to staff members that management cares about maintaining a clean environment.

Staff members are more likely to follow cleaning and maintenance procedures if they understand the importance of these routine functions. Training in cleaning procedures must be systematic to be effective. Training should cover cleanliness standards and recommended methods, products, and equipment used for cleaning and maintenance. Only after proper training can staff members be assigned regular cleaning and maintenance duties. For example, a preparation cook should not be responsible for operating and cleaning a meat slicer until he or she has been properly trained. Proper training, including ongoing refresher training, reduces risks at this control point.

A written cleaning schedule further systematizes this important activity by indicating who is responsible for each cleaning task and how often the task should be performed. The schedule should be based on a survey of cleaning needs. If a survey has never been done, managers, supervisors, and staff members should work together to identify cleaning needs for each area in the food service operation. Questions to answer during the survey include:

- What is to be cleaned or maintained?

- Who is responsible for the cleaning or maintenance?

- When is the area or equipment to be cleaned or maintained?

- What are the safety precautions associated with this cleaning or maintenance procedure?

- How should the cleaned item be stored or protected to prevent recontamination?

- Who is responsible for supervising and checking the cleaning or maintenance effort?

- What must be done to reduce risks during cleaning and maintenance?

Areas which might be covered by the survey include entrance, exit, kitchen, dining, garbage, storage, and restroom areas. Once the survey is completed, a cleaning schedule can be developed. A sample cleaning schedule is presented in Exhibit 1.

Cleaning, Maintenance, and Equipment

Kitchen equipment and utensils must be cleaned and sanitized to prevent cross-contamination. Cleaning and sanitizing tasks can be accomplished manually or mechanically. Manual cleaning and sanitizing is usually used for in-place equipment such as ovens, broilers, griddles, and steam-powered equipment. Most food service businesses also clean and sanitize pots, pans, and utensils (such as mixing bowls, wire whips, and knives) manually. On the other hand, tableware is usually washed and sanitized in a dishwashing machine.

Manual Systems

Manual cleaning and sanitizing of pots, pans, and utensils requires a three-compartment sink large enough to submerse the largest item to be washed, rinsed, and sanitized. The sink area should include adequate space for soiled holding—the accumulation of soiled equipment and utensils. The soiled holding area should be far enough from clean items to prevent cross-contamination. Also, staff members must wash their hands after handling soiled items. If hot water is used for sanitizing, the sanitizing compartment of the sink should be designed with an integral heating device to maintain water temperatures of at least 171°F (77°C) and provided with a basket to allow complete immersion of equipment and utensils into the hot water.

Equipment and utensils should be scraped and pre-soaked before washing to remove large food particles. Washing takes place in the first compartment of the sink. A hot detergent solution (110°F/43°C minimum) is essential for this step. The proper concentration of detergent is economical and protects guests from detergent residue on food-contact surfaces.

Items are rinsed in the second compartment of the sink. Rinsing removes detergent and food particles. Rinse water must be clean and at the proper temperature.

Once the item is washed and rinsed, it is sanitized in the third compartment. There are several methods of manual sanitization. The equipment or utensil can be placed in 170°F (77°C) water for at least 30 seconds. The item may also be exposed to a 50 mg/L chlorine and water solution at 75°F (24°C) or above for at least one minute. Exposing the item to an iodine and water solution of 12.5 mg/L at a temperature of at least 75°F (24°C) for one minute or longer is also an acceptable sanitizing method.

The water used for washing, rinsing, and sanitizing should be changed regularly. Water temperatures must also be monitored with an accurate thermometer. Sanitizer concentrations should be checked with a test kit.

Exhibit 1   Sample Cleaning Schedule

Equipment or Area to Be Cleaned	Person Responsible	Cleaning Frequency	Cleaning Manual Page Reference*
Can Opener	Dishwasher	Daily	
Ceilings	Maintenance Staff	Monthly	
Char-Broiler	Station Cook	Daily Weekly	
Coffee Urn	Server	After Each Brew Daily	
Compartment Steamer	Station Cook Dishwasher	Daily Weekly	
Convection Oven	Station Cook	Daily Weekly	
Conventional Oven	Station Cook	Daily Weekly	
Cutting Boards	Station Cook Pot and Pan Washer	After Each Use Daily	
Dishwashing Machine	Dishwasher	After Each Shift Daily	
Floors	Dishwasher Pot and Pan Washer	As Needed Daily	
Fryer	Station Cook	Daily Weekly	
Griddle	Station Cook	As Needed Daily Weekly	
Grinder	Station Cook Pot and Pan Washer	After Each Use Daily	
Hood/Filters	Pot and Pan Washer Dishwasher	Weekly	
Hot Top Range	Station Cook Pot and Pan Washer	Daily Weekly	
Ice Machine Interior Deliming	Pot and Pan Washer Maintenance Staff	Daily Weekly Per Manufacturer's Recommendations	
Microwave Oven	Station Cook	Daily Weekly	
Mixer	Station Cook	After Each Use Daily	
Mobile Food Warmer	Pot and Pan Washer	After Each Use Weekly	
Mobile Refrigeration Unit	Pot and Pan Washer	After Each Use Weekly	

(continued)

Exhibit 1   *(continued)*

Equipment or Area to Be Cleaned	Person Responsible	Cleaning Frequency	Cleaning Manual Page Reference*
Open Top Range	Station Cook Pot and Pan Washer	Daily Weekly	
Overhead-Fired Broiler	Station Cook	Daily Weekly	
Plate Warmer	Dishwasher	Daily Weekly	
Pot and Pan Sink	Pot and Pan Washer	After Each Shift Daily	
Reach-in Freezer	Station Cook Sous Chef Maintenance Staff	Daily Weekly Monthly	
Reach-in Refrigerator	Station Cook Sous Chef Maintenance Staff	Daily Weekly Monthly	
Refrigerated Drawer	Station Cook Sous Chef Maintenance Staff	Daily Weekly Monthly	
Salamander	Station Cook	Daily Weekly Monthly	
Slicer	Station Cook Pot and Pan Washer	After Each Use Weekly	
Steam-Jacketed Kettle	Station Cook Pot and Pan Washer	Daily Weekly	
Steam Table	Station Cook	After Each Shift Daily	
Tilting Braising Pan	Station Cook	After Each Shift Daily	
Toaster	Server	Daily	
Walk-In Freezer	Sous Chef Maintenance Staff	Daily Weekly Monthly	
Walk-In Refrigerator	Sous Chef Maintenance Staff	Daily Weekly Monthly	
Walls	Dishwasher Pot and Pan Washer Maintenance Staff	Daily Weekly Monthly	
Work Tables	Station Cook	As Needed Daily	

*References are intended to be page numbers in the operation's cleaning manual.

Exhibit 2   Sample Chemical Supplier's Recommended Cleaning Procedures

Equipment Required:
Double compartment plastic pail
Cellulose sponges

Product Recommendation:
_____
_____

Procedure:

1. Immediately after use, take all removable parts to pot-sink for washing and sanitizing according to manual pot-washing instructions.

2. Fill both compartments of pail with warm water. To the wash compartment, add _____ in the ratio of _____ per gallon of water.
   Use separate sponges for wash and rinse compartments.

3. Unplug slicer.
   Besides the electrical hazard, serious injury could result if motor were to start while working near blade.

4. Use wash solution and cellulose sponge to scrub all stationary parts of slicer. Pay particular attention to corners, handles, and hard to get at places.

5. Sanitize, using clean sponge dipped in rinse solution and squeezed nearly dry.
   Dip and wring sponge frequently to be sure sanitizer contacts all surfaces.

6. Reassemble slicer.

7. Replace plug.

8. Return cleaning equipment to proper storage.

Source: DuBois Chemicals, *Sanitation Procedures Manual* (Undated), p. D-41.

All equipment and utensils should be air-dried after sanitizing. Once dry, equipment and utensils should be handled carefully to prevent recontamination of food-contact surfaces. Safe storage of clean, sanitized equipment and utensils is also essential.

Equipment cleaning procedures are often available from manufacturers of cleaning and sanitizing compounds. Exhibit 2 is an example of one company's recommended procedures for cleaning a food slicer.

Mechanical Systems

Most glasses, dishes, and flatware are cleaned and sanitized in a dishwashing machine. There are several types of dishwashing machines. Single-tank, stationary rack machines wash one rack of dishes at a time; each rack is loaded manually. Single-tank machines operate either at single or dual temperatures for wash and rinse cycles. Conveyor machines may have one or more tanks. The conveyor moves dish racks through the machine automatically. A typical warewashing station with a conveyor machine is shown in Exhibit 3.

Flight-type machines also use a conveyor belt. The dishes are loaded directly on the conveyor belt's plastic pegs or bars. Flatware is loaded in racks. This type of machine operates continuously (with a person stationed at each end) and is ideal

Exhibit 3   Typical Warewashing Station—Conveyor Machine

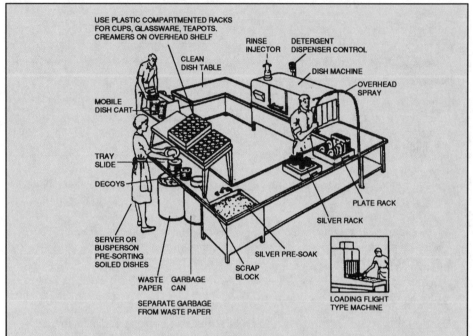

1. Set up a silver pre-soak pan on the soiled dish table. Use a stainless steel or plastic pan. Put a piece of aluminum foil in the bottom, add hot water and use a silver soak product. Change the solution when it becomes dirty.

2. Place glass, cup and bowl racks on the overhead shelf. Make sure that these items are placed in each compartment upside down.

3. Set out decoys on the table so that the buspersons can place dishes all of one kind together.

4. Always knock off excess food soil and paper before racking dishes so that food particles do not enter the wash tank.

5. Rack dishes, all of one kind, together. Then rinse with overhead spray to knock off any remaining heavy food soil.

6. Rack silver in holders with eating end up. Do not place same kind together or they will nest and not wash thoroughly.

FOLLOW LABEL INSTRUCTIONS ON PRODUCT USE AND CONCENTRATION

Source: The Soap and Detergent Association, New York.

for high-volume operations. Carousel-type machines have a circular conveyor belt. Immersion dishwashers clean racked dishes by a process similar to the manual dishwashing system.

It is important to operate dish machines properly. Each staff member responsible for operating the machine should read the manual carefully. Most machines also have exterior data plates which provide basic operating information. Management should establish a cleaning and maintenance schedule based on the manufacturer's recommendations. Regular cleaning and maintenance will ensure optimal performance and minimize time-consuming and costly repairs in the long run.

The basic mechanical warewashing procedure requires ten steps; the following times and temperatures are based on recommendations for a multi-tank conveyor machine:

1. Scrape soiled dishes and pre-soak flatware.
2. Pre-rinse to remove all visible soil.
3. Rack dishes and flatware so water will spray evenly on all surfaces.
4. Wash dishes and flatware in a detergent-water solution at 150°F (66°C) for at least seven seconds.
5. Rinse dishes and flatware in clean water at 160°F (71°C) to 180°F (82°C) for at least seven seconds.
6. Final-rinse dishes and flatware in a sanitizer-water solution at 180°F (82°C) with a maximum conveyor speed of 15 feet (4.6 m) per minute.
7. Air-dry dishes and flatware.
8. Stack clean and sanitized items, being careful not to touch surfaces that will come into contact with food or the guest's mouth.
9. Store dishes and flatware in a clean, dry area.
10. Clean the machine, including the spray arms, trays, tanks, and tables.

As with manual systems, there must be sufficient counter space for the accumulation of soiled tableware. These soiled items must not touch clean and sanitized items. Large food particles should be scraped with a rubber scraper into a disposal or garbage can. Abrasive cleaning pads should not be used for scraping because they can leave behind unsightly scratches that may harbor microorganisms. Decoys (setups of one piece of each type of tableware) make it easier for staff members to pre-sort and rack soiled tableware according to type.

Some operators pre-soak only flatware in order to reduce dish handling and breakage. However, some items, such as glasses used to serve fruit juices, are difficult to clean without pre-soaking. Dishes soiled with eggs, cheese, or sauces are also hard to clean; they may need pre-soaking and, like all tableware, they should be washed as soon as possible after soiling.

Pre-rinsing removes any remaining visible soil. A pressure sprayer located over a garbage disposal can simplify this step. Next, items are racked according to type. Glasses are racked bottom-up, dishes are racked on edge, and flatware is placed in baskets. Specialized racks make the process more efficient. Tableware should be arranged in racks so that the spray can reach all surfaces. Dishes should not be stacked or crowded into the machine. This increases breakage and prevents proper cleaning and sanitizing.

Time and temperature requirements for mechanical wash and rinse cycles vary according to the type of machine (see Exhibit 4). If the machine sanitizes with hot water alone, the final rinse water must be at least 180°F (82°C).

Exhibit 4 Time-Temperature Requirements for Commercial Warewashing Machines

SINGLE TANK STATIONARY RACK TYPES:			
WASH		**FINAL RINSE**	
Minimum Exposure	Minimum Temperature	Minimum Exposure	Minimum Temperature
DUAL TEMPERATURE: 40 sec.	150°F (tank) (66°C)	10 sec.	180°F (manifold) (82°C)
			15 to 25 psi flow pressure
SINGLE TEMPERATURE: 40 sec.	165°F (tank) (74°C)	30 sec.	165°F (tank) (74°C)
	Discharge to waste		Discharge to waste
CHEMICAL SANITIZING: 50 sec.	120°F (tank) (49°C)	20 sec.	120°F (tank) (49°C)
	Discharge to waste		50 mg/L chlorine or other acceptable sanitizing solution

CONVEYOR TYPES					
WASH		**PUMPED RINSE**		**FINAL RINSE**	
Minimum Exposure	Minimum Temperature	Minimum Exposure	Minimum Temperature	Minimum Exposure	Minimum Temperature
					15 to 25 psi flow pressure
SINGLE TANK: 15 sec.	160°F (tank) (71°C)	NOT APPLICABLE		Maximum Conveyor Speed, 7 ft/min. 6 in. wide spray, 5 in. above conveyor	180°F (manifold) (82°C)
MULTIPLE TANK: 7 sec.	150°F (tank) (66°C)	7 sec.	160°F (71°C)	Maximum Conveyor Speed, 15 ft/min. 3 in. wide spray, 5 in. above conveyor	180°F (manifold) (82°C)

NSF Specifications for Various Types of Warewashing Machines

The accompanying chart summarizes the requirements detailed in NSF Standard No. 3 for commercial dishwashing machines[1]. Special equipment differing in design or principle of operation from the machines listed on the chart may not meet the requirements cited there. However, these machines are tested as specials and meet the requirements for soil removal and sanitization of utensils.

1. The figures on the table represent minimum requirements. NSF tests the final rinse flow pressure at 20 psi as an optimum pressure, but allowable flow pressures range from 15 to 25 psi.

2. If the manufacturer's data plate indicates a flow pressure, the machine must carry a gauge valve to measure it. If the data plate does not state a flow pressure, the machine is not required to carry a gauge valve.

3. Temperatures stated on the dish machine data plate are minimums. Except for chemical sanitizing machines, the machine should not heat to more than 15 degrees F. above its minimum temperatures.

[1]For specific machine information, consult the current NSF Food Service Equipment List.

Source: Adapted from National Sanitation Foundation, *Standard No. 3 for Spray-Type Dishwashing Machines.*

Items should be air-dried for at least one minute. A drying agent can be used to minimize water spots. It is important to allow cleaned and sanitized dishes to air-dry thoroughly. Moisture can damage dishes by causing them to stick together. Humidity in the dishroom must be controlled to help speed drying.

After air-drying, the items should be sorted and stacked for storage. Chipped or cracked dishes should be discarded. Staff members who scrape, pre-rinse, and rack soiled tableware should wash their hands before handling clean tableware. Glasses, cups, and flatware may be left in dishwashing racks as long as they are stored in a way that prevents contamination. Tableware should be stored in a clean, dry area.

At the end of each shift, or more frequently if necessary, the dishwashing machine should be disassembled and cleaned. Spray arms and scrap collection trays should be removed and cleaned. Curtains between wash and rinse compartments should be washed, rinsed, sanitized, and dried. Tanks should be drained and the tables and exterior surfaces of the machine should be wiped down. Finally, the detergent and sanitizer dispensers should be refilled as needed.

It is important that food service managers test the operation of commercial dishwashers daily. Some common performance problems and suggested solutions are listed in Exhibit 5. A test kit or other device is needed to accurately measure the mg/L concentration of sanitizing solutions. Regular maintenance is also important. Dishwasher drains, valves, and pumps should be regularly checked for leaks. Nozzles and pipes should be examined for wear and mineral deposits. Detergent concentrations should be checked with a test kit. Temperature measuring devices should be tested for accuracy by running a thermometer through the machine and checking it at each cycle. If the machine is gas powered, the flame should be checked for proper burning color and height. Chains and drive wheels on machines with movable conveyors should be regularly lubricated. Some machine and chemical suppliers provide dish machine service on a contractual basis.

Rising energy costs have prompted many operators to purchase chemical sanitizing machines. Many models are approved by regulatory authorities. Chemical sanitizing machines use lower temperatures, higher water pressure, and longer cycle times than conventional dish machines. Although the final rinse temperature is only 120°F (49°C), tableware is sanitized chemically in the last cycle, usually with iodophors or chlorine solutions. Operations using these low-temperature machines have reported energy savings of as high as 35 to 40%. Convertible high-temperature/low-temperature dish machines are also available. When the high-temperature option is selected, a booster heater provides water at the proper temperature.

Other mechanical warewashing equipment includes pot washers, glass washers (used in bar operations), and under-counter dish machines for room service pantry areas and concierge floors in hotels.

Staff members who operate dishwashing machines should be well trained. Supervision of the warewashing function is important; a dish machine is expensive to purchase and operate. Dish machine and chemical manufacturers usually provide free materials and technical assistance to help train dishwashing staff.

Cleaning and maintenance tools other than warewashing equipment (such as mops and buckets) must be stored so that they are easily accessible and do not contaminate food, utensils, or linens. Such equipment may not be cleaned in food production, handwashing, or warewashing sinks.

Exhibit 5   Common Warewashing Problems

Symptom	Possible Cause	Suggested Solution
Dishes Soiled	Insufficient detergents	Use enough detergent in wash water to ensure complete soil suspension.
	Wash water temperature too low	Keep water temperature within recommended ranges to dissolve food residues and to further facilitate heat accumulation (for sanitization).
	Inadequate wash and rinse times	Allow sufficient time for wash and rinse operations to be effective. (Time should be automatically controlled by timer or by conveyor speed. The timer may need to be reset or the conveyor speed adjusted.)
	Insufficient prescraping	Do a better job of water-scraping dishes prior to washing.
	Improper racking or placings	Rack dishes according to size and type in appropriate rack.
Films	Water hardness	Use an external softening process. Use more detergent to provide internal conditioning. Use a chlorinated cleaner. Check temperature of wash and rinse water. Water maintained above recommended ranges may cause filming.
	Detergent carryover	Maintain adequate pressure and volume of rinse water.
	Improperly cleaned or rinsed equipment	Prevent scale buildup in equipment by adopting frequent and adequate cleaning practices. Maintain adequate water pressure and volume.
Greasy Films	Low pH Insufficient detergent Low water temperatures	Maintain adequate alkalinity to saponify greases. Check amount of detergent, water temperature.
	Improperly cleaned	Unclog all wash and rinse nozzles to provide proper equipment spray action. Clogged rinse nozzles may also interfere with wash tank overflow.
Streaking	Alkalinity in the water	Use an external treatment method to reduce alkalinity.
Spotting	Rinse water hardness	Provide external or internal softening.
	Rinse water temperature too high or too low	Check rinse water temperature. Dishes may be flash drying, or water may be drying on dishes rather than drying off.
	Inadequate time between rinsing and storage	Allow sufficient time for air drying.
Foaming	Detergent	Change to a low sudsing product.
	Water too soft or too hard	Use an appropriate treatment method to adjust the condition of the water.
	Food soil	Adequately remove gross soil before washing. The decomposition of carbohydrates, proteins, or fats may cause foaming during the wash cycle.
	Wash temperature too low	Increase wash temperature.

Source: National Sanitation Foundation, *Cleaning and Sanitizing Workbook.*

Preventive maintenance of all equipment is essential to reduce risks and control long-term costs. Like cleaning activities, maintenance activities should be based on a survey of needs and performed according to a schedule. The schedule should indicate all services and equipment item needs. Equipment maintenance should always be performed according to the manufacturer's recommendations. Maintenance operations should be recorded in a maintenance log, which should list the service, date, and replacement parts, if appropriate. Assigning responsibility for all equipment maintenance to one individual or position is a good control measure. If this is impossible, consider hiring a contract service firm to maintain all equipment.

Pest Control

Insects and rodents are disease-carrying pests that contaminate food products. Some pests contaminate foods with disease agents; a housefly, for example, can carry over six million microbes on its body and many more internally. Other pests (**stored-food insects**) render food products unfit for human consumption. The pests of public health significance are flies, cockroaches, rats, mice, small beetles, and moths.

Insects

The common housefly (*Musca domestica*) has been known to carry typhoid fever, leprosy, amoebic dysentery, tuberculosis, and bubonic plague. Flies eat many of the same foods that humans eat.

The female fly lays about 100 to 120 eggs at a time. In warm, moist, decaying environments, the eggs hatch in as little as eight hours. Within a week or two, the larvae become adult flies. A single fly can produce as many as 14 generations in a single summer season. Exhibit 6 shows the life cycle of a common housefly.

Flies have six legs, each with a claw and a sticky pad. The claws enable flies to cling to rough surfaces, while the sticky pads allow them to walk on smooth surfaces at any angle. Each foot pad is a germ-laden surface that can contaminate food.

A fly can only consume fluids. It draws liquid foods through its proboscis, a fleshy sucking tube at the bottom of its face. In order to eat solid food, a fly must first dissolve the solids by regurgitating some of its stomach fluids. This process can contaminate food products with pathogens.

Cockroaches are ubiquitous and troublesome pests. Four species that account for most cockroach problems in food establishments are shown in Exhibit 7.

The German cockroach (*Blatella germanica*) is the commonest species. It is gray and approximately ¾ of an inch (19 mm) long. It prefers warm, dry areas with ready access to water (such as kitchens, storerooms, and bathrooms). The German cockroach is resistant to most chemical killers.

The brown-banded cockroach (*Supella longipalpa*) is approximately ½ of an inch (13 mm) long and has two brown or yellow bands on its wings. The brown-banded cockroach is found in most parts of the United States and Canada. It prefers warm, dark places and often hides in electric clocks, radios, television sets, and under booth seats.

Exhibit 6 Life Cycle of the Common Housefly

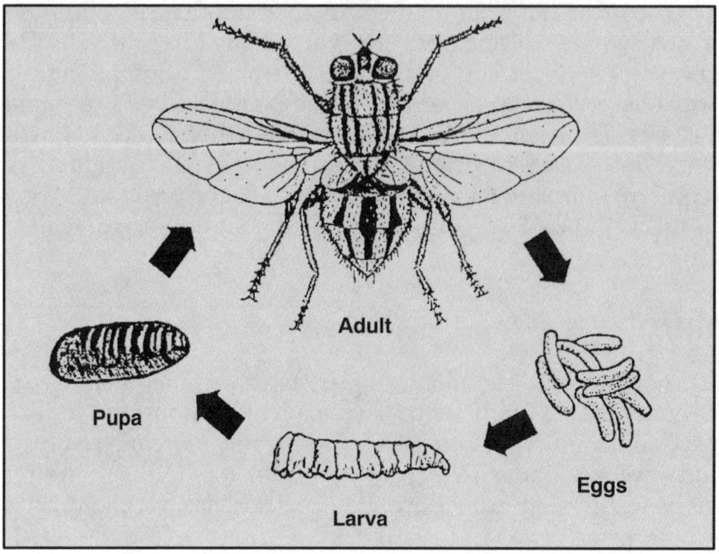

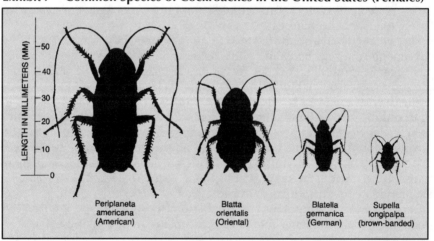

Source: H. D. Pratt, K. S. Littig, and H. G. Scott, *Flies of Public Health Importance.*

Exhibit 7 Common Species of Cockroaches in the United States (Females)

Source: H. D. Pratt, K. S. Littig, and H. G. Scott, *Household and Stored-Food Insects of Public Health Importance.*

The Oriental cockroach (*Blatta orientalis*) is black and approximately ¾ to 1½ inches (19 to 38 mm) long. The Oriental cockroach usually lives in sewers, in cool, damp basements, and under sinks and refrigerators. It has a strong repulsive odor.

The American cockroach (*Periplaneta americana*) is red to dark brown and about 1½ to 2 inches (38 to 51 mm) long. The American cockroach can be found in

Exhibit 8   Common Rodent Pests

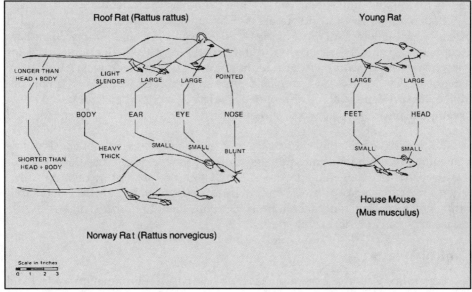

Source: H. D. Pratt and R. Z. Brown, *Biological Factors in Domestic Rodent Control.*

warm, humid environments such as boiler rooms, warm basements, kitchens, and garbage areas. This species consumes sweets and beer, so it may also be attracted to empty beverage bottles and cans.

Beetles and moths are classified as stored-food insects because they destroy stored food products. Some species of beetles attack leather products, woolens, and food products such as flour, spices, cookies, and dried fruits. Other beetles prefer dry grains and vegetables such as corn, rice, peas, beans, and wheat. Moths, commonly known to eat wool, may also damage food; some species destroy wheat, corn, and other grains.

Rodents

Rats and mice carry pathogenic microbes and destroy food products in storage. The roof rat, the Norway rat, and the house mouse are responsible for most rodent problems in food establishments. These three rodents are illustrated in Exhibit 8.

The roof rat (*Rattus rattus*) is either black or brown with a pointed nose and a slender body. The roof rat weighs from 4 to 12 ounces (112 to 336 g) and is 14 to 18 inches (35.6 to 45.7 cm) long, including the tail. It is found in the southeastern and western United States.

The Norway rat (*Rattus norvegicus*) has a blunt nose, a thick, heavy body, and has red to gray-brown fur. It weighs from 10 to 17 ounces (280 to 476 g) and measures 13 to 18 inches (33 to 45.7 cm) in length. The Norway rat is found throughout most of North America.

The house mouse (*Mus musculus*) ranges in color from gray to brown. It has a pointed nose and a small body weighing from $1/2$ to $3/4$ of an ounce (14 to 21 g) and measuring 6 to 7 $^1/_2$ inches (15.2 to 19.1 cm) in length. The house mouse is more widely distributed in the environment than the other two rodents.

Rodents tend to nest in safe areas near food and water. They prefer quiet places like basements. All three of these rodents can climb and jump well and are exceptional swimmers, especially the rats. Their front teeth (incisors), used for gnawing, grow continuously. Rodents gnaw wood, cinder block, aluminum, paperboard, cloth sacks, and even lead pipes to keep their teeth short. If not controlled, these rodents will consume a wide variety of foods. They have been known to eat grain, meat, eggs, potatoes, and even citrus fruits. They often forage for food in garbage.

Rodents have been linked to a variety of human diseases. Salmonellosis can be transmitted through food contaminated by rat or mouse droppings. Rat-bite fever is caused by a pathogenic species of *Streptobacillus* present in rats. All three rodents can carry leptospirosis (Weil's disease) and spread trichinosis by contaminating hog feed. Rats can transmit murine typhus fever to humans, and the house mouse may transmit rickettsial pox.

Control Measures

A successful pest control program has two parts: basic environmental control and effective chemical control. **Basic environmental control** includes methods of keeping rodents and insects out of the food establishment. All materials that serve as food or shelter for pests should either be made pest-resistant or removed from the facility and its immediate vicinity.

Prompt refuse removal—at least twice each week—is critical. Refuse storage areas must be kept clean. Prompt cleanup of spilled food in storage and production areas also minimizes problems. All staff members should be trained to clean as they complete a job.

Doors should be screened and fitted with self-closing devices. Windows should also be screened, and screens should be maintained in a good state of repair. Toilet and lavatory facilities should be kept clean.

Food storage areas must be kept clean as well. Shelves in storage areas should be cleaned at least twice each week. All deliveries should be examined for signs of infestation. Stock rotation (first in, first out) also reduces problems. Opened packages should either be used immediately or their contents stored in covered, dated, and labeled containers. Regular inspections can identify problems before food products become unusable.

Cool, dry storage conditions inhibit insect and rodent breeding. Food products in storage areas should be at least two inches (5.1 cm) from walls and six inches (15.2 cm) from the floor. This reduces harborage areas and improves ventilation. Aisles at least two feet (.6 m) wide also reduce harborage areas and allow for easy cleaning. Floor areas in food storage rooms should be swept and mopped at least twice daily.

Facilities can be made rodent-resistant by closing small openings. A rat, for example, can crawl through a $^1/_2$-inch (1.3 cm) opening, while a mouse can penetrate an opening as small as $^1/_4$ of an inch (.6 cm). Openings around fans, doors, windows, pipes, floor drains, and foundations can be effectively blocked with a combination of brick, mortar, concrete, and galvanized hardware cloth.

Rodent traps are preferable to rodenticides. Snap traps kill or injure mice and rats, while live traps capture and hold live animals for later disposal. Traps can effectively deter expanding rodent populations. Rodent traps should be checked frequently (at least once every 24 hours). Cockroach traps are effective for slight infestations. They can help locate problem areas within the facility.

In addition to basic environmental control, food service operations can control pests with chemicals. Always remember that pesticides are toxic chemicals. If improperly applied, they can be harmful to humans. It is therefore easier and safer to prevent infestation than to try to eliminate pests after they have reproduced unchecked. Pesticides can only be used safely in food establishments by following instructions exactly.

Automatic insecticide dispensers, which spray pesticides at regular intervals, should be installed according to the manufacturer's recommendations. Regulatory authorities approve only certain chemicals for use in these dispensers.

Devices that electrocute flying insects are effective; however, they may only be used if they are positioned so that dead insects do not contaminate food, food-contact surfaces, or clean equipment and utensils. These devices must be fitted with an "escape-resistant" tray which is emptied at least weekly. These devices cannot be used in food storage, preparation, or service areas. There is little scientific data available to support the effectiveness of ultrasonic pest control devices. Most regulatory authorities do not recommend the use of this equipment.

All pesticides used in a food service operation must be clearly labeled and stored in a locked area away from food products and other non-pesticide chemicals (detergents, sanitizers, oven cleaners, and silver polishes, for example).

Some pesticides (restricted-use) can be applied only by certified applicators. General use residual pesticides may be applied to ceilings, floors, and walls. They are not allowed in food storage, production, or service areas. Spot residual pesticides are applied in an area not to exceed two square feet (.19 sq. m) to walls, ceilings, floors, and the undersides of equipment. They are also prohibited near food and for use on utensils and food-contact surfaces. Some pesticides are squirted into cracks and crevices with a special nozzle. In all cases, the exterminator must guard against contaminating food, equipment, or utensils with the pesticide.

An in-house chemical pest control program requires properly trained staff members. It is safer and easier to contract a commercial exterminator who is specially trained to handle toxic chemicals. A professional exterminator can be scheduled for monthly visits or more frequent applications if there is evidence of infestation. Of course, a pest control professional is a waste of money if pests can easily enter, nest, and obtain food in the food establishment. Food establishments should therefore concentrate their efforts on basic environmental control.

Pest control companies fall into one of two general categories: application companies and integrated pest management companies. The integrated pest management company usually works with management on a long-term approach to pest control.

The integrated pest management company usually conducts an audit of the pest population. This audit identifies the pests present, their distribution throughout the facilities, and the factors that contribute to existing and potential problems. The company then presents management with an outline of what is to be done and why it is necessary, including the pesticides to be used and the application time and methods.

The company then applies the selected pesticide and uses a pest monitoring system to measure results, periodically reporting the results to management. These reports help management and the company evaluate the program's effectiveness.

There are several factors to consider when selecting a pest control company. Check with your regulatory authorities and area food service operators for references. Find out how often the company will visit your operation, the extent of chemical application, and the follow-up schedule. It is a good idea to sign a contract that states exactly which services will be performed and how much they will cost. Follow-up inspections should be scheduled at least monthly.

Cleaning, Maintenance, and Change

Cleaning and maintenance technology is evolving rapidly. Technological developments include low-temperature dishwashing machines, new cleaners and sanitizers, and new materials. These advances demand a periodic re-evaluation of the cleaning and maintenance program in a food service business. Managers can keep abreast of changes in cleaning and maintenance technology by reading trade publications, attending trade shows and seminars, and communicating with suppliers.

Other changes include legislation in some countries that require employers to inform their staff members about hazardous chemicals they may need to handle. Many cleaners and sanitizers are included in this category.

Cleaning, Maintenance, and Food Safety

The final control point, cleaning and maintenance, can add to or reduce the risks of running a food establishment. Unsafe chemical handling, storage, and usage can add unnecessary risks.

Staff members are largely responsible for reducing the risks of cleaning and maintaining equipment and inventory. Staff orientation and initial training, followed by ongoing training programs to reinforce critical items, are the keys to reducing risks. Standards established by a cooperative effort between management and staff members help ensure risk reduction. Equipment must be frequently cleaned, sanitized, and maintained. Equipment must also be used correctly in day-to-day operations. The food safety risk management program applied to this control point reduces risks to owners, guests, and staff members alike.

Key Terms

acid-anionic surfactant—Stable sanitizers that have a long shelf life and are active against most microorganisms. They are odorless, non-staining, and effective in hard water, and they have a low toxicity when left as a residual antibacterial film.

basic environmental control—An approach to keeping rodents and insects out of a food establishment, requiring all materials that serve as food or shelter for pests to be made pest-resistant or removed from the facility and its immediate vinicity.

chlorine-based sanitizer—Pathogen-destroying compounds that are active against all microorganisms and spores if used in a concentration of 50 to 100 mg/L (milligrams/liter). They are inexpensive, unaffected by hard water, and do not leave a residue, but have a characteristic chlorine odor and a relatively short shelf life.

cleaning—The removal of soil.

iodine-based sanitizer (iodophor)—Pathogen-destroying compounds that are stable (do not deteriorate easily), have a long shelf life, and will destroy most bacterial cells (but not spores). They are effective in hard water, are non-corrosive, and do not leave a residue or irritate skin, but work somewhat slowly, may stain, and are expensive. They should be applied in a concentration of 12.5 to 25 mg/L (milligrams/liter) for one minute or more at temperatures of 75° to 120°F (24° to 49°C) and a pH of 5.0 or less.

phenolic sanitizer—Pathogen-destroying compounds that act as deodorizers, but have limited applications and should not be used to sanitize food-handling equipment. They work well at pH levels between 6 and 7 and become more stable when combined with synthetic anionics.

quaternary ammonium compounds (QUATS)—Stable sanitizers that have a long shelf life, are active against most microorganisms, work best within a pH range of 9 to 10, and leave a film that controls bacterial growth. Non-corrosive and non-irritating, they eliminate and prevent odors, but destroy some microorganisms slowly and are incompatible with common detergents. They are expensive, and their residue makes them impractical for some uses. Usually applied in concentrations of 180 to 220 mg/L (milligrams/liter) for one minute or longer at temperatures of 75°F (24°C) and above.

sanitizing—The destruction of pathogens that survive the cleaning process. It is necessary because items that look clean are not necessarily sanitary.

sanitizers—Chemical compounds that destroy pathogens.

stored-food insects—Pests that render stored food products unfit for human consumption.

Review Questions

1. What are some of the common types of cleaning agents used in food establishments?

2. How does sanitizing differ from cleaning? Can you identify five types of sanitizers?

3. What are the major safety precautions that must be taken in handling cleaners and sanitizers?

4. Why are written cleaning procedures important?

5. How are pots, pans, and utensils typically cleaned and sanitized?

6. How often should the operation of commercial dishwashers be tested? What types of regular maintenance are required?

7. What are the advantages of using chemical sanitizing machines?

8. What are some of the physical and behavioral characteristics of common pests? What are their preferred environments?

9. A pest control program for food establishments involves what two parts?

10. What are the advantages of contracting with an integrated pest management company?

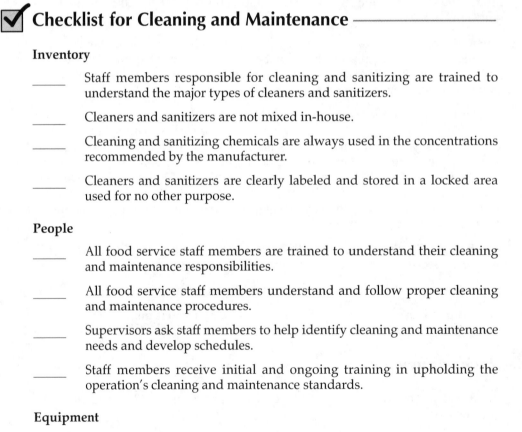

✓ Checklist for Cleaning and Maintenance ———

Inventory

_____ Staff members responsible for cleaning and sanitizing are trained to understand the major types of cleaners and sanitizers.

_____ Cleaners and sanitizers are not mixed in-house.

_____ Cleaning and sanitizing chemicals are always used in the concentrations recommended by the manufacturer.

_____ Cleaners and sanitizers are clearly labeled and stored in a locked area used for no other purpose.

People

_____ All food service staff members are trained to understand their cleaning and maintenance responsibilities.

_____ All food service staff members understand and follow proper cleaning and maintenance procedures.

_____ Supervisors ask staff members to help identify cleaning and maintenance needs and develop schedules.

_____ Staff members receive initial and ongoing training in upholding the operation's cleaning and maintenance standards.

Equipment

_____ Equipment, utensils, and tableware are cleaned, sanitized, stored, and used so as to prevent cross-contamination.

_____ Manual cleaning and sanitizing of equipment and utensils are done in a three-compartment sink.

_____ The manual warewashing area is designed to facilitate holding, scraping and pre-soaking, washing, rinsing, and sanitizing.

_____ Equipment, utensils, and tableware are air-dried before storage.

_____ Equipment, utensils, and tableware are stored in self-draining positions at least six inches (15.2 cm) from the floor.

_____ Staff members understand cleaning procedures for equipment, utensils, and tableware.

_____ Mechanical warewashing equipment is regularly serviced by a qualified person.

_____ Washing, rinsing, and sanitizing times and temperatures are monitored regularly.

_____ All mechanical warewashing equipment (such as pot washers, glass washers, under-counter dish machines) are regularly cleaned and maintained.

_____ Preventive maintenance programs (including schedules) are established and routinely followed.

_____ A separate storage area is maintained for cleaning equipment.

Pest Control

_____ Basic environmental control is used to keep insects and rodents out of the facility.

_____ Effective chemical control is used to rid the facility of insects and rodents.

_____ The pest control company is selected after checking references with the local officials and food service operators.

_____ Contracted chemical control companies are scheduled for follow-up inspections at least monthly.

Food Safety Risk Management Program

_____ Chemicals are carefully handled, stored, and used.

_____ Food service staff members are trained to maintain standards and reduce risks during cleaning and maintenance.

_____ Adequate facilities and equipment are present and used, and are frequently cleaned, sanitized, and maintained to reduce risks at the cleaning and maintenance control point.

Chapter 8 Outline

Competencies

1. Describe floor cleaning methods used in food service operations. (pp. 211–216)

2. Describe cleaning methods for food service walls and ceilings. (pp. 217–221)

3. Identify the most important lighting concerns and the major ventilation problem in food establishments. (pp. 222–223)

4. Explain restrictions on the uses of dressing rooms in food service operations. (p. 223)

5. Summarize major plumbing requirements and concerns in food service operations, and describe basic requirements for toilet and lavatory facilities. (pp. 223–228)

6. Describe requirements for outdoor refuse containers. (pp. 228–234)

Facilities Cleaning and Maintenance

THE CLEANING AND MAINTENANCE of a food service operation's physical facilities is a vitally important part of the operation's food safety risk management program. This chapter includes cleaning and maintenance procedures as well as important facilities design and construction considerations.

In general, building codes dictate the construction and maintenance of physical facilities in a food establishment. Much of the information presented here applies to the dining room—a food establishment's "front of the house." This information is equally applicable to other front-of-the-house areas in lodging operations, such as guestrooms, public restrooms, lobbies, and banquet/meeting rooms.

This chapter also includes an overview of the role of the housekeeping department in the cleaning and maintenance of lodging facilities, followed by a brief discussion of the on-premises laundry.

Floors

There are four basic types of floors: hard floors, resilient floors, wood floors, and carpeting. The selection of floor materials for each area in an operation should be based on how the area will be used. Exhibit 1 presents a breakdown of materials used for hard floors and resilient floors. This exhibit also presents recommendations (not strict rules) on how the various floor materials can be used.

Hard Floors

Hard floor materials include concrete, magnesium oxychloride cement, granolith, marble, terrazzo, ceramic tile, quarry tile, slate, terra cotta, and brick.

Concrete is a mixture of gravel, sand, cement, and water. It is relatively easy and inexpensive to install and maintain. According to government codes, it must be sealed and may also be painted. Magnesium oxychloride cement is a combination of magnesium oxychloride and various other materials. The appearance and durability of this flooring material may vary depending on the fillers used. It must be sealed to protect the surface. Granolith is a mixture of cement and granite chips. It resists abrasion better than concrete.

Exhibit 1   Floor Materials and Their Uses

	FLOOR MATERIAL	RECOMMENDED USES
HARD FLOORS	Brick and Slate	Stair Treads
	Ceramic Tile	Bathroom Kitchen Restroom Utility Room
	Concrete	Basement Garage Laundry Mechanical Room Service Room
	Granolithic	Hallway Lobby
	Magnesite	Hallway Office Workroom
	Marble	Bathroom Lobby Restroom Shower Room Stairs
	Terrazzo	Dressing Room Hallway Kitchen Lobby Utility Room Washroom
RESILIENT FLOORS	Asphalt Tile, Linoleum, Rubber Tile, Vinyl-Asbestos Tile	Lobby Elevator Hallway Office
	Cork	Office Meeting Room
	Vinyl	Elevator Guestroom Hallway Lobby Office
CARPET	Carpet	Dining Room Elevator Guestroom Hallway Lobby Office
WOOD	Wood	Dining Room Meeting Room Elevator

Marble is naturally crystallized limestone. Marble is very durable, but is also expensive and easily stained, and it can be damaged by improper care. Acids should never be used on marble. Terrazzo is a mixture of cement or synthetic plastic and marble or granite chips; it must be sealed. Terrazzo is durable and easy to clean and maintain, but it is expensive. Ceramic tile is a dense, hard material. It is durable, stain-repellent, easy to maintain, and expensive to install.

Quarry tile is usually red or brown. It is porous and requires sealing. Quarry tile is often used in high traffic areas such as kitchens. Slate, terra cotta, and brick are also common natural stone flooring materials.

In general, hard floors are relatively easy to keep clean if they are properly maintained. Most sealed hard floors require daily sweeping with a dry mop or floor brush. These floors may need to be refinished periodically.

Floor finishes provide three benefits: they provide a glossy appearance, they protect the surface of the floor, and they facilitate daily cleaning. Floor finishes should be selected according to the floor manufacturer's recommendations.

Finished floors should be stripped periodically to remove buildup of floor finishing materials. Floors may be stripped by wet or dry methods. Dry stripping combines the mechanical agitation of an abrasive scrubbing compound with a small amount of moisture. The compound is usually applied by means of a floor machine with a pad or brush. As the floor machine agitates the abrasives on the floor, the floor's finish is turned into a powder which can be vacuumed. Dry stripping is faster than wet stripping. However, the combination of agitation and abrasive compounds may damage some floors.

There are two basic methods of wet stripping. The more common method combines machine scrubbing with chemical emulsification. A chemical emulsifier applied to the floor dissolves the old finish. The floor is then machine-scrubbed and the residue removed with a wet vacuum. The emulsifiers are then neutralized and the floor is rinsed.

The other method of wet stripping involves total chemical emulsification of the old finish, eliminating the mechanical scrubbing. The stripping chemical is mopped onto the floor and allowed to completely emulsify the finish. After the finish has been dissolved, it is removed with a wet vacuum. Cleanup operations are faster and less expensive.

The costly procedures of stripping, waxing, and polishing are losing popularity. No-wax hard flooring materials save time and money. A water-dispersed, non-yellowing polymer compound is applied to the surface of the flooring material at the factory. Once installed, the no-wax floor is initially buffed to a high gloss which resists scuffing and marking. Occasional machine buffing with a cleaning/polishing compound maintains the finish and the floor's resistance to marking and scuffing. No-wax floors must be damp-mopped daily.

High-pressure cleaning is often used for irregular surfaces such as those in refuse areas, loading docks, tiled areas, and kitchen areas. The surfaces are cleaned by the force of pressurized water and a chemical added to break down and emulsify the dirt. Drainage is necessary for this method of cleaning.

Resilient Floors

Resilient floors are relatively soft in comparison with hard floors. These floors reduce both noise and staff member fatigue. The resilient category includes floors made of asphalt, linoleum, rubber, vinyl, and cork. Resilient floors usually require sealing.

Asphalt tile is inexpensive and resists moisture, but is easily dented and marked. Some types of asphalt tile contain asbestos, which is illegal in many areas and must be disposed of as hazardous waste. Linoleum is a combination of ground wood or cork, binders, mineral fillers, and oxidized linseed oil bonded to burlap or felt. It is available in sheet or tile form and is moderately priced. Linoleum is durable, but it can be dented.

Rubber tile absorbs sound and provides good traction, even when wet. It is expensive, however, and is easily damaged by oils, detergents, heat, and sunlight. Rubber tile is also susceptible to dents. Vinyl floor coverings are made from a combination of mineral fillers, acetylene, hydrochloric acid, and pigments. Vinyl is an expensive but highly stain-resistant flooring material. It is also available with a no-wax finish.

Cork floors are made from ground cork and resins. This expensive material is difficult to maintain, dents easily, and is frequently damaged by oils or moisture. Cork floors must be sealed with solvent-based epoxy and urethane.

Wood Floors

Wood floors may be constructed of hard or soft woods. They are susceptible to warping if they are exposed to excessive moisture; however, they are durable if properly sealed. Wood floors are potential fire hazards and can be relatively difficult to maintain.

Carpeting

Carpeting, often used in dining and public areas, helps to reduce staff member fatigue, controls noise, and, when installed at entrances, reduces the amount of dirt tracked onto interior floors. Carpeting is made of either natural or synthetic fibers. The type of carpeting selected depends on the traffic in the area to be carpeted. Solid-color carpeting shows traffic patterns in dirt and crushed pile. Patterned carpeting is preferable for high-traffic areas.

Modular carpeting may reduce an operation's overall carpet maintenance costs. Carpet modules or squares can be rotated from high- to low-traffic areas. This rotation results in a better overall appearance and extends the useful life of the carpet.

Proper carpet care is essential to protect this expensive asset. The frequency of carpet cleaning depends on the level of traffic in the area. Carpet cleaning is a labor-intensive task; the cost of labor can be more than 80 percent of the total cost of carpet care. Special equipment such as wet vacuums, steam cleaning or extraction machines, or rotary floor machines might be needed.

Dry carpet cleaning uses a cleaning compound or powder to suspend the dirt so it can be removed by a vacuum. However, this method can create problems. Residue remaining in the carpet pile will attract more soil and may necessitate more frequent cleaning by another method. An advantage of the dry method is that it minimizes the amount of time the carpet is not available for use.

Wet carpet cleaning methods require more labor and more downtime; overnight drying is usually necessary. Wet cleaning that is improperly done can also oversoak carpets, leading to shrinkage, mildew, and residue build-up. All of these conditions may shorten the useful life of the carpeting.

Steam cleaning or water extraction require specialized machinery. Some extraction equipment can be used to dry-vacuum and clean hard floors as well. Because extraction cleaning is hard on carpeting, it should normally be done only once a year.

Some carpet cleaning procedures fall between the dry and wet categories. The dry foam method involves spraying a dry foam carpet shampoo onto the carpet; rotating brushes on the bottom of the rotary floor machine scrub the foam-covered carpet. After the foam dries, heavy vacuuming is required to remove the shampoo residue. Again, any remaining residue will speed resoiling. Dry foam cleaning may also be done by hand.

The bonnet spin pad method is closer to a wet method than a dry method. A rotary floor machine is fitted with a circular abrasive yarn pad. Then the machine scrubs shampoo into the carpet and, in the process, soaks up the dirt in the yarn pad. Unfortunately, this procedure does not effectively achieve deep cleaning. Rotary shampooing—using a bristle brush instead of a pad—is more effective.

Vacuuming is the most important part of overall carpet care. Vacuuming at least once a day prolongs the life of a carpet by removing sand and other substances that can cut or shred carpet fibers. Spots should also be cleaned daily—or when they occur—to minimize staining.

Recommended Floors for Food Establishments

In general, all floor coverings should be non-toxic and able to withstand normal wear. It is important that floor surfaces be maintained in good repair. A smooth, durable floor material (such as sealed concrete, terrazzo, ceramic tile, or durable plastic) is essential in most food service areas. These areas include kitchen, storage, production, and warewashing areas, as well as locker rooms, dressing rooms, and vestibules. Anti-slip floor coverings are a good safety precaution for high-traffic areas, such as those behind the production line and in warewashing stations. Recommended floor finishes are presented in Exhibit 2.

In most cases, red quarry tile with acid-resistant grout is the best choice for flooring material. The tile can be made less slippery by impregnating it with an abrasive material such as carborundum. Poured seamless floors are also acceptable. They must be installed by a specialized contractor, as the quality of the end product depends more on the installation process than the raw materials.

Most building codes prohibit the use of carpeting in floor areas exposed to large amounts of water or grease. Such areas include toilet rooms, dining room service stations, equipment and utensil washing areas, handwashing areas, and food storage and production areas. Carpeting in dining rooms or other public areas must be closely woven and properly installed. Shag carpeting is not permitted because it is difficult to clean and because servers carrying trays of food may stumble easily. Carpeting has to be easily cleanable and maintained in good repair.

Exhibit 2   Recommended Floor Finishes

Food Service Area	Floor Finish			
	Commercial-Grade Vinyl Tile	Quarry Tile	Sealed Concrete	Poured Seamless
Kitchen		X		X
Dry Storage	X	X	X	X
Serving		X	X	X
Restroom	X	X		X
Bar	X	X		X
Janitor Closet		X	X	X

Source: National Sanitation Foundation, *Sanitation Aspects of Food Service Facility Plan Preparation and Review.*

If floors are cleaned with large amounts of water or if they are exposed to fluid waste from equipment, they must have properly installed floor drains with traps. Such floors may only be constructed of terrazzo, ceramic tile, sealed concrete, or other similar materials. The floor should be graded properly to ensure adequate drainage.

Floor mats and duckboards may be used in areas where staff members stand for long periods of time: behind the food production line, in warewashing areas, behind the bar, and in other areas where the floor may be wet. It is essential that mats and duckboards be designed to be removable and be easily cleanable, grease-resistant, and non-absorbent. The use of duckboards as storage racks is prohibited. Duckboards may not be constructed of soft wood.

Codes may specify that the junctures between walls and floors must be covered and sealed if they are likely to get wet. In dry areas, a closed seam no more than $1/32$ of an inch (1.0 mm) is acceptable. Utility pipes and service lines must be installed so as to allow easy floor cleaning. Exposed pipes and sewer lines running horizontally on the floor are prohibited in all new and extensively remodeled food service operations. The objectives of the codes are clear—to prevent the accumulation of soil and to allow easy cleaning and maintenance of all floors in food service facilities.

Codes may recommend only dustless floor cleaning methods for all types of floor surfaces. These include wet cleaning, vacuum cleaning, mopping with treated dustmops, or sweeping with compounds that minimize dust. Wet cleaning equipment (such as mops) must be cleaned and rinsed in a utility sink with a floor drain. Mop water or similar liquid wastes can be disposed of only in a utility sink—not in food preparation areas, food service utensil or equipment washing areas, or lavatories. It is also unsafe and unsightly to pour liquid cleaning waste in parking lots or other exterior surfaces.

Exhibit 3   Characteristic Problems with Walls in Food Establishments

Characteristic	Kitchen Cooking	Kitchen Preparation	Dry Storage	Manual and Mechanical Warewashing	Serving	Restroom	Janitor Closet
Detergents/Chemicals				X		X	X
Dust		X					
Food Acid		X					
Food Splash		X			X		
Grease	X			X			
Heat	X			X			
Impact			X	X	X	X	
Microbial Contamination		X					
Moisture				X		X	X
Rodents/Insects			X	X		X	X
Steam	X						

Source: National Sanitation Foundation, *Sanitation Aspects of Food Service Facility Plan Preparation and Review.*

Walls and Ceilings

All wall coverings must be non-toxic and able to withstand normal wear and tear. Walls, doors, and windows should be designed for easy maintenance. Wall finishes for each area in a food establishment must be selected to withstand the abuses characteristic of that area. Some of these characteristic problems are presented in Exhibit 3.

Many codes suggest that easily cleanable, light-colored, smooth, non-absorbent wall coverings be installed in food storage, food production, equipment and utensil washing, vestibule, and toilet room areas. Recommended wall finishes are presented in Exhibit 4. Most food service facilities have their masonry walls in these areas covered with several coats of epoxy-based paint. It is essential that all holes be filled in before painting to prevent splashed food and bonded dust from accumulating in crevices. Drywall is usually less expensive than masonry but might require more repairs. This is particularly true in high-moisture areas such as the warewashing station. Corner and bumper guards are necessary to protect drywall construction.

Modular, pre-finished wall panels are easy to install and clean. They are usually constructed of fiberglass and are self-extinguishing when exposed to flames. (It is important to check local fire code requirements.) Stainless steel and aluminum are ideal wall finishes, but they are expensive. Ceramic tile and concrete or

Exhibit 4   Recommended Wall Finishes

Food Service Area		Wall Finish				
		Glazed Surface	Block Filled and Epoxy Paint	Drywall Taped Epoxy	Wall Panels	Stainless Steel or Aluminum
Kitchen	Cooking					X
	Food Prep.	X	X	X	X	X
Dry Storage		X	X	X	X	X
Warewashing	Manual	X	X			X
	Mechanical	X	X			X
Serving		X	X	X	X	X
Restroom		X	X	X	X	X
Janitor Closet		X	X	X	X	X

Source: National Sanitation Foundation, *Sanitation Aspects of Food Service Facility Plan Preparation and Review.*

pumice blocks must be glazed. The glaze provides additional protection for walls and ceilings made of these materials.

No exposed wall construction (such as rafters, joists, or studs) is permitted in walk-in refrigeration units, food production areas, equipment or utensil washing areas, vestibules, or toilet rooms. Exposed construction is permitted in other areas, provided that it is surfaced or coated and easy to clean. In some food establishments, these features are part of a rustic decor.

Exposed utility service pipes and lines are permitted in some areas as long as the walls can be cleaned. Unnecessary exposure of utility lines and pipes is prohibited in food production areas, refrigerated storage areas, utensil and equipment washing areas, vestibules, and toilet rooms. Wall attachments (such as light fixtures, decorations, and fans) must be easy to clean and maintain.

Ceilings must be made of non-porous, easily cleanable materials. Recommended materials include plastic-coated fiberboard, epoxy-coated drywall, glazed surfaces, and plastic-laminated panels. No exposed construction is permitted on the ceilings of walk-in refrigeration units, food production areas, equipment and utensil washing areas, vestibules, and toilet rooms. If utility lines and pipes are exposed on the ceiling (in other areas), the ceiling must be easily cleanable. Light fixtures, fans, and other equipment or decorations attached to the ceiling must be in good repair and easily cleanable. Noise control is important, especially in the dishwashing area. Some vinyl-clad fiberboard acoustical tiles are acceptable for use in noisy areas.

Exhibit 5   Sample Room Finish Schedule

Room Finish Schedule										
Room Number	Room Name	Floor Material	Base Material	Wall Finish Material				Ceiling		Remarks
				Top	Bottom	Top	Bottom	Material	Height	

Source: National Sanitation Foundation, *Sanitation Aspects of Food Service Facility Plan Preparation and Review.*

To help food establishment managers prepare and review cleaning and maintenance plans for their facilities, a room finish schedule can be used to specify construction materials. A sample room finish schedule is presented in Exhibit 5.

Walls should be cleaned frequently with a dust mop and washed periodically. Ceilings should be cleaned periodically by washing with a detergent designed for such applications. Walls and ceilings may be washed by hand or with a machine designed for this purpose. The proper cleaners in the right concentration are critical in either case. Thorough rinsing is necessary to remove all soil and residue. Smudges and fingerprints should be wiped off daily with an all-purpose cleaner. Painting should be done by an independent contractor if the establishment has no designated staff member.

Ceilings and walls in dining areas may be constructed or covered with a variety of materials, including wallpaper, fabric, tile, marble, and wood. Most of these materials require special care. They should be cleaned according to the manufacturer's recommendations when possible. Exhibit 6 presents some general guidelines for cleaning various materials.

All floors, walls, and ceilings in the facility must be kept clean and in a state of good repair. These areas should be cleaned when even the slightest amount of food is found on them. General cleanup is permitted during non-rush periods (between meals) and after closing. In some cases, emergency cleaning is necessary; if a cook accidentally spills a gallon of beef stock on the kitchen floor, it must be cleaned up immediately to prevent further accidents. Staff members should be reminded during training to clean when not busy with other responsibilities.

Exhibit 6   How to Care for Materials in Your Building

MATERIAL	ROUTINE CLEANING AND MAINTENANCE
Acoustical Tile	Remove loose dirt or dust with a vacuum or soft brush. A gum eraser will remove most smudges. Soft chalk can cover many stains. More thorough cleaning can be accomplished with wallpaper cleaners or mild soap cleaners. Care must be taken to avoid excessive water and abrasive rubbing action; using a soft sponge is best.
Aluminum	Wash with a mild detergent solution; avoid common alkalies which dull the finish. A fine abrasive may be used periodically; rub in one direction, not in a circle.
Asphalt Tile	Wash with a mild detergent or soap solution; rinse with clean water and dry immediately either with mops or wet/dry vacuums.
Bamboo, Crane, Reed, Wicker, Rattan	Wash with a mild soap or detergent solution; rinse with clear water, dry. Periodic shellacking maintains a natural finish.
Brass	Acidic-type brass cleaners and polishes are used for unfinished brass. Wash lacquered brass with a mild detergent solution, rinse, and wipe dry.
Bronze	Clean with a metal cleaner or polish applied with a soft cloth; work with the grain, covering one small area at a time. Rub statuary finishes periodically with lemon oil on a soft cloth. Then rub briskly with a clean, soft cloth to remove excess oil.
Carpets	All types of carpeting—wool, polyester, nylon, polypropylene, etc.—must be vacuumed regularly to extend their useful life. (Abrasives which are allowed to accumulate in the carpet fibers will actually cut the fibers at the backing.) Also, a daily spotting program ensures prompt removal of spots. Overall cleaning can be accomplished with impregnated granular cleaners, shampoos, or extraction chemicals with a dry residue to prevent rapid resoiling.
Ceramic Tile	Use neutral soap or detergent applied with a sponge, mop, or brush, depending on the stain. Remove excess cleaning solution, rinse with clean water, and thoroughly dry the surface. Avoid alkalies, salts, acids, and abrasive cleaners. These tend to break down the surfaces of glazed and vitreous tiles, and cause problems with the porous cement grout. Some soap cleaners may result in a soap film buildup.
Chromium	Avoid harsh polishes and powders. A damp cloth is usually sufficient, or a mild detergent solution may be used. Then polish with a dry cloth.
Concrete	As soon as the floor can be used, it should be swept clean and a dust seal applied. Old concrete should be thoroughly cleaned and also sealed. Concrete floors can be swept with treated mops, damp-mopped, or scrubbed with a neutral cleaner. Excess solution should be picked up with a squeegee or wet vacuum. Never use acids because concrete dissolves in acidic solutions.
Conductive Floors	These floors are found in hospitals, computer rooms, or anywhere that it is necessary to prevent the building of a static electrical charge on the floor. These floors must be kept *film-free*. This includes coatings, soap films or dust mop dressings, as they will build an insulating residue on the floors. In hospitals, clean with a disinfectant/detergent. In other areas, use a detergent recommended for conductive floors.
Copper	Wash with soap and water, rinse, and dry. Stains and corrosion may be removed with metal polishes. If acidic solutions are used, always rinse thoroughly to avoid excess tarnishing.
Cork Tile	Sweep with a treated mop and buff. Avoid excessive water. If wet cleaning is needed, a mild soap or detergent solution should be applied with a damp mop. Sealed cork floors are preferred as they protect the natural colors of the cork.
Fiberglass	For normal bathtub soils and water conditions, use a multi-purpose alkaline detergent, according to label directions. If the alkaline cleaner does not have built-in disinfectant properties, a liquid or spray disinfectant may be applied to the bath fixture after cleaning. Where hard water is a problem, and accumulated mineral deposits need to be removed, a controlled acid cleaner may be used, containing phosphoric or oxalic acid. Do not use cleaners containing hydrofluoric or hydrochloric acid since these can etch the surface. Solvents such as acetone, xylene, toluene, or turpentine can be used on fiberglass; generally for construction site soils, debris, paint, vinyl adhesives, grease, or tar. Do not allow solvent cleaners to come in contact with drain pipes. Acids and solvents are not recommended for regular cleaning of fiberglass fixtures.
Glass	Wash with a special window cleaning concentrate dissolved in clean water; apply with a window washer's brush; use a squeegee or chamois to dry glass.

Exhibit 6 *(continued)*

Granite	Polished granite may be washed with a detergent solution or applied poultices. Treat unpolished granite with water and sand cleaning at a pressure of 50 psi or less.
Iron	Wash with a soap or detergent solution, rinse, and dry. A phosphoric acid cleaner can also be used. Rinse and dry thoroughly. Rust can be removed with steel wool soaked in mineral spirits. Surfaces that can withstand acid cleaning can be treated with a phosphoric-oxalic acid solution. Rinse thoroughly because oxalic acid is toxic.
Leather Furniture	Wash with a neutral soap or saddle soap. Leather trappings, etc., should be treated with neat's-foot oil to prevent drying and cracking.
Linoleum	Wash with a mild detergent solution; rinse with clear water. Remove water and dry as rapidly as possible. *Avoid* alkaline solutions.
Magnesite	Wash with a neutral detergent; do not use acids or alkaline cleaners. Remove solutions with a wet vacuum; avoid excess water.
Marble	Newly installed marble is best cleaned with a neutral cleaner and clean mops. Marble that has been soiled or stained through neglect has to be cleaned with the poultice method using a powdered abrasive cleaner and hot water. Only mildly alkaline detergent (never acids) should be used on seasoned marble; wash from the bottom up and rinse thoroughly. Then dry either with a chamois or soft cloth to prevent streaking.
Masonry	Steam cleaning with detergents or water and sand cleaning under low pressure may be required for brick, cement block, cinder block, stone and stucco. Interior masonry work may be vacuumed with heavy duty commercial-type machines.
Oil Paintings	Dust *lightly* with a soft dusting brush using extreme care. *Never use water or cleaners.* For badly soiled oil paintings, consult an expert.
Painted Surfaces	Immediately remove spots with a cloth wrung from a detergent solution. Washing should be performed under controlled conditions.
Pewter	Wash with a neutral detergent solution, rinse, and dry with a soft cloth. Apply a commercial silver polish to remove stains or browning.
Porcelain	Use an alkaline detergent; avoid acids, which can dissolve the surface and cause blemishes.
Rubber Tile	Use a mild detergent solution; rinse and remove water promptly.
Slate	Wash with a detergent solution; rinse and dry thoroughly. Chalkboards should *not* be washed on a regular basis; a thin film of chalk dust is best for vision and the care of the board.
Stainless Steel	Wash with a solution of soap or detergent. Rinse thoroughly; dry with a soft cloth. For heavier dirt, or deposits which require scrubbing, there are many specialty products; always rinse and dry, making sure to rub with the grain. Polish with a hydrocarbon-based stainless steel cleaner to prevent fingerprinting and resoiling.
Terra Cotta	Wash with a neutral detergent solution.
Terrazzo	Only neutral detergents should be used. Stains can be removed by the poultice method. Avoid alkaline cleaners as they cause powdering. Avoid using sweeping compounds which contain oil or wax. Acids dissolve the marble chips in terrazzo, soap tends to build up and leave a surface film; steel wool leaves splinters that rust.
Vinyl	Use a neutral detergent solution, rinse, and dry with a wet vacuum.
Wood	Wood floors must be sealed if they are to be maintained properly. Dust mopping and damp mopping sealed floors are usually all that is necessary if a regular maintenance program is followed. Polishing with a floor wax finish may be required. Some of the soft woods can be seriously damaged by strong solutions of soap or detergent and water; oils, grease, and strong alkalies are also harmful. Avoid excessive use of water and always remove water as rapidly as possible.
Vehicles	Trucks should be cleaned with a concentrated alkaline cleaner/degreaser, using high pressure and hot water equipment, to effectively remove road soils, grease, soot, etc.

Source: Adapted from the Soap and Detergent Association, *Programmed Cleaning Guide.*

Lighting and Ventilation

Adequate lighting is essential in all areas of a food establishment. Proper lighting facilitates cleaning and improves safety. Light intensity is measured in units called **footcandles.** One footcandle equals one lumen per square foot (a lumen is a measure of power equal to 0.0015 watt). Footcandles are measured with a light meter.

Codes may recommend at least 10 footcandles (110 lux) at a distance of 30 inches (75 cm) above the floor in all areas and rooms during cleaning. In areas where fresh produce or packaged foods are sold or offered for consumption, in areas used for handwashing, warewashing, and equipment and utensil storage, and in toilet rooms, the minimum is 20 footcandles (220 lux) at the same distance. At least 50 footcandles (540 lux) is required when staff members are working with potentially hazardous foods, or with equipment and utensils that pose safety risks. Most lighting engineers and safety inspectors recommend up to 50 to 70 footcandles of light for kitchen work areas. The objective of these requirements is to provide adequate lighting for cleaning, food storage, food production, and service. It is easier to clean and maintain a well-lit facility. Some areas in the facility (such as walk-in refrigerators and freezers) usually need extra lighting. Adequate exterior lighting renders the establishment more visible and makes guests feel secure as they approach the entrance.

Codes also address protective shielding, coating, or otherwise shatter-resistant bulbs for lighting fixtures. The objective is to prevent broken glass from contaminating food products.

Lighting fixtures, including lamps and shades in dining areas, should be cleaned routinely by dusting or vacuuming, as dust is the primary cause of reduced light intensity. Bulbs or lamps must be replaced promptly when necessary. Small glass fixtures can be removed for cleaning. Large fixtures, including chandeliers, are usually cleaned in place. This difficult job can be performed by an outside contractor.

Ventilation equipment is designed to remove smoke, fumes, condensation, steam, heat, and unpleasant odors from food service kitchens and dining rooms. Sufficient ventilation also helps to maintain comfortable temperatures and minimizes soil buildup on walls, ceilings, and floors. Building codes and health officials may dictate specific ventilation requirements for each area of a food establishment.

The major ventilation problem most food service businesses face is the transfer of unpleasant odors and fumes from the kitchen to public areas such as dining, meeting, and banquet rooms. This problem usually occurs when the kitchen ventilation system is improperly designed, including an inadequate amount of tempered (approximately 70°F [20°C]) makeup air to balance the system. Ventilation in the public areas is usually recirculated through heating and/or air conditioning units. Small percentages of exhausted air are usually replaced with outside fresh air. To avoid this ventilation problem, air from the kitchen must be completely exhausted to the outside and replaced with an equal amount of tempered makeup air. Makeup air intake and exhaust vents must not cause contamination of food.

Regulatory agencies may state that air exhausted from a food service facility cannot create an unlawful discharge or a public health nuisance. All intake and exhaust air ducts must be well maintained to prevent the entrance of dust, dirt, and other contaminants. Regular maintenance also reduces fire hazards and keeps exhaust vents from becoming unsightly; vents dripping with grease are an unappealing sight to guests approaching the building. In new and extensively remodeled buildings, ventilation to the outside is required in all rooms where fumes or obnoxious odors are likely to be created.

Dressing Rooms and Food Service Laundry Facilities

Staff members who wear their uniforms into the building may bring in many contaminants on their apparently clean clothes. Therefore, they should change into the required uniforms at the establishment immediately before they begin work, if possible. If staff members are required to change their clothes at the establishment, the facilities should include an appropriate dressing area. Dressing rooms may not be used for food storage, production, or service, or equipment and utensil washing or storage. The objective of these regulations is to reduce the likelihood of food contamination.

Even if staff members do not change into uniforms after arriving at work, the operation must provide storage facilities for personal belongings (such as coats, shoes, and purses). Locker storage areas must be adequate, secure, orderly, and clean. Lockers may be located in storage areas containing only completely packaged food or packaged single-service articles.

Laundry facilities may be installed in a food establishment if they are used *only* to wash and dry aprons, uniforms, cloths, and linens needed for normal operation. Ideally, laundry facilities should be isolated. However, washers and dryers may be placed in a storage area, provided that the room contains only completely packaged foods or packaged single-service articles. Soiled laundry must be stored in washable laundry bags or non-absorbent containers, and may not be stored in cold food storage rooms. Clean linens and cloths must be stored to prevent contamination.

Cloths used for wiping up food spills cannot be used for other purposes. Dry cloths may be used for wiping food spills from tableware and carryout containers. Moist cloths should be stored in a chemical sanitizer and can be used for wiping spills from food-contact and nonfood-contact surfaces. Cloth gloves must be laundered before being used with a different type of raw animal food such as meat or fish. Once soiled, both gloves and cloths must be properly laundered and dried and stored until used again.

If laundry operations are confined to laundering wiping cloths that are used wet, clean cloths may be stored in a sanitizing solution, air-dried in an area away from food, equipment, and utensil storage areas, or stored moist in the washing machine. (Laundry operations for lodging properties are discussed in the final section of this chapter.)

Plumbing Systems

Hot and cold water of sufficient quantity and pressure is necessary for any food service operation. Water is used for food production, cleaning and sanitizing, and

handwashing. Faulty or careless water hook-ups can contaminate otherwise potable or drinking water. Contaminated water is in turn likely to contaminate food,
equipment, utensils, and people.

In most places, the public water supply is closely monitored. However, some
food service operations may obtain their water from a private source. If water is
supplied privately, it must meet the requirements of applicable laws and be routinely monitored by the supplier in regard to testing (chemical and bacteriological),
treatment, storage, and transport. Bottled drinking water used or sold in a food
establishment must be obtained from approved sources. In rare cases, water may
be transported from the supplier to the operation either as bulk water or as packaged (bottled) water. Bulk water is stored in the operation's closed-water system.

The types and sizes of equipment in the food service operation dictate hot and
cold water requirements. Plumbing codes provide general requirements for water
pressure and usage volume for fixtures and equipment. In general, the volume of
water supplied and its flow pressure must meet the anticipated peak demand and
pressure requirements. Equipment lists in catalogs usually indicate usage pressures and volumes.

If steam comes into contact with food or food-contact surfaces, it must be
potable steam; that is, free from harmful additives or materials. A source of drinking water must also be provided for ice-making equipment.

Regulatory agencies and/or plumbing codes cover the installation requirements of the building's plumbing system. The basic objective of these regulations
is to guard against contamination of the potable water supply. Direct cross-
connections between the potable water supply and a non-potable supply are
prohibited.

Plumbing systems must include devices to prevent indirect cross-connections
caused by backflow and back siphonage. Backflow is a flow reversal due to a
greater pressure in the system compared to the potable water supply. Backflow
usually occurs with a sewage line backup in a food sink. Back siphonage can occur
when the supply pressure is less than the atmospheric pressure. Usually, back
siphonage is caused by a negative pressure on the water supply. This turns an out-
flow source into an intake source. A hose attached to a faucet with its tip submerged in contaminated water can create an indirect cross-connection subject to
back siphonage. Harmful contaminants can be siphoned back into the potable
water supply. An air gap between the water supply inlet and the flood level rim of
the plumbing fixture, equipment, or nonfood equipment must be at least twice the
diameter of the water supply inlet, and cannot be less than 1 inch (25 mm).

If grease traps are part of the plumbing system, they must be easily cleanable.
Garbage grinders and disposers must be properly installed. Drains are an important component of the plumbing system. Indirect drains are essential to prevent
the backup of sewage into sinks used to clean food, utensils, equipment, or tools.
Strict observance of this part of the plumbing codes serves to eliminate faulty
plumbing installations and to provide a source of safe drinking water to the public.

Sewage and other liquid waste must be removed from the premises
promptly and properly. Sewage is usually removed through a public system. In
some areas, an on-site private system for the elimination of sewage and liquid

waste is permitted, although some localities limit the capacity of these systems. Such systems require a permit. Care in the disposal of sewage and liquid waste will prevent the contamination of potable water, equipment, utensils, and food.

Toilet and Lavatory Facilities

The installation, number, convenience, and accessibility of toilet and lavatory facilities are strictly defined in plumbing codes. Toilet facilities must be available for all staff members and guests; usually, staff members should not share restroom facilities with guests if the seating capacity exceeds 50 people in the serving area. Toilet rooms should be completely enclosed and fitted with tight-fitting, self-closing doors which should be kept closed except during cleaning and to assist the handicapped. Each toilet must have a supply of toilet tissue. Fixtures should, like all areas of the facility, be clean and well maintained.

Lavatories (i.e., sinks) may be located either in or immediately adjacent to toilet rooms. Handwashing sinks may not be used for food production or equipment and utensil washing. Each lavatory must have hot and cold running water. A 15-second minimum water flow is required on all metered self-closing or slow-closing faucets.

Each lavatory must be stocked with liquid or powdered handwashing soap or detergent. Handwashing facilities must also have a continuous towel system, single-use paper towels, or heated air-drying devices. Air-drying devices are the most sanitary. If disposable paper towels are used, a waste receptacle is necessary. All equipment in the lavatory must be easy to clean and maintain.

Dispensing systems for restroom supplies (towels, tissue, and soap) can discourage waste and help control costs. Toilet tissue dispensers with the capacity for a reserve roll are best. Fully automatic paper towel dispensers control usage with a timed delay and thus minimize waste.

Liquid soap dispensers are widely used in public restrooms today. These dispensers usually hold approximately one pint (500 ml) to one quart (1 liter) of soap—enough for 1,000 to 3,000 washings. Liquid soap dispensers should be self-cleaning and checked periodically for leaks or clogs. Powdered soap dispensers are also available. Bar soaps, although acceptable for staff member handwashing stations, may be inappropriate for public restrooms because they may become mushy, brittle, or dirty. They may also leave an unsightly residue on lavatories.

The importance of adequate lavatory facilities in a food establishment is obvious: food service staff members are continually touching food and food-contact surfaces. To ensure proper handwashing, an operation must have proper facilities.

A clean and well-maintained public restroom is very important. Many people feel that the condition of the restroom reflects the general level of food safety in a food service or lodging property. Staff members should check restrooms according to a set schedule. A form for this purpose is presented in Exhibit 7.

The cleanliness of guestroom bathrooms and public restrooms is critical to a successful food safety risk management program in lodging properties. If these facilities are not cleaned correctly, a buildup of pathogens can occur in corners, junctions, spaces between the sink and counter and floor and toilet, and

Exhibit 7   Restroom Inspection Report Form

Date	Time	Condition(s) Requiring Action	Time Action Taken	Staff Member's Initials	Supervisor's Initials

hard-to-reach corners in the bathtub or shower. The pathogens can make people ill. Pathogens can be transferred to guests who place makeup, toothbrushes, or shaving equipment on counters that have not been properly cleaned.

Restroom cleaners containing detergents and quaternary ammonium compounds can be used on all restroom surfaces. An outline of the critical steps involved in restroom cleaning follows:

1. Turn on all lights and the ventilating fan.

2. Flush the toilet. After it has refilled, pour cleaner-detergent into the toilet bowl.

3. Wash the tub area, tile walls, tub enclosure, and shower curtain to remove soap film and hair. Flush the tracks and guides free of soapy water and hair if there is a glass or plastic tub enclosure.

4. Clean the tub fixtures. Make certain there is no ring around the tub or marks near the drain. If the tub has a pop-up stopper, remove it and clean it thoroughly. Polish it dry.

5. Clean the lavatory. Flush soap dishes with hot water. Remove, clean, and polish pop-up stoppers.

6. Wash off counter and tile splash-areas and all fixtures.

7. With a clean damp cloth, dust light fixtures, the door (including the top of the door), all exposed piping, the top of the tub enclosure, and the shower curtain rod.

8. Clean and polish mirrors with glass cleaner.

9. Clean the toilet by swabbing the bowl thoroughly, including around and under the rim. Clean outer areas and all fixtures.

10. Rinse your hands in the lavatory and dry with a clean cloth.

11. Dry the lavatory, counter, and fixtures.

12. Replace supplies (soap, towels, paper products).

13. Clean the floor, starting at the corner of the room and finishing at the door.

14. Always clean from top to bottom so you are not resoiling surfaces already cleaned.

When used frequently and properly, this system of restroom cleaning is effective and economical; it reduces labor and eliminates a buildup of pathogenic organisms.

Cleaning and Maintaining Furniture, Glass, and Decorative Items

Many decorative items are used to enhance an operation's image and ambiance. The frequency of cleaning and maintenance depends on the item and its use.

Curtains, draperies, and upholstered furniture can add a great deal to the ambiance of a food establishment or lodging property. In most cases, careful vacuuming will prolong the life of these items. Some fabrics may be handwashed when soiled, while other fabrics must be dry-cleaned. Because of the variety of fabrics used for these items, it is best to follow the manufacturer's cleaning recommendations.

Hot solvent cleaning can be used to clean silks, crushed velvet, and other fine fabrics. This method minimizes color bleeding and shrinkage. Portable equipment is used for in-place cleaning of curtains, draperies, and upholstered furniture. The equipment resembles a miniature water extraction unit.

A dry foam soil extractor may be used to shampoo and remove spills from upholstery. The machine loosens dirt and the attached vacuum removes the soil. The equipment can also be used to clean carpeted stairs. Some upholstery fabrics can be made soil-resistant by applying a protective coating after cleaning.

Blinds and shades should be vacuumed or dusted frequently. Some metal and plastic surfaces can be washed with a mild detergent solution and rinsed with clean water. Cloth or fabric materials may require specialized cleaning chemicals and procedures.

Glass is relatively easy to clean and maintain, and the necessary equipment and supplies are relatively inexpensive. Squeegees come in a variety of sizes. Brass models with hardwood handles are more durable than aluminum models. An ammonia-water solution cleans glass effectively. Alcohol may be added to the water as an anti-freeze when cleaning windows at temperatures below freezing. Commercial glass cleaners are also effective.

Periodic, scheduled cleaning of glass surfaces is necessary to prevent excessive soil buildup. Some establishments contract their outdoor window cleaning to professional companies. This reduces the safety risks for the operation's own staff members.

Plant care programs are essential for establishments using live plants to enhance decor. A typical plant care program includes watering, periodic trimming and grooming, fertilizing, insect and disease control, and replacement of unhealthy plants.

Interior plants should be selected and placed according to the individual plant's requirements. Each species may have slightly different needs for water, air, light, humidity, nutrients, grooming, and transplanting. In most cases, light should be continuous for 12 to 14 hours daily. A minimum intensity of 50 foot-candles is generally recommended. Ideal temperatures range from 70° to 75°F (21° to 24°C). Indoor plants usually come from tropical environments; therefore, they prefer humid air.

Most plants prefer soil that is barely moist throughout at all times. Potting soil is a lightweight soil that drains quickly; it is cleaner and contains more nutrients than outdoor soil. Indoor plants should be fed lightly with fertilizer about three times annually. Many properties contract their plant care to an outside company. This ensures that the plants are always healthy and attractive.

Refuse Storage and Disposal

Food contamination and pest problems can be prevented by the proper storage and disposal of refuse. Refuse is solid waste not carried through the sewage system. Refuse is often stored outdoors before removal. Containers used for this purpose must be insect- and rodent-resistant, durable, non-absorbent, leak-proof, easily cleanable, and maintained in good repair. Refuse containers should be lined with wet-strength paper or plastic bags. Bags alone should not be used for outdoor refuse storage because they are not pest-resistant. Outdoor receptacles must have tight-fitting doors or lids.

A food establishment's refuse facilities must be of adequate capacity. Refuse containers not in use should be stored outdoors on a rack or in a storage box at least 18 inches (46 cm) off the ground. Refuse containers should be cleaned regularly to prevent insect and rodent infestation. Containers can be cleaned effectively with a combination of detergent and hot water or steam.

Refuse must be removed from the premises frequently to prevent odor and pest problems. Outdoor refuse storage areas must be clean and well-maintained. Enclosures must be made of durable, easily cleanable materials. Outdoor refuse storage areas must have a smooth, non-absorbent base (such as asphalt or concrete) that is sloped to drain.

Many large food service operations use trash compactors. Such equipment can reduce solid waste bulk by up to 75 percent. Some compactors automatically deodorize and apply insecticides to solid waste. Liquid waste generated by a compactor should be disposed of as sewage. Suitable facilities with hot water are also required for compactors.

Recycling is an important consideration for more and more food service operators. Fast-food operations are often accused of generating large amounts of paper, plastic, and polystyrene refuse. Many chains have responded by reducing the weight and thickness of their containers or by completely changing the materials used. Recycled paper can be used for cash receipts, order pages for servers, and placemats.

Recycling will increasingly be required of food service operators. Protection from insects and rodents is critical during storage of recyclables. Recyclables must be regularly removed from the premises of a food establishment. They can be temporarily stored in portable receptacles or removed with transport vehicles. Food service operators would be wise to make a positive difference in their communities through the use of recycling.

Exterior Cleaning and Maintenance

Exterior masonry surfaces are typically brick, concrete block, stucco, stone, or a combination of these materials. These surfaces are porous and attract water, dirt, and scale. Cleaning such surfaces is difficult but important. Cleaning methods vary according to the climate, the type and condition of the masonry, and the design of the building. (Exhibit 6 includes cleaning procedures for some of these surfaces.)

Exterior masonry cleaners are frequently applied with spray guns and hoses. During cleaning operations, glass and aluminum exterior surfaces, as well as plants and shrubs, must be protected. Damaged masonry surfaces can be repaired and waterproofed with special chemical compounds. These applications not only enhance the exterior appearance of the building, they also prolong its life and increase its value.

Clean parking lots and sidewalks contribute to a positive first impression as guests approach the facility. These surfaces should be easy to maintain and should not cause dust problems. The type of outdoor cleaning equipment to select depends on the area to be cleaned, surface characteristics, the type of debris to be removed, the frequency of cleaning, and the financial resources available. A number of different types of sweeping machines are available. Air-recycling machines create an air blast with a fan to loosen debris. The debris is pulled up through a hose and deposited in a collection tank. Broom-vacuum machines loosen debris with a rotating broom and deposit it into a hopper. Push vacuum machines are walk-behind units used primarily to clean large outdoor surfaces. They function much like regular vacuum cleaners.

Ice and snow melting compounds play an important role in exterior building maintenance in certain climates. These compounds are only effective if the bulk of the snow has already been removed. Snow removal can be expensive, but it is necessary for the sake of appearance and safety. Many operations contract snow removal to an outside company rather than purchasing the equipment and having a regular staff member do it.

The three major types of ice and snow melting compounds are rock salt, calcium chloride, and pre-formulated chemicals. These compounds should always be used according to the manufacturer's directions.

Rock salt is relatively abundant and inexpensive. This compound lowers the freezing point of water; however, it is ineffective at temperatures below 0°F

(–18°C). Rock salt leaves behind a powdered residue which may soil carpeting near entrances. Rock salt can also be corrosive to metals containing iron.

Calcium chloride compounds create an intense heat and absorb moisture; thus they are effective at temperatures below 0°F (–18°C). However, these compounds can destroy animal and plant life, concrete, carpeting, fabrics, and metal surfaces. Calcium chloride may irritate the skin, so gloves should be worn when using this chemical. Calcium chloride compounds are more expensive than rock salt.

Pre-formulated chemicals are the most expensive ice and snow removal compounds. They are also the safest. They melt snow and ice quickly, are non-toxic, and are non-corrosive to metals and fabrics. They are also effective at temperatures below 0°F (–18°C).

The selection of ice and snow melting compounds should be based on the requirements of the individual operation. The compounds should be stored in low-moisture areas and applied with caution.

Cleaning and Maintenance in Lodging Operations

As pointed out at the beginning of this chapter, much of the discussion of the cleaning and maintenance of food service facilities applies to lodging operations as well. The rest of this chapter is devoted exclusively to special cleaning and maintenance considerations for lodging establishments. We will consider the role of the housekeeping department in the cleaning and maintenance of hotels and lodging properties, and then briefly discuss on-premises laundry facilities.

The Housekeeping Department

The housekeeping department of a modern lodging property does more than just clean; it provides a pleasant, clean, and comfortable environment in which guests can feel secure and satisfied. Housekeeping staff members should be made aware of their vital contribution to the property's overall image and their tremendous impact on guest satisfaction. By consistently exceeding guest expectations, an efficient housekeeping department encourages guests and their acquaintances to return to the property, stimulating both repeat business and positive word-of-mouth referrals.

The **executive housekeeper** is in charge of the housekeeping department of a lodging property, and is a member of the management team. Although department organization and operations vary with the size and individual needs of a property, housekeeping is a 24-hour effort in many properties.

Consider a 400-room hotel that can accommodate 900 guests. In addition to its guestrooms, the hotel has two restaurants, a large lobby area, four banquet/conference rooms, and an outdoor pool and courtyard area. The equipment requirements of this property are staggering. The housekeeping department alone requires thirty vacuum cleaners, two wet vacuums, one extractor, three carpet shampooers, several portable cleaning units for upholstery, and a floor-cleaning machine. The department also needs a large inventory of cleaning chemicals, room supplies, and cleaning accessories.

The hotel also requires a large housekeeping staff. The executive housekeeper is in charge of four supervisors; each supervisor oversees 100 guestrooms. The department also includes 70 room attendants and 20 laundry operators. The on-premises laundry processes over 150,000 pounds (68,100 kg) of linens each month from the rooms and food and beverage departments—over 900 tons (816,000 kg) in an average year. The cost of supplies (cleaning chemicals, equipment, room supplies) and labor for the housekeeping department exceeds half a million dollars annually.

In some lodging properties, a room attendant cleans 15 to 18 guestrooms in an eight-hour shift. The supervisor spot-checks cleaned guestrooms. The supervisor is also usually responsible for distributing supplies and training new staff members. The housekeeping staff may also assist the food and beverage department in preparing meeting and banquet rooms.

What makes an efficient housekeeping department? Six basics of housekeeping management have been identified in progressive and successful lodging operations; these fundamentals form the core of a lodging property's housekeeping program:

1. Contact with top management on a regular basis

2. Development of supervisors' leadership skills

3. Training of supervisors and staff members

4. Motivation of supervisors and staff members

5. Providing the necessary equipment and supplies

6. Measuring the efficiency of the overall effort

The six basics of housekeeping management provide a realistic set of objectives for any lodging property.

Housekeeping tasks should be performed when business is the slowest. For example, public areas are usually cleaned late at night. Guestrooms, on the other hand, are usually cleaned by mid-afternoon because they must be ready for assignment to guests, who generally arrive in the afternoon or early evening.

Waste Collection and Disposal

One of the main functions of the housekeeping department is the collection and disposal of litter and waste. A lodging property typically uses a variety of receptacles for this purpose.

Cigarettes are usually disposed of in some type of urn. Self-closing urns are best because they are attractive and minimize fire hazards. Water-quenching urns are also effective; however, they are difficult to refill, may cause odor problems, and are subject to corrosion. Granular-filled urns, which contain stone chips or sand, are another alternative. However, if these urns tip over, the stone chips or sand may damage carpets and floors. Urns should be placed near telephones, elevators, drinking fountains, restrooms, and in landings, foyers, and lobby areas. Their contents should only be emptied into metal containers.

Waste receptacles should be located near entrances, exits, and on terraces. Outside receptacles must be covered to protect them from the elements. Guest-room wastebaskets should be conveniently located. Waste receptacles should be seamless to reduce odors and facilitate cleaning. Plastic film liners protect waste receptacles and make them easier to empty.

Waste may be collected from urns and receptacles and placed on a custodial cart or in a plastic drum on wheels. Some operations use litter vacuums that shred waste, depositing it in a collection bag. Once collected, waste must be disposed of properly.

The On-Premises Laundry

Many hospitality properties operate their own **on-premises laundry (OPL)**. The OPL should be designed and operated according to the specific needs of the property. The following list suggests some important planning considerations:

- Property size and level of service

- The maximum amount of laundry (output) the OPL will be expected to handle

- The amount of space allocated to the OPL

- How much and what kind of equipment to purchase

- Valet laundry service for guests

The OPL launders primarily linens—bedding, towels, and dining room linens. Linens may be made of all-natural fabrics (such as cotton and wool) or synthetic fabrics (such as nylon and polyester). Most properties select a polyester/cotton blend, since this fabric offers most of the comfort of all-natural fabrics but is easier to care for. Regardless of the fabric, linens should be laundered according to the manufacturer's instructions.

Exhibit 8 shows the flow of linens through a property. In a lodging property, linens are collected in guestrooms, guest bathrooms, public restrooms, and dining areas. Housekeeping staff members place soiled guestroom linens into soiled-linen bags. Buspersons or servers usually collect soiled linens in food service outlets. It is important to keep tableware out of the bags, since it can stain linens permanently. Linens are transported to the OPL either by hand or on carts. Linens should never be dragged across the floor.

Once inside the OPL, linens are sorted by the color and type of fabric and degree of soiling. Cleaning rags should be washed separately because they are more heavily soiled than bed sheets. Fabric color, type, and soil will determine the washing process, washing time, water temperature, amount of agitation, and proper chemicals. Wash cycles may include as many as nine steps.

In addition to water and detergent, several chemicals are commonly used in OPLs. These include fabric brighteners, bleaches, mildewcides, fabric softeners, starches, antichlors (which remove bleach), alkalies (detergent boosters), and sours (which neutralize residual alkalinity). These chemicals are inventory resources that must be handled carefully, used according to manufacturer's recommendations, and controlled in the same way as food and beverage inventory items.

Exhibit 8   Flow of Laundry Through a Hotel or Food Service Operation

Source: *On Premises Laundry Procedures in Hotels, Motels, Healthcare Facilities, and Restaurants* (St. Paul, Minn.: Ecolab, Institutional Products Division), undated.

Staff training is the key to success in the OPL. Training should include safety, equipment operation, and inventory handling. Regular equipment inspection should also be included. Periodic retraining for everyone helps ensure that standards are being maintained. Retraining reinforces earlier training and demonstrates the property's commitment to safety and other standards. Training materials should be presented to staff members in a language they can understand. With the rising number of non-English-speaking staff members in hospitality properties, multi-lingual training programs are becoming a necessity. Chemical and equipment suppliers can often help with training programs.

Equipment resources in an OPL are a major investment. This equipment may include washers, dryers, steam cabinets and tunnels, ironers and pressing machines, folding machines, and rolling/holding equipment. Each specialized piece of equipment must be regularly serviced as part of a preventive maintenance program.

Facilities and Food Safety

Facilities represent the greatest dollar investment in assets by a hospitality establishment. These assets can become liabilities if a realistic food safety risk management program is not developed, implemented, and monitored.

The cleaning and maintenance of all areas of hospitality facilities must receive a high priority after the facilities are properly designed and constructed. Surfaces (such as floors, walls, and ceilings) must be regularly cleaned and maintained. The food safety risk management program must also address lighting, ventilation, plumbing systems, and decorative lighting. Dressing rooms and laundries have unique considerations, as does the exterior of the facilities.

By establishing procedures in each area of the facilities, managers can reduce risks and maximize the return on investment in relation to these assets.

Key Terms

executive housekeeper—The person in charge of a housekeeping department in a lodging property; a member of the management team.

footcandle—Unit of light intensity; measured with a light meter. One foot candle equals one lumen per square foot (a lumen is a measure of power equal to 0.0015 watt).

hard floor—A floor constructed of one of the following: concrete, magnesium oxychloride cement, granolith, marble, terrazzo, ceramic tile, quarry tile, slate, terra cotta, or brick; generally relatively easy to keep clean if properly maintained.

modular carpeting—Carpet modules or squares that can be rotated from high- to low-traffic areas, resulting in a better overall appearance and extending the useful life of the carpet; may reduce an operation's overall carpet maintenance costs.

on-premises laundry (OPL)—Washing and drying facilities housed in a hospitality operation.

resilient floor—A relatively soft floor made of asphalt, linoleum, rubber, vinyl, or cork; reduces noise and staff member fatigue; usually requires sealing.

Review Questions

1. What types of floors are recommended for food establishments?

2. Why should wall coverings or finishes in food production areas be light-colored, smooth, and non-absorbent?

3. How is lighting intensity measured?

4. Ventilation serves what purposes in a food establishment? What is the major ventilation problem in most restaurants?

5. Laundry facilities may be installed in a food establishment to wash what types of items?

6. What are some of the cleaning and maintenance requirements for toilet and lavatory facilities?

7. What types of care do window blinds and shades require?

8. What are the cleaning and maintenance requirements for containers used for outdoor storage of refuse?

9. The selection of outdoor cleaning equipment should be based on what factors?

10. An on-premises laundry for a lodging operation requires what five planning considerations?

Checklist for Facilities Cleaning and Maintenance

General

_____ Facilities are constructed and maintained in accordance with government codes and ordinances.

_____ A room finish schedule is submitted to local health officials when renovations or new facility construction is planned.

_____ Cleaning takes place when the least amount of food is exposed.

_____ Staff members are trained to clean when not busy with other responsibilities.

Floors, Walls, and Ceilings

_____ Floors, ceilings, and walls are properly constructed and maintained in good repair.

_____ A regular cleaning and maintenance program is established for walls and ceilings.

_____ Anti-slip floor coverings are used where permitted.

_____ Dustless methods of floor cleaning are used.

_____ Floor materials in each area are selected according to the area's planned use.

_____ Floor maintenance methods are based on the characteristics of the materials.

_____ High-pressure cleaning is used for floors with irregular surfaces.

_____ Selection of floor-cleaning chemicals is based on the floor manufacturer's recommendations.

Lighting and Ventilation

_____ Utilities are installed to minimize the likelihood of contamination and soil buildup.

_____ Adequate lighting is present in all areas of the facility, and light fixtures are cleaned and maintained regularly.

_____ Light bulbs and tubes are shielded in food storage, production, service, or display areas and in equipment and utensil cleaning and storage areas.

_____ Ventilation equipment is available and used to remove smoke, fumes, steam, condensation, excessive heat, vapors, and obnoxious odors.

_____ Ventilation systems are present and meet all regulatory authority requirements.

_____ Kitchen and serving area ventilation systems are coordinated.

Dressing Rooms and Laundry Facilities

_____ Dressing and locker rooms are not used for food storage, preparation, or service, or equipment and utensil washing or storage.

_____ Laundry facilities are installed and operated according to established standards.

Plumbing Systems

_____ Water in the proper quantity, quality, and temperature is available for normal operations.

_____ Liquid waste and sewage are removed promptly and properly.

_____ The building's plumbing system meets all applicable codes.

_____ The plumbing system is designed and maintained to prevent backflow and back siphonage.

_____ Toilet facilities and lavatories are regularly inspected, cleaned, and maintained, and meet all applicable codes.

_____ Staff members are assigned to check the condition of public restrooms frequently throughout the day.

_____ Restroom supplies are checked regularly and replaced when necessary.

Decorative Items

_____ Draperies and upholstery are vacuumed regularly to prolong their useful lives.

_____ Fabrics are cleaned according to the manufacturer's recommendations.

_____ Glass and windows are cleaned regularly.

_____ A contract service is used for exterior window cleaning.

_____ The plant care program covers watering, trimming, fertilizing, and insect and disease control.

_____ Plants are healthy, properly shaped, and attractive.

Refuse Storage and Disposal

_____ Refuse containers are durable, easy to clean, and pest-resistant.

_____ Outdoor refuse containers are kept covered.

_____ Refuse containers are cleaned and maintained at regular intervals.

_____ Refuse recycling is evaluated and implemented when appropriate.

Exterior Cleaning and Maintenance

_____ Cleaning methods selected for exterior building surfaces are suited to the climate, the type and condition of the materials, and the building design.

_____ Parking lots and sidewalks are regularly cleaned and maintained.

_____ Ice and snow melting compounds are used during the winter to maintain the attractiveness and safety of the property's sidewalks and entrance areas.

Housekeeping

_____ Housekeeping staff members are aware that they are part of the property's public relations efforts.

_____ The six basics of housekeeping management are used to evaluate the department's efficiency and effectiveness.

_____ Housekeeping activities take place when business is slowest.

_____ Chemicals used in public areas work safely and rapidly and dry quickly.

Waste Collection and Disposal

_____ Urns and waste receptacles are conveniently located and properly maintained.

_____ Urns and waste receptacles are emptied regularly and their contents disposed of properly.

On-Premises Laundry (OPL)

_____ The OPL is planned according to its expected output, space, services provided, equipment, and the size of the property.

_____ Linens are selected and maintained using manufacturer's instructions.

_____ Laundry chemicals are handled carefully and used in the proper amounts.

Food Safety Risk Management Program

_____ All areas of the facilities are designed, constructed, cleaned, and maintained in accordance with applicable laws.

Index